Essays,
Speeches &
Public Letters

WILLIAM FAULKNER

ESSAYS, SPEECHES & PUBLIC LETTERS

UPDATED, WITH MATERIAL NEVER
BEFORE COLLECTED IN ONE VOLUME

Edited by James B. Meriwether

THE MODERN LIBRARY

NEW YORK

LIBRARY OF CONGRESS CATALOGING-IN-PUBLICATION DATA
Faulkner, William, 1897–1962.
Essays, speeches & public letters / by William Faulkner ; edited by James B.
Meriwether.—[rev., 2nd ed.]
p.   cm.
Includes bibliographical references.
ISBN 0-8129-7137-X
I. Title: Essays, speeches, and public letters. II. Meriwether,
James B. III. Title.

PS3511.A86A6 2004
818'.5208—dc22   2003044278

WILLIAM FAULKNER

William Faulkner was born in New Albany, Mississippi, on September 25, 1897. His family was rooted in local history: his great-grandfather, a Confederate colonel and railroad builder, was assassinated by a former partner in 1889, and his grandfather was a wealthy lawyer and banker. When Faulkner was five his parents moved to Oxford, Mississippi, where he was educated in local schools, dropping out of high school in 1915, early in his senior year. Rejected for pilot training in the U.S. Army, he joined the Royal Air Force in 1918, but the war ended when he was still in training in Toronto. After the war, he took some classes at the University of Mississippi and worked for a time at the university post office. Mostly, however, he educated himself by wide reading.

Faulkner had begun writing poems when he was a schoolboy, and in 1924 he published a poetry collection, *The Marble Faun.* His literary aspirations were fueled by his close friendship with Sherwood Anderson, whom he met during a stay in New Orleans. Faulkner's first novel, *Soldiers' Pay,* was published in 1926, followed a year later by *Mosquitoes,* a literary satire. His next book, *Flags in the Dust,* was heavily cut and rearranged at the publisher's in-

sistence and appeared finally as *Sartoris* in 1929. In the
meantime he had completed *The Sound and the Fury*, and
when it appeared at the end of 1929 he had finished
Sanctuary and was ready to begin writing *As I Lay Dying*.
That same year he married Estelle Oldham, recently di-
vorced from Cornell Franklin, whom he had courted a
decade and a half earlier.

Although Faulkner gained literary acclaim from these
and subsequent novels—*Light in August* (1932), *Pylon*
(1935), *Absalom, Absalom!* (1936), *The Unvanquished*
(1938), *The Wild Palms* (1939), *The Hamlet* (1940), and
Go Down, Moses (1942)—and continued to publish stories
regularly in magazines, he was unable to support himself
solely by writing fiction. He worked as a screenwriter for
MGM, Twentieth Century-Fox, and Warner Bros., forming a close relationship with director Howard Hawks,
with whom he worked on *To Have and Have Not*, *The Big
Sleep*, and *Land of the Pharaohs*, among other films.

In 1944 all but one of Faulkner's novels were out of
print, and his personal life was at low ebb. Before the war
he had been discovered by Sartre and others in the
French literary world. In the postwar period his reputation rebounded, as Malcolm Cowley's anthology *The
Portable Faulkner* brought him fresh attention in America,
and the immense esteem in which he was held in Europe
consolidated his worldwide stature.

Faulkner wrote seventeen books set in the mythical
Yoknapatawpha County, home of the Compson family
of *The Sound and the Fury*. "No land in all fiction lives
more vividly in its physical presence than this county of
Faulkner's imagination," Robert Penn Warren wrote in
an essay on Cowley's anthology. "The descendants of the
old families, the descendants of bushwhackers and car-
petbaggers, the swamp rats, the Negro cooks and farm

hands, the bootleggers and gangsters, tenant farmers, college boys, county-seat lawyers, country storekeepers, peddlers—all are here in their fullness of life and their complicated interrelations."

In 1950 Faulkner was awarded the Nobel Prize for Literature. In his later novels—*Intruder in the Dust* (1948), *Requiem for a Nun* (1951), *A Fable* (1954), *The Town* (1957), *The Mansion* (1959), and *The Reivers* (1962)—he continued to explore what he had called "the problems of the human heart in conflict with itself," but did so in the context of Yoknapatawpha's increasing connection with the modern world.

He died of a heart attack on July 6, 1962.

Foreword

James B. Meriwether

The first edition of this collection was published by Random House on January 7, 1966. Intended to be as complete a collection as possible of the nonfiction prose that Faulkner had published or planned to publish, it contained sixty-three different pieces. Since then, a number of new items have turned up that I would have included in the original edition had I known about them, and still others have become available that belong here. In all, thirty-nine new items are added to this edition.

The editorial principles of this new edition remain the same, as do the categories of the pieces. To avoid an awkward number of subdivisions, I have stretched the definition of Public Letters to include dust-jacket blurbs and newspaper ads and announcements and have included Drama with the Book Reviews. Several corrections of errors in texts in the first edition have been silently made, and the endnotes of others have been expanded where new information has become available.

Included here are the six reviews that Faulkner contributed to the University of Mississippi undergraduate newspaper, *The Mississippian,* in 1920, 1921, and 1922. Carvel Collins republished them in *William Faulkner: Early*

Prose and Poetry, Boston, 1962, a volume long out of print. Collins also edited *William Faulkner: New Orleans Sketches,* New York, 1968, which included as an appendix Faulkner's 1925 essay on Sherwood Anderson. Although that volume has recently been reprinted by the University Press of Mississippi, the Anderson essay has been included here because it so obviously belongs with Faulkner's other 1925 critical pieces.*

❈ ❈ ❈

Readers of William Faulkner's fiction know its extraordinary variety. To take only three examples from among his best work: Could three great novels, written by one author, over a span of less than a decade and a half, differ more from one another than do *The Sound and the Fury, Absalom, Absalom!,* and *Go Down, Moses*? On a much smaller scale, the same variety is to be found in his nonfiction prose. Such major pieces as the essays "Mississippi," "On Privacy," and "On Fear," and the Foreword to *The Faulkner Reader,* are small-scale masterpieces—and are strikingly different from one another. Or take the speeches: the Nobel Prize, Pine Manor, and Delta Council addresses are probably the best and, again, are very different. One can also learn a great deal about William Faulkner's intelligence, knowledge, imagination, talent, and sense of humor by observing in the differences of any

---

* In *Selected Letters of William Faulkner,* edited by Jospeh Blotner, New York, 1977, there are six public letters that would have been included in this collection had they not been available there. In order to make this volume as comprehensive a record as possible of Faulkner's nonfiction prose writings, I list here the recipients and page numbers of those letters: Sven Ahmen, pp. 308–309; Random House, p. 371; Bob Flautt, pp. 389–390; W. C. Neill, pp. 390–391; Secretary of Junior Chamber of Commerce, Batesville, pp. 401–402; selected writers, pp. 403–404.

one speech from all the others not only the variety of his interests and the strength of his beliefs but also how aware he is of his particular audience and of how he appears to that audience. Even the most minor pieces, like many of his letters to the editors of various periodicals, display the same variety, the same sorts of differences—for example, see the letters to the editors of the *New York Times*, December 26, 1954, the Memphis *Commercial Appeal*, March 20, 1955, and the *Oxford Eagle*, October 15, 1960.

This collection is indeed a highly significant part of Faulkner's oeuvre. As the novelist and critic George Garrett emphasized in his review of the original edition of this book, Faulkner's essays were "written like everything else he wrote, as a part of his whole life's work. . . ." And he goes on to say that these essays, and many of the other pieces in the volume, "are couched in his own style and vocabulary, one which was designed not to sound like a great deal of other contemporary criticism and certainly not to partake of the accepted and debased jargon of any critical school. . . . Moreover, one must be aware of the relationship of one piece to another and to the whole of his work." (*Shenandoah*, Spring 1966; another excerpt from the review is quoted on the front cover of this book. More of Garrett's distinguished Faulkner criticism appears in the "Southern Literature and William Faulkner" section of Garrett's *The Sorrows of Fat City: A Selection of Literary Essays and Reviews*, University of South Carolina Press, 1992.)

In 1976, the novelist and critic Warren Beck published one of the finest, most massive, and—inexplicably—most neglected of all the books of Faulkner criticism, entitled, with misleading modesty, *Faulkner: Essays* (University of Wisconsin Press). His scattered remarks about the Nobel Prize address stand out as a superb example of what can be learned about Faulkner, the writer of fiction, from his nonfiction prose, and how closely related his nonfiction is to his novels and stories. He called it "Faulkner's profound humanistic declaration . . . an artist's credo that could have stood as a preface to any of his novels. . . ." This speech, he said, "defined in large and lasting terms . . . the artist's role in the modern world, according to the august concepts upon which he based a dedication to his calling," and it declared "what his fiction had implied throughout, his position as committed humanistic realist." Carefully choosing his audience, Faulkner addressed younger writers, and did so "with concern not just for literature's future but for his ongoing service . . . by warning and heartening, linking courage and compassion as proved human values in a formidably restive world," speaking "out of his gathered convictions and invincible stamina. . . ." The phrasing of the address "echoes his lifetime fictional attempt to present the subjective existential reality of human beings in their struggling toward self-possession and integrity, still tempted to indifference, slackening into ambivalence, yet rousing themselves to moral assertion based on 'the old verities.' "

Everything in this collection of his nonfiction prose, then, is revelatory of Faulkner the artist and Faulkner the man. The pieces, in showing us some of what this immensely dedicated, immensely complex, and deeply secretive writer chose to reveal about himself publicly during the last four decades of his career, permit us to understand, a little better, the man and his work.

Acknowledgments

My most grateful thanks are due to Jill Faulkner Summers, executrix of the estate of William Faulkner, for her permissions, and her encouragement. To my editor at Random House, Danielle Durkin, thanks are also due for her encouragement, her patience, and her copyediting skills.

—September 30, 2003

CONTENTS

BIOGRAPHICAL NOTE   v

FOREWORD   ix

ACKNOWLEDGMENTS   xiii

EDITOR'S PREFACE TO THE FIRST EDITION   xxiii

ESSAYS, SPEECHES & PUBLIC LETTERS

1 ESSAYS

    A Note on Sherwood Anderson, 1953   3

    Mississippi, 1954   11

    A Guest's Impression of New England, 1954   44

    An Innocent at Rinkside, 1955   48

    Kentucky: May: Saturday, 1955   52

    On Privacy, 1955   62

    Impressions of Japan, 1955   76

    To the Youth of Japan, 1955   82

    Letter to a Northern Editor, 1956   86

    On Fear: Deep South in Labor: Mississippi, 1956   92

    A Letter to the Leaders in the Negro Race, 1956   107

    Albert Camus, 1961   113

II SPEECHES

Funeral Sermon for Mammy Caroline Barr,
February 4, 1940   117

Upon Receiving the Nobel Prize for Literature, 1950   119

To the Graduating Class, University High School, 1951   122

Upon Being Made an Officer of the Legion of Honor,
1951   125

To the Delta Council, 1952   126

To the Graduating Class, Pine Manor Junior College,
1953   135

Upon Receiving the National Book Award for Fiction, 1955   143

To the Southern Historical Association, 1955   146

Upon Receiving the Silver Medal of the Athens Academy,
1957   152

To the American Academy of Arts and Letters
in Presenting the Gold Medal for Fiction
to John Dos Passos, 1957   153

To the Raven, Jefferson, and ODK Societies of the
University of Virginia, 1958   155

To the English Club of the University of Virginia, 1958   160

To the U. S. National Commission for UNESCO, 1959   166

To the American Academy of Arts and Letters upon
Acceptance of the Gold Medal for Fiction, 1962   168

III INTRODUCTIONS

FOREWORD TO *Sherwood Anderson & Other Famous
Creoles*, 1926   173

INTRODUCTION TO THE MODERN LIBRARY EDITION
OF *Sanctuary*, 1932   176

FOREWORD TO *The Faulkner Reader*, 1954   179

IV BOOK REVIEWS

The Road Back, BY ERICH MARIA REMARQUE, 1931   185

Test Pilot, BY JIMMY COLLINS, 1935   188

The Old Man and the Sea, BY ERNEST HEMINGWAY, 1952   193

V PUBLIC LETTERS

TO THE BOOK EDITOR OF THE *Chicago Tribune,*
JULY 16, 1927   197

TO THE PRESIDENT OF THE LEAGUE OF AMERICAN WRITERS,
1938   198
TO THE EDITOR OF THE MEMPHIS *Commercial Appeal,*
JULY 12, 1941   199
"HIS NAME WAS PETE," *Oxford Eagle,* AUGUST 15, 1946   200
TO THE EDITOR OF THE *Oxford Eagle,* MARCH 13, 1947   202
TO THE EDITOR OF THE MEMPHIS *Commercial Appeal,*
MARCH 26, 1950   203
TO THE EDITOR OF THE MEMPHIS *Commercial Appeal,*
APRIL 9, 1950   205
TO THE SECRETARY OF THE AMERICAN ACADEMY OF ARTS
AND LETTERS, JUNE 12, 1950   206
"TO THE VOTERS OF OXFORD," SEPTEMBER 1950   207
TO THE EDITOR OF THE *Oxford Eagle,* SEPTEMBER 14, 1950   208
TO THE EDITOR OF *Time,* NOVEMBER 13, 1950   210
STATEMENT TO THE PRESS ON THE WILLIE MCGEE CASE,
MEMPHIS *Commercial Appeal,* MARCH 27, 1951   211
TO THE EDITOR OF THE *New York Times,*
DECEMBER 26, 1954   212
TO THE EDITOR OF THE MEMPHIS *Commercial Appeal,*
FEBRUARY 20, 1955   214
TO THE EDITOR OF THE MEMPHIS *Commercial Appeal,*
MARCH 20, 1955   215
TO THE EDITOR OF THE *New York Times,* MARCH 25, 1955   217
TO THE EDITOR OF THE MEMPHIS *Commercial Appeal,*
APRIL 3, 1955   218
TO THE EDITOR OF THE MEMPHIS *Commercial Appeal,*
APRIL 10, 1955   220
TO THE EDITOR OF THE MEMPHIS *Commercial Appeal,*
APRIL 17, 1955   221
PRESS DISPATCH ON THE EMMETT TILL CASE,
SEPTEMBER 9, 1955   222
TO THE EDITOR OF *Life,* MARCH 26, 1956   224
TO THE EDITOR OF THE *Reporter,* APRIL 19, 1956   225
TO THE EDITOR OF *Time,* APRIL 23, 1956   226
TO THE EDITOR OF *Time,* DECEMBER 10, 1956   227
TO THE EDITOR OF THE *New York Times,* DECEMBER 16, 1956 227
TO THE EDITOR OF *Time,* FEBRUARY 11, 1957   228

TO THE EDITOR OF THE MEMPHIS *Commercial Appeal*,
    SEPTEMBER 15, 1957   229
TO THE EDITOR OF THE *New York Times*, OCTOBER 13, 1957   230
NOTICE, *Oxford Eagle*, SEPTEMBER 24, 1959   231
"NOTICE," *Oxford Eagle*, OCTOBER 15, 1959   232
TO THE EDITOR OF THE *New York Times*, AUGUST 28, 1960   232

New Material for This Revised Edition

VI ESSAYS
Verse, Old and Nascent: A Pilgrimage, 1924   237
On Criticism, 1925   242
Sherwood Anderson, 1925   246
Literature and War, 1925   254
And Now What's To Do, 1925   256
The Composition, Editing, and Cutting of *Flags in
    the Dust*, c. 1928   260
Mac Grider's Son, 1934   264
Note on *A Fable*, c. 1953   270

VII SPEECHES
Funeral Sermon for Mammy Caroline Barr
    February 5, 1940   275
Address to the Congrès pour la Liberté de la Culture,
    1952   277
Address at the American Literature Seminar, Nagano,
    1955   279
Address upon Receiving the Andrés Bello Award,
    Caracas, 1961   283
Address at the Teatro Municipal, Caracas, 1961   285

VIII INTRODUCTIONS
Two Introductions to *The Sound and the Fury*   289
    Oxford, Mississippi, August 19, 1933   289
    Oxford, Mississippi, 1946   296
Prefatory Note to "Appendix: Compson, 1699–1945,"
    1946   301

IX BOOK AND DRAMA REVIEWS

In April Once, BY W. A. PERCY, 1920   307

Turns and Movies, BY CONRAD AIKEN, 1921   309

Aria da Capo: A Play in One Act, BY EDNA ST. VINCENT
MILLAY, 1922   312

American Drama: Eugene O'Neill, 1922   314

American Drama: Inhibitions, 1922   317

Linda Condon—Cytherea—The Bright Shawl, BY JOSEPH
HERGESHEIMER, 1922   321

Ducdame, BY JOHN COWPER POWYS, 1925   323

Test Pilot, BY JIMMY COLLINS (The uncut text), 1935   328

X PUBLIC LETTERS

TO THE NEW ORLEANS *Times-Item,* APRIL 4, 1925   337

TO THE EDITOR OF THE MEMPHIS *Commercial Appeal,*
FEBRUARY 15, 1931   338

BLURB FOR *Men in Darkness,* BY JAMES HANLEY, 1932   344

BLURB AND PROMOTIONAL USE OF LETTER TO CLIFTON
CUTHBERT, 1933   344

CLASSIFIED AD IN THE MEMPHIS *Commercial Appeal,*
JANUARY 22, 1936   345

INSCRIPTION ON THE MONUMENT TO LAFAYETTE COUNTY'S
WORLD WAR II DEAD, 1947   346

TO THE MEMPHIS *Commercial Appeal,* APRIL 30, 1950   347

BLURB FOR *The End of the Affair,* BY GRAHAM GREENE, 1955   349

DRAFT OF SEPTEMBER 15, 1957, LETTER TO THE MEMPHIS
Commercial Appeal   350

ESTATE ADMINISTRATOR'S NOTICE IN THE *Oxford
Eagle,* 1960   352

Editor's Preface
to the First Edition

At one time William Faulkner planned a book of five or six related essays, to be called *The American Dream*. But he wrote only two chapters of it, "On Privacy" and "On Fear," in 1955 and 1956. And apparently he never considered a more miscellaneous collection of his essays, though in the latter part of his career he did some of his best writing in that form. Presumably, had he approved and helped put together such a volume, it would have been selective, a smaller and more unified collection than this. But in the absence of any instruction from him, it seems best now to make of this book as complete a record as possible of Faulkner's mature achievement in the field of non-fiction prose.

His earliest literary essays and book reviews, written while he was still a student and apprentice poet, are omitted here, as are a few fragmentary or unpublished "public" letters. Otherwise this collection includes the text of all Faulkner's mature articles, speeches, book reviews, introductions to books, and letters intended for publication. Most of the pieces are from the latter part of his career, and many of them reflect the increased sense of his responsibility as a public figure which Faulkner showed after he won the Nobel Prize for Literature in 1950. And although some of his writing in this field was occasional, written to order and to meet a deadline, because he needed the money, there is no hackwork here. Faulkner did not accept commissions he did not find attractive and think he could execute well.

❈ ❈ ❈

To establish the text, Faulkner's original typescripts and correspondence with his editors and agents were consulted whenever possible. If the text printed here depends upon such authority, it is indicated in the footnote at the end of each selection, which gives the original place and date of its publication.

In addition a number of editorial corrections have been silently made. Within some of the pieces a greater degree of consistency was imposed upon the original system of indention, punctuation, and quotation marks. Book and periodical titles have all been put into italics, titles of parts of books or contributions to periodicals have been put within quotation marks. Headings of letters have been made uniform. A number of obvious typing and printer's errors have been corrected. On the other hand I have retained, where I was aware of them, Faulkner's habitual, intentional, or idiosyncratic archaisms and innovations of spelling, punctuation, and construction.

J.B.M.

ONE

Essays

A Note on
Sherwood Anderson*

ONE DAY during the months while we walked and talked in New Orleans—or Anderson talked and I listened—I found him sitting on a bench in Jackson Square, laughing with himself. I got the impression that he had been there like that for some time, just sitting alone on the bench laughing with himself. This was not our usual meeting place. We had none. He lived above the Square, and without any especial prearrangement, after I had had something to eat at noon and knew that he had finished his lunch too, I would walk in that direction and if I did not meet him already strolling or sitting in the Square, I myself would simply sit down on the curb where I could see his doorway and wait until he came out of it in his bright, half-racetrack, half-Bohemian clothes.

This time he was already sitting on the bench, laughing. He told me what it was at once: a dream: he had dreamed the night before that he was walking for miles along country roads, leading a horse which he was trying to swap for a night's sleep—not for a simple bed for the night, but for the sleep itself; and with me to listen now, went on from there, elaborating it, building it into a work of art with the same tedious (it had the appearance of fumbling but actually it wasn't: it was seeking, hunting) almost excruciating patience and humility with which he did all his writing, me listening and believing no word of it: that is, that it had been any dream dreamed in sleep. Because I knew better. I knew that he had invented it, made it; he had made most of it or at least some of it while I was there watching and listening to him. He didn't know why he had been compelled, or anyway needed, to claim it had been a dream, why there had to be that connection with dream and sleep, but I did. It was because he had written his whole biography into an anecdote or perhaps a parable: the horse (it had been a racehorse at first, but now it was a working horse, plow carriage and saddle, sound and strong and valuable, but without recorded pedigree) representing the vast rich strong docile sweep of the Mississippi Valley, his own America, which he in his bright blue racetrack shirt and vermilion-mottled Bohemian Windsor tie, was offering with humor and patience and humility, but mostly with patience and humility, to swap for his own dream of purity and integrity and hard and unremitting work and accomplishment, of which *Winesburg, Ohio* and *The Triumph of the Egg* had been symptoms and symbols.

He would never have said this, put it into words, himself. He may never have been able to see it even, and he certainly would have denied it, probably pretty violently, if I had tried to point it out to him. But this would not have been for the reason that it might not have been true, nor for the reason that, true or not, he would not have believed it. In fact, it would have made little difference whether it was true or not or whether he believed it or not. He would have repudiated it for the reason which was the great tragedy of his character. He expected people to make fun of, ridicule him. He expected people nowhere near his equal in stature or accomplishment or wit or anything else, to be capable of making him appear ridiculous.

That was why he worked so laboriously and tediously and indefatigably at everything he wrote. It was as if he said to himself: 'This anyway will, shall, must be invulnerable.' It was as though he wrote not even out of the consuming unsleeping appeaseless thirst for glory for which any normal artist would destroy his aged mother, but for what to him was more important and urgent: not even for mere truth, but for purity, the exactitude of purity. His was not the power and rush of Melville, who was his grandfather, nor the lusty humor for living of Twain, who was his father; he had nothing of the heavy-handed disregard for nuances of his older brother, Dreiser. His was that fumbling for exactitude, the exact word and phrase within the limited scope of a vocabulary controlled and even repressed by what was in him almost a fetish of simplicity, to milk them both dry, to seek always to penetrate to thought's uttermost end. He worked so hard at this that it finally became just style: an end instead of a means: so that he presently came to believe that, provided he kept the style pure and intact and unchanged and inviolate, what the style contained would have to be first rate: it couldn't help but be first rate, and therefore himself too.

At this time in his life, he had to believe this. His mother had been a bound girl, his father a day laborer; this background had taught him that the amount of security and material success which he had attained was, must be, the answer and end to life. Yet he gave this up, repudiated and discarded it at a later age, when older in years than most men and women who make that decision, to dedicate himself to art, writing. Yet, when he made the decision, he found himself to be only a one- or two-book man. He had to believe that, if only he kept that style pure, then what the style contained would be pure too, the best. That was why he had to defend the style. That was the reason for his hurt and anger at Hemingway about Hemingway's *The Torrents of Spring,* and at me in a lesser degree since my fault was not full book-length but instead was merely a privately-printed and -subscribed volume which few people outside our small New Orleans group would ever see or hear about, because of the book of Spratling's caricatures which we titled *Sherwood Anderson & Other Famous Creoles* and to which I wrote an introduction in Anderson's primer-like style. Neither of us—Hemingway or I—could have touched, ridiculed, his work itself. But we had made his style look ridiculous; and by that time, after *Dark Laughter,* when he had reached the point where he should have stopped writing, he had to defend that style at all costs because he too must have known by then in his heart that there was nothing else left.

The exactitude of purity, or the purity of exactitude: whichever you like. He was a sentimentalist in his attitude toward people, and quite often incorrect about them. He believed in people, but it was as though only in theory. He expected the worst from them, even while each time he was prepared again to be disappointed or even hurt, as if it had never happened before, as though the only people he could really trust, let himself go with, were the ones of his own invention, the figments and symbols of his own fumbling dream. And he was sometimes a sentimentalist in his writing (so was Shakespeare sometimes) but he was never impure in it. He never scanted it, cheapened it, took the easy way; never failed

to approach writing except with humility and an almost
religious, almost abject faith and patience and willingness to surrender, relinquish himself to and into it. He
hated glibness; if it were quick, he believed it was false
too. He told me once: 'You've got too much talent. You
can do it too easy, in too many different ways. If you're
not careful, you'll never write anything.' During those
afternoons when we would walk about the old quarter, I
listening while he talked to me or to people—anyone,
anywhere—whom we would meet on the streets or the
docks, or the evenings while we sat somewhere over a
bottle, he, with a little help from me, invented other
fantastic characters like the sleepless man with the horse.
One of them was supposed to be a descendant of Andrew
Jackson, left in that Louisiana swamp after the Battle of
Chalmette, no longer half-horse half-alligator but by
now half-man half-sheep and presently half-shark, who—
it, the whole fable—at last got so unwieldy and (so we
thought) so funny, that we decided to get it onto paper
by writing letters to one another such as two temporarily
separated members of an exploring-zoological expedition
might. I brought him my first reply to his first letter. He
read it. He said:

'Does it satisfy you?'

I said, 'Sir?'

'Are you satisfied with it?'

'Why not?' I said. 'I'll put whatever I left out into
the next one.' Then I realised that he was more than
displeased: he was short, stern, almost angry. He said:

'Either throw it away, and we'll quit, or take it back
and do it over.' I took the letter. I worked three days
over it before I carried it back to him. He read it again,
quite slowly, as he always did, and said, 'Are you satisfied now?'

'No sir,' I said. 'But it's the best I know how to do.'

'Then we'll pass it,' he said, putting the letter into his pocket, his voice once more warm, rich, burly with laughter, ready to believe, ready to be hurt again.

I learned more than that from him, whether or not I always practised the rest of it anymore than I have that. I learned that, to be a writer, one has first got to be what he is, what he was born; that to be an American and a writer, one does not necessarily have to pay lip-service to any conventional American image such as his and Dreiser's own aching Indiana or Ohio or Iowa corn or Sandburg's stockyards or Mark Twain's frog. You had only to remember what you were. 'You have to have somewhere to start from: then you begin to learn,' he told me. 'It dont matter where it was, just so you remember it and aint ashamed of it. Because one place to start from is just as important as any other. You're a country boy; all you know is that little patch up there in Mississippi where you started from. But that's all right too. It's America too; pull it out, as little and unknown as it is, and the whole thing will collapse, like when you prize a brick out of a wall.'

'Not a cemented, plastered wall,' I said.

'Yes, but America aint cemented and plastered yet. They're still building it. That's why a man with ink in his veins not only still can but sometimes has still got to keep on moving around in it, keeping moving around and listening and looking and learning. That's why ignorant unschooled fellows like you and me not only have a chance to write, they must write. All America asks is to look at it and listen to it and understand it if you can. Only the understanding aint important either: the important thing is to believe in it even if you dont understand it, and then try to tell it, put it down. It wont ever be quite right, but there is always next time; there's always more ink and paper, and something else to try to understand and tell. And that one probably wont be exactly right either, but there is a next time to that one, too. Because tomorrow America is going to be something different, something more and new to watch and listen to and try to understand; and, even if you cant understand, believe.

To believe, to believe in the value of purity, and to believe more. To believe not in just the value, but the necessity for fidelity and integrity; lucky is that man whom the vocation of art elected and chose to be faithful to it, because the reward for art does not wait on the postman. He carried this to extremes. That of course is impossible on the face of it. I mean that, in the later years when he finally probably admitted to himself that only the style was left, he worked so hard and so laboriously and so self-sacrificingly at this, that at times he stood a little bigger, a little taller than it was. He was warm, generous, merry and fond of laughing, without pettiness and jealous only of the integrity which he believed to be absolutely necessary in anyone who approached his craft; he was ready to be generous to anyone, once he was convinced that that one approached his craft with his own humility and respect for it. During those New Orleans days and weeks, I gradually became aware that here was a man who would be in seclusion all forenoon—working. Then in the afternoon he would appear and we would walk about the city, talking. Then in the evening we would meet again, with a bottle now, and now he would really talk; the world in minuscule would be there in whatever shadowy courtyard where glass and bottle clinked and the palms hissed like dry sand in whatever moving air. Then tomorrow forenoon and he would be secluded again—working; whereupon I said to myself, 'If this is what it takes to be a novelist, then that's the life for me.'

So I began a novel, *Soldiers' Pay*. I had known Mrs Anderson before I knew him. I had not seen them in some time when I met her on the street. She commented on my absence. I said I was writing a novel. She asked if I wanted Sherwood to see it. I answered, I dont remember exactly what, but to the effect that it would be all right with me if he wanted to. She told me to bring it to her when I finished it, which I did, in about two months. A few days later, she sent for me. She said, 'Sherwood says he'll make a swap with you. He says that if he doesn't have to read it, he'll tell Liveright (Horace Liveright: his own publisher then) to take it.'

'Done,' I said, and that was all. Liveright published the book and I saw Anderson only once more, because the unhappy caricature affair had happened in the meantime and he declined to see me, for several years, until one afternoon at a cocktail party in New York; and again there was that moment when he appeared taller, bigger than anything he ever wrote. Then I remembered *Winesburg, Ohio* and *The Triumph of the Egg* and some of the pieces in *Horses and Men,* and I knew that I had seen, was looking at, a giant in an earth populated to a great—too great—extent by pygmies, even if he did make but the two or perhaps three gestures commensurate with gianthood.

[*Atlantic,* June 1953; the text printed here has been taken from Faulkner's typescript.]

※ ※ ※

Mississippi

MISSISSIPPI begins in the lobby of a Memphis, Tennessee hotel and extends south to the Gulf of Mexico. It is dotted with little towns concentric about the ghosts of the horses and mules once tethered to the hitch-rail enclosing the county courthouse and it might almost be said to have only those two directions, north and south, since until a few years ago it was impossible to travel east or west in it unless you walked or rode one of the horses or mules; even in the boy's early manhood, to reach by rail either of the adjacent county towns thirty miles away to the east or west, you had to travel ninety miles in three different directions on three different railroads.

In the beginning it was virgin—to the west, along the Big River, the alluvial swamps threaded by black almost motionless bayous and impenetrable with cane and buckvine and cypress and ash and oak and gum; to the east, the hardwood ridges and the prairies where the Appalachian mountains died and buffalo grazed; to the south, the pine barrens and the moss-hung liveoaks and the greater swamps less of earth than water and lurking with alligators and water moccasins, where Louisiana in its time would begin.

And where in the beginning the predecessors crept with their simple artifacts, and built the mounds and vanished, bequeathing only the mounds in which the succeeding recordable Algonquian stock would leave the

skulls of their warriors and chiefs and babies and slain
bears, and the shards of pots, and hammer- and arrow-
heads and now and then a heavy silver Spanish spur.
There were deer to drift in herds alarmless as smoke
then, and bear and panther and wolves in the brakes and
bottoms, and all the lesser beasts—coon and possum and
beaver and mink and mushrat (not muskrat: mushrat);
they were still there and some of the land was still virgin
in the early nineteen hundreds when the boy himself began to hunt. But except for looking occasionally out
from behind the face of a white man or a Negro, the
Chickasaws and Choctaws and Natchez and Yazoos were
as gone as the predecessors, and the people the boy crept
with were the descendants of the Sartorises and De
Spains and Compsons who had commanded the Manassas and Sharpsburg and Shiloh and Chickamauga regiments, and the McCaslins and Ewells and Holstons and
Hogganbecks whose fathers and grandfathers had
manned them, and now and then a Snopes too because
by the beginning of the twentieth century Snopeses were
everywhere: not only behind the counters of grubby little side street stores patronised mostly by Negroes, but
behind the presidents' desks of banks and the directors'
tables of wholesale grocery corporations and in the
deaconries of Baptist churches, buying up the decayed
Georgian houses and chopping them into apartments
and on their death-beds decreeing annexes and baptis-
mal fonts to the churches as mementos to themselves or
maybe out of simple terror.

They hunted too. They too were in the camps where
the De Spains and Compsons and McCaslins and Ewells
were masters in their hierarchial turn, shooting the does
not only when law but the Master too said not, shooting
them not even because the meat was needed but leaving

the meat itself to be eaten by scavengers in the woods, shooting it simply because it was big and moving and alien, of an older time than the little grubby stores and the accumulating and compounding money; the boy a man now and in his hierarchial turn Master of the camp and coping, having to cope, not with the diminishing wilderness where there was less and less game, but with the Snopeses who were destroying that little which did remain.

These elected the Bilboes and voted indefatigably for the Vardamans, naming their sons after both; their origin was in bitter hatred and fear and economic rivalry of the Negroes who farmed little farms no larger than and adjacent to their own, because the Negro, remembering when he had not been free at all, was therefore capable of valuing what he had of it enough to struggle to retain even that little and had taught himself how to do more with less: to raise more cotton with less money to spend and food to eat and fewer or inferior tools to work with: this, until he, the Snopes, could escape from the land into the little grubby side street stores where he could live not beside the Negro but on him by marking up on the inferior meat and meal and molasses the price which he, the Negro, could not even always read.

In the beginning, the obsolescent, dispossessed tomorrow by the already obsolete: the wild Algonquian—Chickasaw and Choctaw and Natchez and Pascagoula—looking down from the tall Mississippi bluffs at a Chippeway canoe containing three Frenchmen—and had barely time to whirl and look behind him at a thousand Spaniards come overland from the Atlantic Ocean, and for a little while longer had the privilege of watching an ebb-flux-ebb-flux of alien nationalities as rapid as the magician's spill and evanishment of inconstant cards:

the Frenchman for a second, then the Spaniard for perhaps two, then the Frenchman for another two and then the Spaniard again and then the Frenchman again for that last half-breath before the Anglo-Saxon, who would come to stay, to endure: the tall man roaring with Protestant scripture and boiled whiskey, Bible and jug in one hand and like as not an Indian tomahawk in the other, brawling, turbulent, uxorious and polygamous: a married invincible bachelor without destination but only motion, advancement, dragging his gravid wife and most of his mother-in-law's kin behind him into the trackless wilderness, to spawn that child behind a log-crotched rifle and then get her with another one before they moved again, and at the same time scattering his inexhaustible other seed in three hundred miles of dusky bellies: without avarice or compassion or forethought either: felling a tree which took two hundred years to grow, to extract from it a bear or a capful of wild honey.

He endured, even after he too was obsolete, the younger sons of Virginia and Carolina planters coming to replace him in wagons laden with slaves and indigo seedlings over the very roads he had hacked out with little else but the tomahawk. Then someone gave a Natchez doctor a Mexican cotton seed (maybe with the boll-weevil already in it since, like the Snopes, he too has taken over the southern earth) and changed the whole face of Mississippi, slaves clearing rapidly now the virgin land lurking still (1850) with the ghosts of Murrell and Mason and Hare and the two Harpes, into plantation fields for profit where he, the displaced and obsolete, had wanted only the bear and the deer and the sweetening for his tooth. But he remained, hung on still; he is still there even in the boy's middle-age, living in a log or plank or tin hut on the edge of what remains of the fading wilderness, by and on the tolerance and sometimes even the bounty of the plantation owner to whom, in his intractable way and even with a certain dignity and independence, he is a sycophant, trapping coons and muskrats, now that the bear and the panther are almost gone too, improvident still, felling still the two-hundred-year-old tree even though it has only a coon or a squirrel in it now.

Manning, when that time came, not the Manassas and Shiloh regiments but confederating into irregular bands and gangs owning not much allegiance to anyone or anything, unified instead into the one rite and aim of stealing horses from Federal picket-lines; this in the intervals of raiding (or trying to) the plantation house of the very man to whom he had been the independent sycophant and intended to be again, once the war was over and presuming that the man came back from his Sharpsburg or Chickamauga majority or colonelcy or whatever it had been; trying to, that is, until the major's or colonel's wife or aunt or mother-in-law, who had buried the silver in the orchard and still held together a few of the older slaves, fended him off and dispersed him, and when necessary even shot him, with the absent husband's or nephew's or son-in-law's hunting gun or dueling pistols,—the women, the indomitable, the undefeated, who never surrendered, refusing to allow the Yankee *minie* balls to be dug out of portico column or mantelpiece or lintel, who seventy years later would get up and walk out of *Gone with the Wind* as soon as Sherman's name was mentioned; irreconcilable and enraged and still talking about it long after the weary exhausted men who had fought and lost it gave up trying to make them hush: even in the boy's time the boy himself knowing about Vicksburg and Corinth and exactly where his grandfather's regiment had been at First Manassas before he remembered hearing very much about Santa Claus.

In those days (1901 and -2 and -3 and -4) Santa Claus occurred only at Christmas, not like now, and for the rest of the year children played with what they could find or contrive or make, though just as now, in '51 and -2 and -3 and -4, they still played, aped in miniature, what they had been exposed to, heard or seen or been moved by most. Which was true in the child's time and case too: the indomitable unsurrendered old women holding together still, thirty-five and forty years later, a few of the old house slaves: women too who, like the white ones, declined, refused to give up the old ways and forget the old anguishes. The child himself remembered one of them: Caroline: free these many years but who had declined to leave. Nor would she ever accept in full her weekly Saturday wages, the family never knew why unless the true reason was the one which appeared: for the simple pleasure of keeping the entire family reminded constantly that they were in arrears to her, compelling the boy's grandfather then his father and finally himself in his turn to be not only her banker but her book-keeper too, having got the figure of eighty-nine dollars into her head somehow or for some reason, and though the sum itself altered, sometimes more and sometimes less and sometimes it would be she herself who would be several weeks in arrears, it never changed: one of the children, white or Negro, liable to appear at any time, usually when most of the family would be gathered at a meal, with the message: 'Mammy says to tell you not to forget you owe her eighty-nine dollars.'

To the child, even at that time, she seemed already older than God, calling his grandsire 'colonel' but never the child's father nor the father's brother and sister by anything but their christian names even when they themselves had become grandparents: a matriarch with a score of descendants (and probably half that many more whom she had forgotten or outlived), one of them a boy too, whether a great grandson or merely a grandson even she did not remember, born in the same week with the white child and both bearing the same (the white child's grandsire's) name, suckled at the same black breast and sleeping and eating together and playing together the game which was the most important thing the white child knew at that time since at four and five and six his world was still a female world and he had heard nothing else that he could remember: with empty spools and chips and sticks and a scraped trench filled with well-water for the River, playing over again in miniature the War, the old irremediable battles—Shiloh and Vicksburg, and Brice's Crossroads which was not far from where the child (both of them) had been born, the boy because he was white arrogating to himself the right to be the Confederate General—Pemberton or Johnston or Forrest—twice to the black child's once, else, lacking that once in three, the black one would not play at all.

Not the tall man, he was still the hunter, the man of the woods; and not the slave because he was free now; but that Mexican cotton seed which someone had given the Natchez doctor clearing the land fast now, plowing under the buffalo grass of the eastern prairies and the brier and switch-cane of the creek- and river-bottoms of the central hills and deswamping that whole vast flat alluvial Delta-shaped sweep of land along the Big River, the Old Man: building the levees to hold him off the land long enough to plant and harvest the crop: he taking another foot of scope in his new dimension for every

foot man constricted him in the old: so that the steamboats carrying the baled cotton to Memphis or New Orleans seemed to crawl along the sky itself.

And little steamboats on the smaller rivers too, pene-
trating the Tallahatchie as far up as Wylie's Crossing
above Jefferson. Though most of the cotton from that
section, and on to the east to that point of no economic
return where it was more expedient to continue on east
to the Tombigbee and then south to Mobile, went the
sixty miles overland to Memphis by mule and wagon;
there was a settlement—a tavern of sorts and a smithy and
a few gaunt cabins—on the bluff above Wylie's, at the
exact distance where a wagon or a train of them loaded
with cotton either starting or resuming the journey in
the vicinity of Jefferson, would have to halt for the
night. Or not even a settlement but rather a den, whose
denizens lurked unseen by day in the brakes and thickets
of the river bottom, appearing only at night and even
then only long enough to enter the tavern kitchen where
the driver of the day's cotton wagon sat unsuspecting before the fire, whereupon driver wagon mules and cotton
and all would vanish: the body into the river probably
and the wagon burned and the mules sold days or weeks
later in a Memphis stockyard and the unidentifiable cotton already on its way to the Liverpool mill.

At the same time, sixteen miles away in Jefferson,
there was a pre-Snopes, one of the tall men actually, a
giant of a man in fact: a dedicated lay Baptist preacher
but furious not with a furious unsleeping dream of paradise nor even for universal Order with an upper-case O,
but for simple civic security. He was warned by everyone
not to go in there because not only could he accomplish
nothing, he would very likely lose his own life trying it.
But he did go, alone, talking not of gospel nor God nor

even virtue, but simply selected the biggest and boldest
and by appearance anyway the most villainous there and
said to him: 'I'll fight you. If you lick me, you take what
money I have. If I lick you, I baptise you into my
church': and battered and mauled and gouged that one
into sanctity and civic virtue then challenged the next
biggest and most villainous and then the next; and the
following Sunday baptised the entire settlement in the
river, the cotton wagons now crossing on Wylie's hand-
powered ferry and passing peacefully and unchallenged
on to Memphis until the railroads came and took the
bales away from them.

That was in the seventies. The Negro was a free
farmer and a political entity now; one, he could not sign
his name, was Federal marshal at Jefferson. Afterward he
became the town's official bootlegger (Mississippi was
one of the first to essay the noble experiment, along with
Maine), resuming—he had never really quitted it—his
old allegiance to his old master and gaining his professional name, Mulberry, from the huge old tree behind
Doctor Habersham's drugstore, in the gallery-like tun-
nels among the roots of which he cached the bottled
units of his commerce.

Soon he (the Negro) would even forge ahead in that
economic rivalry with Snopes which was to send Snopes
in droves into the Ku Klux Klan—not the old original
one of the war's chaotic and desperate end which, measured against the desperate times, was at least honest and
serious in its desperate aim, but into the later base one of
the twenties whose only kinship to the old one was the
old name. And a little money to build railroads with
was in the land now, brought there by the man who in
'66 had been a carpet-bagger but who now was a citizen;
his children would speak the soft consonantless Negro

tongue as the children of parents who had lived below the Potomac and Ohio Rivers since Captain John Smith, and their children would boast of their Southern heritage. In Jefferson his name was Redmond. He had found the money with which Colonel Sartoris had opened the local cottonfields to Europe by building his connecting line up to the main railroad from Memphis to the Atlantic Ocean—narrow gauge, like a toy, with three tiny locomotives like toys too, named after Colonel Sartoris's three daughters, each with its silver-plated oilcan engraved with the daughter's christian name: like toys, the standard-sized cars jacked up at the junction then lowered onto the narrow trucks, the tiny locomotive now invisible ahead of its charges so that they appeared in process of being snatched headlong among the fields they served by an arrogant plume of smoke and the arrogant shrieking of a whistle—who, after the inevitable quarrel, finally shot Colonel Sartoris dead on a Jefferson street, driven, everyone believed, to the desperate act by the same arrogance and intolerance which had driven Colonel Sartoris's regiment to demote him from its colonelcy in the fall elections after Second Manassas and Sharpsburg.

So there were railroads in the land now; now couples who had used to go overland by carriage to the River landings and the steamboats for the traditional New Orleans honeymoon, could take the train from almost anywhere. And presently pullmans too, all the way from Chicago and the Northern cities where the cash, the money was, so that the rich Northerners could come down in comfort and open the land indeed: setting up with their Yankee dollars the vast lumbering plants and mills in the southern pine section, the little towns which had been hamlets without change or alteration for fifty

years, booming and soaring into cities overnight above
the stump-pocked barrens which would remain until in
simple economic desperation people taught themselves
to farm pine trees as in other sections they had already
learned to farm corn and cotton.

And Northern lumber mills in the Delta too: the mid-
twenties now and the Delta booming with cotton and
timber both. But mostly booming with simple money:
increment a troglodyte which had fathered twin troglo-
dytes: solvency and bankruptcy, the three of them
booming money into the land so fast that the problem
was how to get rid of it before it whelmed you into suf-
focation. Until in something almost resembling self-
defense, not only for something to spend it on but to bet
the increment from the simple spending on, seven or
eight of the bigger Delta towns formed a baseball league,
presently raiding as far away—and successfully too—for
pitchers and short-stops and slugging outfielders, as the
two major leagues, the boy, a young man now, making
acquaintance with this league and one of the big Northern lumber companies not only coincidentally with one
another but because of one another.

At this time the young man's attitude of mind was
that of most of the other young men in the world who
had been around twenty-one years of age in April, 1917,
even though at times he did admit to himself that he was
possibly using the fact that he had been nineteen on that
day as an excuse to follow the avocation he was coming
more and more to know would be forever his true one:
to be a tramp, a harmless possessionless vagabond. In any
case, he was quite ripe to make the acquaintance, which
began with that of the lumber company which at the
moment was taking a leisurely bankruptcy in a town
where lived a lawyer who had been appointed the ref-

eree in the bankruptcy: a family friend of the young man's family and older than he, yet who had taken a liking to the young man and so invited him to come along for the ride too. His official capacity was that of interpreter, since he had a little French and the defuncting company had European connections. But no interpreting was ever done since the entourage did not go to Europe but moved instead into a single floor of a Memphis hotel, where all—including the interpreter—had the privilege of signing chits for food and theatre tickets and even the bootleg whiskey (Tennessee was in its dry mutation then) which the bellboys would produce, though not of course at the discreet and innocent-looking places clustered a few miles away just below the Mississippi state line, where roulette and dice and blackjack were available.

Then suddenly Mr Sells Wales was in it too, bringing the baseball league with him. The young man never did know what connection (if any) Mr Wales had with the bankruptcy, nor really bothered to wonder, let alone care and ask, not only because he had developed already that sense of *noblesse oblige* toward the avocation which he knew was his true one, which would have been reason enough, but because Mr Wales himself was already a legend in the Delta. Owner of a plantation measured not in acres but in miles and reputedly sole owner of one of the league baseball teams or anyway most of its players, certainly of the catcher and the base-stealing shortstop and the .340 hitting outfielder ravished or pirated it was said from the Chicago Cubs, his ordinary costume seven days a week was a two- or three-days' beard and muddy high boots and a corduroy hunting coat, the tale, the legend telling of how he entered a swank St Louis hotel in that costume late one night and demanded a

room of a dinner jacketed clerk, who looked once at the
beard and the muddy boots but probably mostly at Mr
Wales's face and said they were filled up: whereupon Mr
Wales asked how much they wanted for the hotel and
was told, superciliously, in tens of thousands, and—so
told the legend—drew from his corduroy hip a wad of
thousand dollar bills sufficient to have bought the hotel
half again at the price stated and told the clerk he
wanted every room in the building vacated in ten minutes.

That one of course was apocryphal, but the young
man himself saw this one: Mr Wales and himself having
a leisurely breakfast one noon in the Memphis hotel
when Mr Wales remembered suddenly that his private
ball club was playing one of its most important games at
a town about sixty miles away at three oclock that afternoon and telephoned to the railroad station to have a
special train ready for them in thirty minutes, which it
was: an engine and a caboose: reaching Coahoma about
three oclock with a mile still to the ball park: a man
(there were no taxis at the station at that hour and few
in Mississippi anywhere at that time) sitting behind the
wheel of a dingy though still sound Cadillac car, and Mr
Wales said:

'What do you want for it?'

'What?' the man in the car said.

'Your automobile,' Mr Wales said.

'Twelve fifty,' the man said.

'All right,' Mr Wales said, opening the door.

'I mean twelve hundred and fifty dollars,' the man
said.

'All right,' Mr Wales said, then to the young man:
'Jump in.'

'Hold up here, mister,' the man said.

'I've bought it,' Mr Wales said, getting in too. 'The ball park,' he said. 'Hurry.'

The young man never saw the Cadillac again, though he became quite familiar with the engine and caboose during the next succeeding weeks while the league pennant race waxed hotter and hotter, Mr Wales keeping the special train on call in the Memphis yards as twenty-five years earlier a city-dwelling millionaire might have hacked a carriage and pair to his instant nod, so that it seemed to the young man that he would barely get back to Memphis to rest before they would be rushing once more down the Delta to another baseball game.

'I ought to be interpreting, sometime,' he said once.

'Interpret, then,' Mr Wales said. 'Interpret what this goddamn cotton market is going to do tomorrow, and we can both quit chasing this blank blank sandlot ball team.'

The cotton seed and the lumber mills clearing the rest of the Delta too, pushing what remained of the wilderness further and further southward into the V of Big River and hills. When the young man, a youth of sixteen and seventeen then, was first accepted into that hunting club of which he in his hierarchial time would be Master, the hunting grounds, haunt of deer and bear and wild turkey, could be reached in a single day or night in a mule-drawn wagon. Now they were using automobiles: a hundred miles then two hundred southward and still southward as the wilderness dwindled into the confluence of the Yazoo River and the big one, the Old Man.

The Old Man: all his little contributing streams levee-ed too, along with him, and paying none of the dykes any heed at all when it suited his mood and fancy, gathering water all the way from Montana to Pennsyl-

vania every generation or so and rolling it down the artificial gut of his victims' puny and baseless hoping, piling
the water up, not fast: just inexorable, giving plenty of
time to measure his crest and telegraph ahead, even
warning of the exact day almost when he would enter the
house and float the piano out of it and the pictures off the
walls, and even remove the house itself if it were not
securely fastened down.

Inexorable and unhurried, overpassing one by one his
little confluent feeders and shoving the water into them
until for days their current would flow backward, upstream: as far upstream as Wylie's Crossing above Jefferson. The little rivers were dyked too but back here was
the land of individualists: remnants and descendants of
the tall men now taken to farming, and of Snopeses who
were more than individualists: they were Snopeses, so
that where the owners of the thousand-acre plantations
along the Big River confederated as one man with sandbags and machines and their Negro tenants and wage-
hands to hold the sandboils and the cracks, back here the
owner of the hundred or two hundred acre farm pa-
trolled his section of levee with a sandbag in one hand
and his shotgun in the other, lest his upstream neighbor
dynamite it to save his (the upstream neighbor's) own.

Piling up the water while white man and Negro
worked side by side in shifts in the mud and the rain,
with automobile headlights and gasoline flares and kegs
of whiskey and coffee boiling in fifty-gallon batches in
scoured and scalded oil-drums; lapping, tentative, almost
innocently, merely inexorable (no hurry, his) among
and beneath and between and finally over the frantic
sandbags, as if his whole purpose had been merely to
give man another chance to prove, not to him but to
man, just how much the human body could bear, stand,

endure; then, having let man prove it, doing what he could have done at any time these past weeks if so minded: removing with no haste nor any particular malice or fury either, a mile or two miles of levee and coffee drums and whiskey kegs and gas flares in one sloughing collapse, gleaming dully for a little while yet among the parallel cotton middles until the fields vanished along with the roads and lanes and at last the towns themselves.

Vanished, gone beneath one vast yellow motionless expanse, out of which projected only the tops of trees and telephone poles and the decapitations of human dwelling-places like enigmatic objects placed by inscrutable and impenetrable design on a dirty mirror; and the mounds of the predecessors on which, among a tangle of moccasins, bear and horses and deer and mules and wild turkeys and cows and domestic chickens waited patient in mutual armistice; and the levees themselves, where among a jumble of uxorious flotsam the young continued to be born and the old to die, not from exposure but from simple and normal time and decay, as if man and his destiny were in the end stronger even than the river which had dispossessed him, inviolable by and invincible to, alteration.

Then, having proved that too, he—the Old Man—would withdraw, not retreat: subside, back from the land slowly and inexorably too, emptying the confluent rivers and bayous back into the old vain hopeful gut, but so slowly and gradually that not the waters seemed to fall but the flat earth itself to rise, creep in one plane back into light and air again: one constant stain of yellow-brown at one constant altitude on telephone poles and the walls of gins and houses and stores as though the line had been laid off with a transit and painted in one gigantic unbroken brush-stroke, the earth itself one alluvial inch higher, the rich dirt one inch deeper, drying into long cracks beneath the hot fierce glare of May: but not for long, because almost at once came the plow, the plowing and planting already two months late but that did not matter: the cotton man-tall once more by August and whiter and denser still by picking-time, as if the Old Man said, 'I do what I want to, when I want to. But I pay my way.'

And the boats, of course. They projected above that yellow and liquid plane and even moved upon it: the skiffs and skows of fishermen and trappers, the launches of the United States Engineers who operated the Levee Commission, and one small shallow-draught steamboat steaming in paradox among and across the cotton fields themselves, its pilot not a riverman but a farmer who knew where the submerged fences were, its masthead lookout a mechanic with a pair of pliers to cut the telephone wires to pass the smokestack through: no paradox really, since on the River it had resembled a house to begin with, so that here it looked no different from the baseless houses it steamed among, and on occasion even strained at top boiler pressure to overtake like a mallard drake after a fleeing mallard hen.

But these were not enough, very quickly not near enough; the Old Man meant business indeed this time. So now there began to arrive from the Gulf ports the shrimp trawlers and pleasure cruisers and Coast Guard cutters whose bottoms had known only salt water and the mouths of tidal rivers, to be run still by their salt water crews but conned by the men who knew where the submerged roads and fences were for the good reason that they had been running mule-plow furrows along them or up to them all their lives, sailing among the swollen carcasses of horses and mules and deer and cows and sheep to pluck the Old Man's patient flotsam, black and white, out of trees and the roofs of gins and cotton sheds and floating cabins and the second storey windows of houses and office buildings; then—the salt-water men, to whom land was either a featureless treeless salt-marsh or a snake- and alligator-infested swamp impenetrable with trumpet vine and Spanish moss; some of whom had never even seen the earth into which were driven the spiles supporting the houses they lived in—staying on even after they were no longer needed, as though waiting to see emerge from the water what sort of country it was which bore the economy on which the people—men and women, black and white, more of black than white even, ten to one more—lived whom they had saved; seeing the land for that moment before mule and plow altered it right up to the water's receding edge, then back into the River again before the trawlers and cruisers and cutters became marooned into canted and useless rubble too along with the ruined hencoops and cowsheds and priv- ies; back onto the Old Man, shrunken once more into his normal banks, drowsing and even innocent-looking, as if it were something else beside he who had changed, for a little time anyway, the whole face of the adjacent earth.

They were homeward bound now, passing the river towns, some of which were respectable in age when south Mississippi was a Spanish wilderness: Greenville and Vicksburg, Natchez and Grand- and Petit Gulf (vanished now and even the old site known by a differ- ent name) which had known Mason and one at least of the Harpes and from or on which Murrell had based his abortive slave insurrection intended to efface the white people from the land and leave him emperor of it, the land sinking away beyond the levee until presently you could no longer say where water began and earth stopped: only that these lush and verdant sunny savannahs would no longer bear your weight. The rivers flowed no longer west, but south now, no longer yellow or brown, but black, threading the miles of yellow salt marsh from which on an off-shore breeze mosquitoes came in such clouds that in your itching and burning anguish it would seem to you you could actually see them in faint adumbration crossing the earth, and met tide and then the uncorrupted salt: not the Gulf quite yet but at least the Sound behind the long barrier of the islands—Ship and Horn and Petit Bois, the trawler and cruiser bottoms home again now among the lighthouses and channel markers and shipyards and drying nets and processing plants for fish.

The man remembered that from his youth too: one summer spent being blown innocently over in catboats since, born and bred for generations in the north Mississippi hinterland, he did not recognise the edge of a squall until he already had one. The next summer he returned because he found that he liked that much water, this time as a hand in one of the trawlers, remembering: a four-gallon iron pot over a red bed of charcoal on the foredeck, in which decapitated shrimp boiled among handsful of salt and black pepper, never emptied, never washed and constantly renewed, so that you ate them all day long in passing like peanuts; remembering: the predawn, to be broken presently by the violent near-subtropical yellow-and-crimson day almost like an audible explosion, but still dark for a little while yet, the dark ship creeping onto the shrimp grounds in a soundless sternward swirl of phosphorus like a drowning tumble of fireflies, the youth lying face down on the peak staring into the dark water watching the disturbed shrimp burst outward-shooting in fiery and fading fans like the trails of tiny rockets.

He learned the barrier islands too; one of a crew of five amateurs sailing a big sloop in off-shore races, he learned not only how to keep a hull on its keel and moving but how to get it from one place to another and bring it back: so that, a professional now, living in New Orleans he commanded for pay a power launch belonging to a bootlegger (this was the twenties), whose crew consisted of a Negro cook-deckhand-stevedore and the bootlegger's younger brother: a slim twenty-one or -two year old Italian with yellow eyes like a cat and a silk shirt bulged faintly by an armpit-holstered pistol too small in calibre to have done anything but got them all killed, even if the captain or the cook had dreamed of resisting or resenting trouble if and when it came, which the captain or the cook would extract from the holster and hide at the first opportunity (not concealed really: just dropped into the oily bilge under the engine, where, even though Pete soon discovered where it would be, it was safe because he refused to thrust his hand and arm into the oil-fouled water but instead merely lay about the cockpit, sulking); taking the launch across Pontchartrain and down the Rigolets out to the Gulf, the Sound, then lying-to with no lights showing until the Coast Guard cutter (it ran almost on schedule; theirs was a job too even if it was, comparatively speaking, a hopeless one) made its fast haughty eastward rush, going, they always like to believe, to Mobile, to a dance, then by compass on to the island (it was little more than a sandspit bearing a line of ragged and shabby pines thrashing always in the windy crash and roar of the true Gulf on the other side of it) where the Caribbean schooner would bury the

casks of green alcohol which the bootlegger's mother
back in New Orleans would convert and bottle and label
into scotch or bourbon or gin. There were a few wild
cattle on the island which they would have to watch for,
the Negro digging and Pete still sulking and refusing to
help at all because of the pistol, and the captain watching for the charge (they couldn't risk showing a light)
which every three or four trips would come—the gaunt
wild half-seen shapes charging suddenly and with no
warning down at them as they turned and ran through
the nightmare sand and hurled themselves into the
dinghy, to pull along parallel to the shore, the animals
following, until they had tolled them far enough away
for the Negro to go back ashore for the remaining casks.
Then they would heave-to again and lie until the cutter
passed back westward, the dance obviously over now, in
the same haughty and imperious rush.

That was Mississippi too, though a different one from
where the child had been bred; the people were Catho-
lics, the Spanish and French blood still showed in the
names and faces. But it was not a deep one, if you did not
count the sea and the boats on it: a curve of beach, a thin
unbroken line of estates and apartment hotels owned
and inhabited by Chicago millionaires, standing back to
back with another thin line, this time of tenements inhabited by Negroes and whites who ran the boats and
worked in the fish-processing plants.

Then the Mississippi which the young man knew began: the fading purlieus inhabited by a people whom
the young man recognised because their like was in his
country too: descendants, heirs at least in spirit, of the
tall men, who worked in no factories and farmed no land
nor even truck patches, living not out of the earth but
on its denizens: fishing guides and individual profes-

sional fishermen, trappers of muskrats and alligator hunters and poachers of deer, the land rising now, once more earth instead of half water, vista-ed and arras-ed with the long leaf pines which northern capital would convert into dollars in Ohio and Indiana and Illinois banks. Though not all of it. Some of it would alter hamlets and villages into cities and even build whole new ones almost overnight, cities with Mississippi names but patterned on Ohio and Indiana and Illinois because they were bigger than Mississippi towns, rising, standing today among the tall pines which created them, then tomorrow (that quick, that fast, that rapid) among the stumpy pockage to which they were monuments. Because the land had made its one crop: the soil too fine and light to compete seriously in cotton: until people discovered that it would grow what other soils would not: the tomatoes and strawberries and the fine cane for sugar: not the sorghum of the northern and western counties which people of the true cane country called hog-feed, but the true sweet cane which made the sugar house molasses.

Big towns, for Mississippi: cities, we called them: Hattiesburg, and Laurel, and Meridian, and Canton; and towns deriving by name from further away than Ohio: Kosciusko named after a Polish general who thought that people should be free who wanted to be, and Egypt because there was corn there when it was nowhere else in the bad lean times of the old war which the old women had still never surrendered, and Philadelphia where the Neshoba Indians whose name the county bears still remain for the simple reason that they did not mind living in peace with other people, no matter what their color or politics. This was the hills now: Jones

County which old Newt Knight, its principal proprietor and first citizen or denizen, whichever you liked, seceded from the Confederacy in 1862, establishing still a third republic within the boundaries of the United States until a Confederate military force subdued him in his embattled log-castle capital; and Sullivan's Hollow: a long narrow glen where a few clans or families with North Ireland and Highland names feuded and slew one another in the old pre-Culloden fashion yet banding together immediately and always to resist any outsider in the pre-Culloden fashion too: vide the legend of the revenue officer hunting illicit whiskey stills, captured and held prisoner in a stable and worked in traces as the pair to a plow-mule. No Negro ever let darkness catch him in Sullivan's Hollow. In fact, there were few Negroes in this country at all: a narrow strip of which extended up into the young man's own section: a remote district there through which Negroes passed infrequently and rapidly and only by daylight.

It is not very wide, because almost at once there begins to the east of it the prairie country which sheds its water into Alabama and Mobile Bay, with its old tight intermarried towns and plantation houses columned and porticoed in the traditional Georgian manner of Virginia and Carolina in place of the Spanish and French influence of Natchez. These towns are Columbus and Aberdeen and West Point and Shuqualak, where the good quail shooting is and the good bird dogs are bred and trained—horses too: hunters; Dancing Rabbit is here too, where the treaty dispossessing them of Mississippi was made between the Choctaws and the United States; and in one of the towns lived a kinsman of the young man, dead now, rest him: an invincible and in-

corrigible bachelor, a leader of cotillions and an inveter-
ate diner-out since any time an extra single man was
needed, any hostess thought of him first.

But he was a man's man too, and even more: a young
man's man, who played poker and matched glasses with
the town's young bachelors and the apostates still young
enough in time to still resist the wedlock; who walked
not only in spats and a stick and yellow gloves and a
Homburg hat, but an air of sardonic and inviolable
atheism too, until at last he was forced to the final desperate resort of prayer: sitting after supper one night
among the drummers in the row of chairs on the sidewalk before the Gilmer Hotel, waiting to see what (if
anything) the evening would bring, when two of the
young bachelors passing in a Model T Ford stopped and
invited him to drive across the line into the Alabama
hills for a gallon of moonshine whiskey. Which they did.
But the still they sought was not in hills because these
were not hills: it was the dying tail of the Appalachian
mountain range. But since the Model T's engine had to
be running fast anyway for it to have any headlights, going up the mountain was an actual improvement, especially after they had to drop to low gear. And coming
from the generation before the motor car, it never occurred to him that coming back down would be any
different until they got the gallon and had a drink from
it and turned around and started back down. Or maybe
it was the whiskey, he said, telling it: the little car rushing faster and faster behind a thin wash of light of about
the same volume that two lightning bugs would have
made, around the plunging curves which, the faster the
car ran, became only the more frequent and sharp and
plunging, whipping around the nearly right-angle bends
with a rock wall on one hand and several hundred feet of

vertical and empty night on the other, until at last he prayed; he said: 'Lord, You know I haven't worried You in over forty years, and if You'll just get me back to Columbus I promise never to bother You again.'

And now the young man, middleaged now or anyway middleaging, is back home too where they who altered the swamps and forests of his youth, have now altered the face of the earth itself; what he remembered as dense river bottom jungle and rich farm land, is now an artificial lake twenty-five miles long: a flood control project for the cotton fields below the huge earth dam, with a few more outboard-powered fishing skiffs on it each year, and at last a sailboat. On his way in to town from his home the middleaging (now a professional fiction-writer: who had wanted to remain the tramp and the possessionless vagabond of his young manhood but time and success and the hardening of his arteries had beaten him) man would pass the back yard of a doctor friend whose son was an undergraduate at Harvard. One day the undergraduate stopped him and invited him in and showed him the unfinished hull of a twenty-foot sloop, saying, 'When I get her finished, Mr Bill, I want you to help me sail her.' And each time he passed after that, the undergraduate would repeat: 'Remember, Mr Bill, I want you to help me sail her as soon as I get her in the water:' to which the middleaging would answer as always: 'Fine, Arthur. Just let me know.'

Then one day he came out of the postoffice: a voice called him from a taxicab, which in small Mississippi towns was any motor car owned by any footloose young man who liked to drive, who decreed himself a taxicab as Napoleon decreed himself emperor; in the car with the driver was the undergraduate and a young man whose father had vanished recently somewhere in the West out of the ruins of the bank of which he had been president, and a fourth young man whose type is universal: the town clown, comedian, whose humor is without viciousness and quite often witty and always funny. 'She's in the water, Mr Bill,' the undergraduate said. 'Are you ready to go now?' And he was, and the sloop was too; the undergraduate had sewn his own sails on his mother's machine; they worked her out into the lake and got her on course all tight and drawing, when suddenly it seemed to the middleaging that part of him was no longer in the sloop but about ten feet away, looking at what he saw: a Harvard undergraduate, a taxi-driver, the son of an absconded banker and a village clown and a middleaged novelist sailing a home-made boat on an artificial lake in the depths of the north Mississippi hills: and he thought that that was something which did not happen to you more than once in your life.

Home again, his native land; he was born of it and his bones will sleep in it; loving it even while hating some of it: the river jungle and the bordering hills where still a child he had ridden behind his father on the horse after the bobcat or fox or coon or whatever was ahead of the belling hounds and where he had hunted alone when he got big enough to be trusted with a gun, now the bottom of a muddy lake being raised gradually and steadily every year by another layer of beer cans and bottle caps and lost bass plugs—the wilderness, the two weeks in the woods, in camp, the rough food and the rough sleeping, the life of men and horses and hounds among men and horses and hounds, not to slay the game but to pursue it, touch and let go, never satiety—moved now even further away than that down the flat Delta so that the mile-long freight trains, visible for miles across the fields where the cotton is mortgaged in February,

planted in May, harvested in September and put into
the Farm Loan in October in order to pay off February's
mortgage in order to mortgage next year's crop, seem to
be passing two or even three of the little Indian-named
hamlets at once over the very ground where, a youth
now capable of being trusted even with a rifle, he had
shared in the yearly ritual of Old Ben: the big old bear
with one trap-ruined foot who had earned for himself a
name, a designation like a living man through the legend of the deadfalls and traps he had wrecked and the
hounds he had slain and the shots he had survived, until
Boon Hogganbeck, the youth's father's stable foreman,
ran in and killed it with a hunting knife to save a hound
which he, Boon Hogganbeck, loved.

But most of all he hated the intolerance and injustice:
the lynching of Negroes not for the crimes they committed but because their skins were black (they were becoming fewer and fewer and soon there would be no
more of them but the evil would have been done and
irrevocable because there should never have been any);
the inequality: the poor schools they had then when
they had any, the hovels they had to live in unless they
wanted to live outdoors: who could worship the white
man's God but not in the white man's church; pay taxes
in the white man's courthouse but couldn't vote in it or
for it; working by the white man's clock but having to
take his pay by the white man's counting (Captain Joe
Thoms, a Delta planter though not one of the big ones,
who after a bad crop year drew a thousand silver dollars
from the bank and called his five tenants one by one into
the dining room where two hundred of the dollars were
spread carelessly out on the table beneath the lamp, saying: 'Well, Jim, that's what we made this year.' Then the
Negro: 'Gret God, Cap'n Joe, is all that mine?' And

Captain Thoms: 'No no, just half of it is yours. The other half belongs to me, remember.'); the bigotry which could send to Washington some of the senators and congressmen we sent there and which could erect in a town no bigger than Jefferson five separate denominations of churches but set aside not one square foot of ground where children could play and old people could sit and watch them.

But he loves it, it is his, remembering: the trying to, having to, stay in bed until the crack of dawn would bring Christmas and of the other times almost as good as Christmas; of being waked at three oclock to have breakfast by lamplight in order to drive by surrey into town and the depot to take the morning train for the three or four days in Memphis where he would see automobiles, and the day in 1910 when, twelve years old, he watched John Moisant land a bicycle-wheeled aileronless (you warped the whole wing-tip to bank it or hold it level) Bleriot monoplane on the infield of the Memphis race-track and knew forever after that someday he too would have to fly alone; remembering: his first sweetheart, aged eight, plump and honey-haired and demure and named Mary, the two of them sitting side by side on the kitchen steps eating ice cream; and another one, Minnie this time, grand-daughter of the old hillman from whom, a man himself now, he bought moonshine whiskey, come to town at seventeen to take a job behind the soda counter of the drug store, watching her virginal and innocent and without self-consciousness pour Coca-Cola syrup into the lifted glass by hooking her thumb through the ring of the jug and swinging it back and up in one unbroken motion onto her horizontal upper arm exactly as he had seen her grandfather pour whiskey from a jug a thousand times.

Even while hating it, because for every Joe Thoms with two hundred silver dollars and every Snopes in a hooded nightshirt, somewhere in Mississippi there was this too: remembering: Ned, born in a cabin in the back yard in 1865, in the time of the middleaged's great-grandfather and had outlived three generations of them, who had not only walked and talked so constantly for so many years with the three generations that he walked and talked like them, he had two tremendous trunks filled with the clothes which they had worn—not only the blue brass-buttoned frock coat and the plug hat in which he had been the great-grandfather's and the grandfather's coachman, but the broadcloth frock coats which the great-grandfather himself had worn, and the pigeon-tailed ones of the grandfather's time and the short coat of his father's which the middleaged could re-member on the backs for which they had been tailored, along with the hats in their eighty years of mutation too: so that, glancing idly up and out the library window, the middleaged would see that back, that stride, that coat and hat going down the drive toward the road, and his heart would stop and even turn over. He (Ned) was eighty-four now and in these last few years he had begun to get a little mixed up, calling the middleaged not only 'Master' but sometimes 'Master Murry', who was the middleaged's father, and 'Colonel' too, coming once a week through the kitchen and in to the parlor or per-haps already found there, saying: 'Here's where I wants to lay, right here where I can be facing out that window. And I wants it to be a sunny day, so the sun can come in on me. And I wants you to preach the sermon. I wants you to take a dram of whiskey for me, and lay yourself back and preach the best sermon you ever preached.'

And Caroline too, whom the middleaged had inher-

ited too in his hierarchial turn, nobody knowing anymore exactly how many more years than a hundred she
was but not mixed up, she: who had forgotten nothing,
calling the middleaged 'Memmy' still, from fifty-odd
years ago when that was as close as his brothers could
come to 'William'; his youngest daughter, aged four and
five and six, coming in to the house and saying, 'Pappy,
Mammy said to tell you not to forget you owe her eighty-
nine dollars.'

'I wont,' the middleaged would say. 'What are you all
doing now?'

'Piecing a quilt,' the daughter answered. Which they
were. There was electricity in her cabin now, but she
would not use it, insisting still on the kerosene lamps
which she had always known. Nor would she use the
spectacles either, wearing them merely as an ornament
across the brow of the immaculate white cloth—head-
rag—which bound her now hairless head. She did not
need them: a smolder of wood ashes on the hearth winter and summer in which sweet potatoes roasted, the five-
year-old white child in a miniature rocking chair at one
side of it and the aged Negress, not a great deal larger, in
her chair at the other, the basket bright with scraps and
fragments of cloth between them and in that dim light
in which the middleaged himself could not have read his
own name without his glasses, the two of them with in-
finitesimal and tedious and patient stitches annealing
the bright stars and squares and diamonds into another
pattern to be folded away among the cedar shavings in
the trunk.

Then it was the Fourth of July, the kitchen was closed
after breakfast so the cook and houseman could attend a
big picnic; in the middle of the hot morning the aged
Negress and the white child gathered green tomatoes

from the garden and ate them with salt, and that afternoon beneath the mulberry tree in the back yard the
two of them ate most of a fifteen-pound chilled water-
melon, and that night Caroline had the first stroke. It
should have been the last, the doctor thought so too.
But by daylight she had rallied, and that morning the
generations of her loins began to arrive, from her own
seventy and eighty year old children, down through their
great- and twice-great-grandchildren—faces which the
middleaged had never seen before until the cabin would
no longer hold them: the women and girls sleeping on
the floor inside and the men and boys sleeping on the
ground in front of it, Caroline herself conscious now and
presently sitting up in the bed: who had forgotten nothing: matriarchial and imperial, and more: imperious:
ten and even eleven oclock at night and the middleaged
himself undressed and in bed, reading, when sure enough
he would hear the slow quiet stockinged or naked feet
mounting the back stairs; presently the strange dark face
—never the same one of two nights ago or the two or
three nights before that—would look in the door at him,
and the quiet, courteous, never servile voice would say:
'She want the ice cream.' And he would rise and dress
and drive in to the village; he would even drive through
the village although he knew that everything there will
have long been closed and he would do what he had
done two nights ago: drive thirty miles on to the arterial
highway and then up or down it until he found an open
drive-in or hot-dog stand to sell him the quart of ice
cream.

But that stroke was not the one; she was walking
again presently, even, despite the houseman's standing
order to forestall her with the automobile, all the way in
to town to sit with his, the middleaging's, mother, talk-

ing, he liked to think, of the old days of his father and himself and the three younger brothers, the two of them two women who together had never weighed two hundred pounds in a house roaring with five men: though they probably didn't since women, unlike men, have learned how to live uncomplicated by that sort of sentimentality. But it was as if she knew herself that the summer's stroke was like the throat-clearing sound inside the grandfather clock preceding the stroke of midnight or of noon, because she never touched the last unfinished quilt again. Presently it had vanished, no one knew where, and as the cold came and the shortening days she began to spend more and more time in the house, not her cabin but the big house, sitting in a corner of the kitchen while the cook and houseman were about, then in the middleaging's wife's sewing room until the family gathered for the evening meal, the houseman carrying her rocking chair into the dining room to sit there while they ate: until suddenly (it was almost Christmas now) she insisted on sitting in the parlor until the meal was ready, none knew why, until at last she told them, through the wife: 'Miss Hestelle, when them niggers lays me out, I want you to make me a fresh clean cap and apron to lay in.' That was her valedictory; two days after Christmas the stroke came which was the one; two days after that she lay in the parlor in the fresh cap and apron she would not see, and the middleaging did indeed lay back and preach the sermon, the oration, hoping that when his turn came there would be someone in the world to owe him the sermon which all owed to her who had been, as he had been from infancy, within the scope and range of that fidelity and that devotion and that rectitude.

Loving all of it even while he had to hate some of it

because he knows now that you dont love because: you love despite; not for the virtues, but despite the faults.

[*Holiday,* April 1954; the text printed here has been taken from Faulkner's typescript.]

✿ ✿ ✿

A Guest's Impression
of New England

———————

IT IS NOT the country which impressed this one. It is the people—the men and women themselves so individual, who hold individual integration and privacy as high and dear as they do liberty and freedom; holding these so high that they take it for granted that all other men and women are individuals, too, and treat them as such, doing this simply by letting them alone with absolute and complete dignity and courtesy.

Like this. One afternoon (it was October, the matchless Indian summer of New England) Malcolm Cowley and I were driving through back roads in western Connecticut and Massachusetts. We got lost. We were in what a Mississippian would call mountains but which New Englanders call hills; the road was not getting worse yet: just hillier and lonelier and apparently going nowhere save upward, toward a range of hills. At last, just as we were about to turn back, we found a house, a mailbox, two men, farmers or in the costume of farmers —sheep-lined coats and caps with earflaps tied over the crown—standing beside the mailbox, and watching us quietly and with perfect courtesy as we drove up and stopped.

'Good afternoon,' Cowley said.

'Good afternoon,' one of the men said.

'Does this road cross the mountain?' Cowley said.

'Yes,' the man said, still with that perfect courtesy.

'Thank you,' Cowley said and drove on, the two men still watching us quietly—for perhaps fifty yards, when Cowley braked suddenly and said, 'Wait,' and backed the car down to the mailbox again where the two men still watched us. 'Can I get over it in this car?' Cowley said.

'No,' the same man said. 'I dont think you can.' So we turned around and went back the way we came.

That's what I mean. In the West, the Californian would have been a farmer only by hobby, his true dedication and calling being that of a car trader, who would assure us that our car could not possibly make the crossing but that he had not only a car that could make it, but the only car west of the Rocky Mountains that could do it; in the Central States and the East we would have been given directions to circumvent the mountain, based on obscure third-count road forks and distant houses with lightning rods on the northeast chimney and creek crossings where if you looked carefully you could discern the remains of bridges vanished these forty years ago, which Gabriel himself could not have followed; in my own South the two Mississippians would have adopted us before Cowley could have closed his mouth and put the car in motion again, saying (one of them; the other would already be getting into the car): 'Why sure, it wont be no trouble at all; Jim here will go with you and I'll telephone across the mountain for my nephew to meet you with his truck where you are stuck; it'll pull you right on through and he'll even have a mechanic waiting with a new crankcase.'

But not the New Englander, who respects your right to privacy and free will by telling, giving you only and exactly what you asked for, and no more. If you want to try to take your car over that road, that's your business and not his to ask you why. If you want to wreck it and spend the night on foot to the nearest lighted window or disturbed watchdog, that's your business, too, since it's your car and your legs, and if you had wanted to know if *the car* could cross the mountain, you would have asked that. Because he is free, private, not made so by the stern and rockbound land—the poor thin soil and the hard long winters—on which his lot was cast, but on the contrary: having elected deliberately of his own volition that stern land and weather because he knew he was tough enough to cope with them; having been bred by the long tradition which sent him from old worn-out Europe so he could be free; taught him to believe that there is no valid reason why life should be soft and docile and amenable, that to be individual and private is the thing and that the man who cannot cope with any environment anywhere had better not clutter the earth to begin with.

To stand out against that environment which has done its worst to him, and failed, leaving him not only superior to it but its master, too. He quits it occasionally of course, but he takes it with him, too. You will find him in the Middle West, you will find him in Burbank and Glendale and Santa Monica in sunglasses and straw sandals and his shirt-tail outside his pants. But open the aloha bed-jacket and scratch him a little and you will find the thin soil and the rocks and the long snow and the man who had not at all been driven from his birthplace because it had beaten him at last, but who had left it because he himself was the victor and the spirit was gone with his cooling and slowing blood, and now is simply using that never-never land of mystics and astrologers and fire-worshippers and raw-carrot fiends as a hobby for his declining years.

[*New England Journeys Number 2,* Dearborn, Michigan, 1954; the punctuation of the text printed here has been corrected from an unrevised Faulkner typescript.]

¤ ¤ ¤

An Innocent at Rinkside

THE VACANT ICE looked tired, though it shouldn't have.
They told him it had been put down only ten minutes
ago following a basket-ball game, and ten minutes after
the hockey match it would be taken up again to make
room for something else. But it looked not expectant
but resigned, like the mirror simulating ice in the Xmas
store window, not before the miniature fir trees and
reindeer and cosy lamplit cottage were arranged upon it,
but after they had been dismantled and cleared away.

Then it was filled with motion, speed. To the innocent, who had never seen it before, it seemed discorded
and inconsequent, bizarre and paradoxical like the frantic darting of the weightless bugs which run on the surface of stagnant pools. Then it would break, coalesce
through a kind of kaleidoscopic whirl like a child's toy,
into a pattern, a design almost beautiful, as if an in-
spired choreographer had drilled a willing and patient
and hard-working troupe of dancers—a pattern, design
which was trying to tell him something, say something to
him urgent and important and true in that second before, already bulging with the motion and the speed, it
began to disintegrate and dissolve.

Then he learned to find the puck and follow it. Then
the individual players would emerge. They would not
emerge like the sweating barehanded behemoths from
the troglodyte mass of football, but instead as fluid and

fast and effortless as rapier-thrusts or lightning—Richard with something of the passionate glittering fatal alien quality of snakes, Geoffrion like an agile ruthless precocious boy who maybe couldn't do anything else but then he didn't need to; and others—the veteran Laprade, still with the know-how and the grace. But he had time too now, or rather time had him, and what remained was no longer expendable that recklessly, heedlessly, successfully; not enough of it left now to buy fresh passion and fresh triumph with.

Excitement: men in rapid hard close physical conflict, not just with bare hands, but armed with the knife-blades of skates and the hard fast deft sticks which could break bones when used right. He had noticed how many women were among the spectators, and for just a moment he thought that perhaps this was why—that here actual male blood could flow, not from the crude impact of a heavier fist but from the rapid and delicate stroke of weapons, which like the European rapier or the Frontier pistol, reduced mere size and brawn to its proper perspective to the passion and the will. But only for a moment because he, the innocent, didn't like that idea either. It was the excitement of speed and grace, with the puck for catalyst, to give it reason, meaning.

He watched it—the figure-darted glare of ice, the concentric tiers rising in sections stipulated by the hand-lettered names of the individual fan-club idols, vanishing upward into the pall of tobacco smoke trapped by the roof—the roof which stopped and trapped all that intent and tense watching, and concentrated it downward upon the glare of ice frantic and frenetic with motion; until the by-product of the speed and the motion—their violence—had no chance to exhaust itself upward into space and so leave on the ice only the swift glittering changing pattern. And he thought how perhaps something is happening to sport in America (assuming that by definition sport is something you do yourself, in solitude or not, because it is fun), and that something is the roof we are putting over it and them. Skating, basketball, tennis, track meets and even steeple-chasing have moved indoors; football and baseball function beneath covers of arc lights and in time will be rain- and cold-proofed too. There still remain the proper working of a fly over trout water or the taking of a rise of birds in front of a dog or the right placing of a bullet in a deer or even a bigger animal which will hurt you if you dont. But not for long: in time that will be indoors too beneath lights and the trapped pall of spectator tobacco, the concentric sections bearing the name and device of the lion or the fish as well as that of the Richard or Geoffrion of the scoped rifle or 4-ounce rod.

But (to repeat) not for long, because the innocent did not quite believe that either. We—Americans—like to watch; we like the adrenalic discharge of vicarious excitement or triumph or success. But we like to do also: the discharge of the personal excitement of the triumph and the fear to be had from actually setting the horse at the stone wall or pointing the over-canvassed sloop or finding by actual test if you can line up two sights and one buffalo in time. There must have been little boys in that throng too, frantic with the slow excruciating passage of time, panting for the hour when they would be Richard or Geoffrion or Laprade—the same little Negro boys whom the innocent has seen shadow-boxing in front of a photograph of Joe Louis in his own Mississippi town—the same little Norwegian boys he watched staring up the snowless slope of the Holmenkollen jump one July day in the hills above Oslo.

Only he (the innocent) did wonder just what a professional hockey-match, whose purpose is to make a decent and reasonable profit for its owners, had to do with our National Anthem. What are we afraid of? Is it our national character of which we are so in doubt, so fearful that it might not hold up in the clutch, that we not only dare not open a professional athletic contest or a beauty-pageant or a real-estate auction, but we must even use a Chamber of Commerce race for Miss Sewage Disposal or a wildcat land-sale, to remind us that that liberty gained without honor and sacrifice and held without constant vigilance and undiminished honor and complete willingness to sacrifice again at need, was not worth having to begin with? Or, by blaring or chanting it at ourselves every time ten or twelve or eighteen or twenty-two young men engage formally for the possession of a puck or a ball, or just one young woman walks across a lighted platform in a bathing-suit, do we hope to so dull and eviscerate the words and tune with repetition, that when we do hear it we will not be disturbed from that dream-like state in which 'honor' is a break and 'truth' an angle?

[*Sports Illustrated,* January 24, 1955; the text printed here has been taken from Faulkner's typescript.]

✖ ✖ ✖

Kentucky:
May: Saturday

Three Days to the Afternoon

THREE DAYS BEFORE

THIS SAW BOONE: the bluegrass, the virgin land rolling westward wave by dense wave from the Allegheny gaps, unmarked then, teeming with deer and buffalo about the salt licks and the limestone springs whose water in time would make the fine bourbon whiskey; and the wild men too—the red men and the white ones too who had to be a little wild also to endure and survive and so mark the wilderness with the proofs of their tough survival—Boonesborough, Owenstown, Harrod's and Harbuck's Stations; Kentucky: the dark and bloody ground.

And knew Lincoln too, where the old weathered durable rail fences enclose the green and sacrosanct pace of rounded hills long healed now from the plow, and big old trees to shade the site of the ancient one-room cabin in which the babe first saw light; no sound there now but such wind and birds as when the child first faced the road which would lead to fame and martyrdom—unless perhaps you like to think that the man's voice is somewhere there too, speaking into the scene of his own na-

tivity the simple and matchless prose with which he reminded us of our duties and responsibilities if we wished
to continue as a nation.

And knew Stephen Foster and the brick mansion of
his song; no longer the dark and bloody ground of memory now, but already my old Kentucky home.

TWO DAYS BEFORE

Even from just passing the stables, you carry with you
the smell of liniment and ammonia and straw—the
strong quiet aroma of horses. And even before we reach
the track we can hear horses—the light hard rapid thud
of hooves mounting into crescendo and already fading
rapidly on. And now in the gray early light we can see
them, in couples and groups at canter or hand-gallop
under the exercise boys. Then one alone, at once furious
and solitary, going full out, breezed, the rider hunched
forward, excrescent and precarious, not of the horse
but simply (for the instant) with it, in the conventional
posture of speed—and who knows, perhaps the two of
them, man and horse both: the animal dreaming, hoping that for that moment at least it looked like Whirl-
away or Citation, the boy for that moment at least that
he was indistinguishable from Arcaro or Earl Sande,
perhaps feeling already across his knees the scented
sweep of the victorious garland.

And we ourselves are on the track now, but carefully
and discreetly back against the rail out of the way: now
we are no longer a handful clotting in a murmur of fur-
longs and poles and tenths of a second, but there are a
hundred of us now and more still coming, all craning to
look in one direction into the mouth of the chute. Then

it is as if the gray, overcast, slightly moist post-dawn air itself had spoken above our heads. This time the exercise boy is a Negro, moving his mount at no schooled or calculated gait at all, just moving it rapidly, getting it off the track and out of the way, speaking not to us but to all circumambience: man and beast either within hearing: "Y'awl can git out of the way too now; here's the big horse coming."

And now we can all see him as he enters the chute on a lead in the hand of a groom. The groom unsnaps the lead and now the two horses come on down the now empty chute toward the now empty track, out of which the final end of the waiting and the expectation has risen almost like an audible sound, a suspiration, a sigh.

Now he passes us (there are two of them, two horses and two riders, but we see only one), not just the Big Horse of professional race argot because he does look big, bigger than we know him to be, so that most of the other horses we have watched this morning appear dwarfed by him, with the small, almost gentle, head and the neat small feet and the trim and delicate pasterns which the ancient Arab blood has brought to him, the man who will ride him Saturday (it is Arcaro himself) hunched like a fly or a cricket on the big withers. He is not even walking. He is strolling. Because he is looking around. Not at us. He has seen people; the sycophant adulant human roar has faded behind his drumming feet too many times for us to hold his attention. And not at track either because he has seen track before and it usually looks like this one does from this point (just entering the backstretch): empty. He is simply looking at this track, which is new to him, as the steeplechase rider walks on foot the new course which he will later ride.

He—they—go on, still walking, vanishing at last behind the bulk of the tote board on the other side of the infield; now the glasses are trained and the stop watches appear, but nothing more until a voice says: "They took him in to let him look at the paddock." So we breathe again for a moment.

Because we have outposts now: a scattering of people in the stands themselves who can see the gate, to warn us in time. And do, though when we see him, because of the bulk of the tote board, he is already in full stride, appearing to skim along just above the top rail like a tremendous brown hawk in the flattened bottom of his stoop, into the clubhouse turn still driving; then something seems to happen; not a falter nor check though it is only afterward that we realize that he has seen the gate back into the chute and for an instant thought, not "Does Arcaro want us to go back in there?" but "Do I want to turn off here?" deciding in the next second (one of them: horse or man) no, and now driving again, down to us and past us as if of his own intention he would make up the second or two or three which his own indecision had cost him, a flow, rush, the motion at once long and deliberate and a little ungainly; a drive and power; something a little rawboned, not graceless so much as too busy to bother with grace, like the motion of a big working hunter, once again appearing to skim along just above the top rail like the big diminishing hawk, inflexible and undeviable, voracious not for meat but for speed and distance.

ONE DAY BEFORE

Old Abe's weathered and paintless rails are now the white panels of millionaires running in ruler-straight

lines across the green and gentle swell of the Kentucky
hills; among the ordered and parklike groove the mares
with recorded lineages longer than most humans know
or bother with stand with foals more valuable head for
economic head than slum children. It rained last night;
the gray air is still moist and filled with a kind of lumi-
nousness, lambence, as if each droplet held in airy suspension still its molecule of light, so that the statue
which dominated the scene at all times anyway now
seems to hold dominion over the air itself like a dim sun,
until, looming and gigantic over us, it looks like gold—
the golden effigy of the golden horse, "Big Red" to the
Negro groom who loved him and did not outlive him
very long, Big Red's effigy of course, looking out with
the calm pride of the old manly warrior kings, over the
land where his get still gambol as infants, until the Saturday afternoon moment when they too will wear the
mat of roses in the flash and glare of magnesium; not
just his own effigy, but symbol too of all the long recorded line from Aristides through the Whirlaways and
Count Fleets and Gallant Foxes and Citations: epiphany
and apotheosis of the horse.

THE DAY

Since daylight now we have moved, converged, toward, through the Georgian-Colonial sprawl of the en-
trance, the throne's anteroom, to bear our own acolytes'
office in that ceremonial.

Once the horse moved man's physical body and his
household goods and his articles of commerce from one
place to another. Nowadays all it moves is a part or the

whole of his bank account, either through betting on it or trying to keep owning and feeding it.

So, in a way, unlike the other animals which he has domesticated—cows and sheep and hogs and chickens and dogs (I don't include cats; man has never tamed cats)—the horse is economically obsolete. Yet it still endures and probably will continue to as long as man himself does, long after the cows and sheep and hogs and chickens, and the dogs which control and protect them, are extinct. Because the other beasts and their guardians merely supply man with food, and someday science will feed him by means of synthetic gases and so eliminate the economic need which they fill. While what the horse supplies to man is something deep and profound in his emotional nature and need.

It will endure and survive until man's own nature changes. Because you can almost count on your thumbs the types and classes of human beings in whose lives and memories and experience and glandular discharge the horse has no place. These will be the ones who don't like to bet on anything which involves the element of chance or skill or the unforeseen. They will be the ones who don't like to watch something in motion, either big or going fast, no matter what it is. They will be the ones who don't like to watch something alive and bigger and stronger than man, under the control of puny man's will, doing something which man himself is too weak or too inferior in sight or hearing or speed to do.

These will have to exclude even the ones who don't like horses—the ones who would not touch a horse or go near it, who have never mounted one nor ever intend to; who can and do and will risk and lose their shirts on a horse they have never seen.

So some people can bet on a horse without ever seeing one outside a Central Park fiacre or a peddler's van. And perhaps nobody can watch horses running forever, with a mutuel window convenient, without making a bet. But it is possible that some people can and do do this.

So it is not just betting, the chance to prove with money your luck or what you call your judgment, that draws people to horse races. It is much deeper than that. It is a sublimation, a transference: man, with his admiration for speed and strength, physical power far beyond what he himself is capable of, projects his own desire for physical supremacy, victory, onto the agent—the baseball or football team, the prize fighter. Only the horse race is more universal because the brutality of the prize fight is absent, as well as the attenuation of football or baseball —the long time needed for the orgasm of victory to occur, where in the horse race it is a matter of minutes, never over two or three, repeated six or eight or ten times in one afternoon.

4:29 P.M.

And this too: the song, the brick mansion, matched to the apotheosis: Stephen Foster as handmaiden to the Horse as the band announces that it is now about to be the one thirty minutes past 4 o'clock out of all possible 4 o'clocks on one Saturday afternoon out of all possible Saturday afternoons. The brazen chords swell and hover and fade above the packed infield and the stands as the ten horses parade to post—the ten animals which for the next two minutes will not just symbolize but bear the burden and be the justification, not just of their individual own three years of life, but of the generations of selection and breeding and training and care which brought them to this one triumphant two minutes where one will be supreme and nine will be supreme failures—brought to this moment which will be supreme for him, the apex of his life which, even counted in lustra, is only twenty-one years old, the beginning of manhood. Such is the price he will pay for the supremacy; such is the gamble he will take. But what human being would refuse that much loss, for that much gain, at twenty-one?

Only a little over two minutes: one simultaneous metallic clash as the gates spring. Though you do not really know what it was you heard: whether it was that metallic crash, or the simultaneous thunder of the hooves in that first leap or the massed voices, the gasp, the exhalation—whatever it was, the clump of horses indistinguishable yet, like a brown wave dotted with the bright silks of the riders like chips flowing toward us along the rail until, approaching, we can begin to distinguish individuals, streaming past us now as individual horses—horses which (including the rider) once stood about eight feet tall and ten feet long, now look like arrows twice that length and less than half that thickness, shooting past and bunching again as perspective diminishes, then becoming individual horses once more around the turn into the backstretch, streaming on, to bunch for the last time into the homestretch itself, then again individuals, individual horses, the individual horse, the Horse: 2:01:4/5 minutes.

And now he stands beneath the rose escarpment above the flash and glare of the magnesium and the whirring film of celluloid immortality. This is the moment, the peak, the pinnacle; after this, all is ebb. We who watched have seen too much; expectation, the glandular pressure, has been too high to long endure; it is evening, not only of the day but the emotional capacity too; Boots and Saddles will sound twice more and condensations of light and movement will go through the motions of horses and jockeys again. But they will run as though in dream, toward anticlimax; we must turn away now for a little time, even if only to assimilate, get used to living with, what we have seen and experienced. Though we have not yet escaped that moment. Indeed, this may be the way we will assimilate and endure it: the voices, the talk, at the airports and stations from which we scatter back to where our old lives wait for us, in the aircraft and trains and buses carrying us back toward the old comfortable familiar routine like the old comfortable hat or coat: porter, bus driver, pretty stenographer who has saved for a year, scanted Christmas probably, to be able to say "I saw the Derby," the sports editor who, having spent a week talking and eating and drinking horse and who now wants only to get home and have a double nightcap and go to bed, all talking, all with opinions, valid and enduring:

"That was an accident. Wait until next time."

"What next time? What horse will they use?"

"If I had been riding him, I would have rode him different."

"No, no, he was ridden just right. It was that little shower of rain made the track fast like California."

"Or maybe the rain scared him, since it don't rain in L.A.? Maybe when he felt wet on his feet he thought he was going to sink and he was just jumping for dry land, huh?"

And so on. So it is not the Day after all. It is only the eighty-first one.

[*Sports Illustrated,* May 16, 1955]

❅ ❅ ❅

On Privacy

(The American Dream: What Happened to It?)

THIS WAS the American Dream: a sanctuary on the earth for individual man: a condition in which he could be free not only of the old established closed-corporation hierarchies of arbitrary power which had oppressed him as a mass, but free of that mass into which the hierarchies of church and state had compressed and held him individually thralled and individually impotent.

A dream simultaneous among the separate individuals of men so asunder and scattered as to have no contact to match dreams and hopes among the old nations of the Old World which existed as nations not on citizenship but subjectship, which endured only on the premise of size and docility of the subject mass; the individual men and women who said as with one simultaneous voice: 'We will establish a new land where man can assume that every individual man—not the mass of men but individual men—has inalienable right to individual dignity and freedom within a fabric of individual courage and honorable work and mutual responsibility.'

Not just an idea, but a condition: a living human condition designed to be coeval with the birth of America itself, engendered created and simultaneous with the very air and word America, which at that one stroke, one instant, should cover the whole earth with one simultaneous suspiration like air or light. And it was, it did: radiating outward to cover even the old weary repudiated still-thralled nations, until individual men everywhere, who had no more than heard the name, let alone knew where America was, could respond to it, lifting up not only their hearts but the hopes too which until now they did not know—or anyway dared not remember—that they possessed.

A condition in which every man would not only not be a king, he wouldn't even want to be one. He wouldn't even need to bother to need to be the equal of kings because now he was free of kings and all their similar congeries; free not only of the symbols but of the old arbitrary hierarchies themselves which the puppet-symbols represented—courts and cabinets and churches and schools—to which he had been valuable not as an individual but only as that integer, his value compounded in that immutable ratio to his sheer mindless numbers, that animal increase of his will-less and docile mass.

The dream, the hope, the condition which our forefathers did not bequeath to us, their heirs and assigns, but rather bequeathed us, their successors, to the dream and the hope. We were not even given the chance then to accept or decline the dream, for the reason that the dream already owned and possessed us at birth. It was not our heritage because we were its, we ourselves heired in our successive generations to the dream by the idea of the dream. And not only we, their sons born and bred in America, but men born and bred in the old alien repudiated lands, also felt that breath, that air, heard that promise, that proffer that there was such a thing as hope for individual man. And the old nations themselves, so old and so long-fixed in the old concepts of man as to have thought themselves beyond all hope of change, making oblation to that new dream of that new concept of man by gifts of monuments and devices to mark the portals of that inalienable right and hope: 'There is room for you here from about the earth, for all ye individually homeless, individually oppressed, individually unindividualised.'

A free gift left to us by those who had mutually travailed and individually endured to create it; we, their successors, did not even have to earn, deserve it, let alone win it. We did not even need to nourish and feed it. We needed only to remember that, living, it was therefore perishable and must be defended in its crises. Some of us, most of us perhaps, could not have proved by definition that we knew exactly what it was. But then, we didn't need to: who no more needed to define it than we needed to define that air we breathed or that word, which, the two of them, simply by existing simultaneously—the breathing of the American air which made America—together had engendered and created the dream on that first day of America as air and motion created temperature and climate on the first day of time.

Because that dream was man's aspiration in the true meaning of the word aspiration. It was not merely the blind and voiceless hope of his heart: it was the actual inbreathe of his lungs, his lights, his living and unsleeping metabolism, so that we actually lived the Dream. We did not live *in* the dream: we lived the Dream itself, just as we do not merely live *in* air and climate, but we live Air and Climate; we ourselves individually representative of the Dream, the Dream itself actually audible in the strong uninhibited voices which were not afraid to speak *cliché* at the very top of them, giving to the *cliché*-avatars of 'Give me liberty or give me death' or 'This to be self-evident that all individual men were created equal in one mutual right to freedom' which had never lacked for truth anyway, assuming that hope and dignity are truth, a validity and immediacy absolving them even of *cliché*.

That was the Dream: not man created equal in the sense that he was created black or white or brown or yellow and hence doomed irrevocably to that for the remainder of his days—or rather, not doomed with equality but blessed with equality, himself lifting no hand but instead lying curled and drowsing in the warm and airless bath of it like the yet-wombed embryo; but liberty in which to have an equal start at equality with all other men, and freedom in which to defend and preserve that equality by means of the individual courage and the honorable work and the mutual responsibility. Then we lost it. It abandoned us, which had supported and protected and defended us while our new nation of new concepts of human existence got a firm enough foothold to stand erect among the nations of the earth, demanding nothing of us in return save to remember always that, being alive, it was therefore perishable and so must be held always in the unceasing responsibility and vigilance of courage and honor and pride and humility. It is gone now. We dozed, slept, and it abandoned us. And in that vacuum now there sound no longer the strong loud voices not merely unafraid but not even aware that fear existed, speaking in mutual unification of one mutual hope and will. Because now what we hear is a cacophony of terror and conciliation and compromise babbling only the mouthsounds; the loud and empty words which we have emasculated of all meaning whatever—freedom, democracy, patriotism—with which, awakened at last, we try in desperation to hide from ourselves that loss.

Something happened to the Dream. Many things did. This, I think, is a symptom of one of them.

About ten years ago a well-known literary critic and essayist, a good friend of long standing, told me that a wealthy widely-circulated weekly pictorial magazine had offered him a good price to write a piece about me—not about my work or works, but about me as a private citizen, an individual. I said No, and explained why: my belief that only a writer's works were in the public domain, to be discussed and investigated and written about, the writer himself having put them there by submitting them for publication and accepting money for them; and therefore he not only would but must accept whatever the public wished to say or do about them from praise to burning. But that, until the writer committed a crime or ran for public office, his private life was his own; and not only had he the right to defend his privacy, but the public had the duty to do so since one man's liberty must stop at exactly the point where the next one's begins; and that I believed that anyone of taste and responsibility would agree with me.

But the friend said No. He said: 'You are wrong. If I do the piece, I will do it with taste and responsibility. But if you refuse me, sooner or later someone will do it who will not bother about taste or responsibility either, who will care nothing about you or your status as a writer, an artist, but only as a commodity: merchandise: to be sold, to increase circulation, to make a little money.'

'I dont believe it,' I said. 'Until I commit a crime or

announce for office, they cant invade my privacy after I ask them not to.'

'They not only can,' he said, 'but once your European reputation gets back here and makes you financially worth it, they will. Wait and see.'

I did. I did both. Two years ago, by mere chance during a talk with an editor in the house which publishes my books, I learned that the same magazine had already set on foot the same project which I had declined eight years before; I dont know whether the publishers were formally notified or if they just heard about it by chance too, as I did. I said No again, recapitulating the same reasons which I still believed were not even arguable by anyone possessing the power of the public press, since the qualities of taste and responsibility would have to be inherent in that power for it to be valid and allowed to endure. The editor interrupted.

'I agree with you,' he said. 'Besides, you dont need to give me reasons. The simple fact that you dont want it done is enough. Shall I attend to it for you?' So he did, or tried to. Because my critic friend was still right. Then I said,

'Try them again. Say "I ask you: please dont." ' Then I submitted the same *I ask you: please dont* to the writer who was to do the piece. I dont know whether he was a staff writer designated to the job, or whether he volunteered for it or perhaps himself sold his employers on the idea. Though my recollection is that his answer implied 'I've got to, If I refuse they will fire me.' Which is probably correct, since I got the same answer from a staff-member of another magazine on the same subject. And if that was so, if the writer, a member of the craft he served, was victim too of that same force of which I was victim—that irresponsible use which is therefore misuse and which in its turn is betrayal, of that power called Freedom of the Press which is one of the most potent and priceless of the defenders and preservers of human dignity and rights—then the only defense left me was to refuse to co-operate, have anything to do with the project at all. Though by now I knew that that would not save me, that nothing I could do would stop them.

Perhaps they—the writer and his employer—didn't believe me, could not believe me. Perhaps they dared not believe me. Perhaps it is impossible now for any American to believe that anyone not hiding from the police could actually not want, as a free gift, his name and photograph in any printed organ, no matter how base or modest or circumscribed in circulation. Though perhaps the matter never reached this point: that both of them— the publisher and the writer—knew from the first, whether I did or not, that the three of us, the two of them and their victim, were all three victims of that fault (in the sense that the geologist uses the term) in our American culture which is saying to us daily: 'Beware!', the three of us faced as one not with an idea, a principle of choice between good and bad taste or responsibility or lack of it, but with a fact, a condition in our American life before which all three of us were (at that moment) helpless, at that moment doomed.

So the writer came with his group, force, crew, and got his material where and how he could and departed and published his article. But that's not the point. The writer is not to be blamed since, empty-handed, he would (if my recollection is right) have been fired from the job which deprived him of the right to choose between good and bad taste. Nor the employer either since, to hold his (the employer's) precarious own in a craft can compel even him, head and chief of one of its integral components, to serve the mores of the hour in order to survive among his rival ones.

It's not what the writer said, but that he said it. That he—they—published it, in a recognised organ which, to be and remain recognised, functions on the assumption of certain inflexible standards; published it not only over the subject's protests but with complete immunity to them; an immunity not merely assumed to itself by the organ but an immunity already granted in advance by the public to which it sold its wares for a profit. The terrifying (not shocking; we cannot be shocked by it since we permitted its birth and watched it grow and condoned and validated it and even use it individually for our own private ends at need) thing is that it could have happened at all under those conditions. That it could have happened at all with its subject not even notified in advance. And even when he, the victim, was warned by accident in advance, he was still completely helpless to prevent it. And even after it was done, the victim had no recourse whatever since, unlike sacrilege and obscenity, we have no laws against bad taste, perhaps because in a democracy the majority of the people who make the laws dont recognise bad taste when they see it, or perhaps because in our democracy bad taste has been converted into a marketable and therefore taxable and therefore lobbyable commodity by the merchandising federations which at the same simultaneous time create the market (not the appetite: that did not need creating: only pandering to) and the product to serve it, and bad taste by simple solvency was purified of bad taste and absolved. And even if there had been grounds for recourse, the matter would still have remained on the black side of the ledger since the publisher could charge the judgment and costs to operating loss and the increased sales from the publicity to capital investment.

The point is that in America today any organization or group, simply by functioning under a phrase like Freedom of the Press or National Security or League Against Subversion, can postulate to itself complete immunity to violate the individualness—the individual privacy lacking which he cannot be an individual and lacking which individuality he is not anything at all worth the having or keeping—of anyone who is not himself a member of some organization or group numerous enough or rich enough to frighten them off. That organization will not be of writers, artists, of course; being individuals, not even two artists could ever confederate, let alone enough of them. Besides, artists in America dont have to have privacy because they dont need to be artists as far as America is concerned. America doesn't need artists because they dont count in America; artists have no more place in American life than the employers of the weekly pictorial magazine staff-writers have in the private life of a Mississippi novelist. But there are the other two occupations which are valuable to American life, which require, demand privacy in order to endure, live. These are science and the humanities, the scientists and the humanitarians: the pioneers in the science of endurance and mechanical craftsmanship and self-discipline and skill like Colonel Lindbergh who was compelled at last to repudiate it by the nation and culture one of whose mores was an inalienable right to violate his privacy instead of an inviolable duty to defend it, the nation which assumed an inalienable right to arrogate to itself the glory of his renown yet which had neither the power to protect his children nor the responsibility to shield his grief; the pioneers in the simple science of saving the nation like Doctor Oppenheimer who was harassed and impugned through those same mores until all privacy was stripped from him and there remained only the qualities of individualism whose possession we boast since they alone differ us from animals—gratitude for kindness, fidelity to friendship, chivalry toward women and the capacity to love—before which even his officially vetted harassers were impotent, turning away themselves (one hopes) in shame, as though the whole business had had nothing whatever to do with loyalty or disloyalty or security or insecurity, but was simply to batter and strip him completely naked of the privacy lacking which he could never have become one of that handful of individuals capable of serving the nation at a moment when apparently nobody else was, and so reduce him at last to one more identityless integer in that identityless anonymous unprivacied mass which seems to be our goal.

And even that is only a point of departure. Because the sickness itself goes much further back. It goes back to that moment in our history when we decided that the old simple moral verities over which taste and responsibility were the arbiters and controls, were obsolete and to be discarded. It goes back to that moment when we repudiated the meaning which our fathers had stipulated for the words 'liberty' and 'freedom' on and by and to which they founded us as a nation and dedicated us as a people, ourselves in our time keeping only the mouthsounds of them. It goes back to the moment when we substituted license in the place of liberty—license for any action which kept within the proscription of laws promulgated by confederations of the practitioners of the license and the harvesters of the material benefits. It goes back to that moment when in place of freedom we substituted immunity for any action to any recourse, provided merely that the act be performed beneath the aegis of the empty mouthsound of freedom.

At which instant truth vanished too. We didn't abolish truth; even we couldn't do that. It simply quit us, turned its back on us, not in scorn nor even contempt nor even (let us hope) despair. It just simply quit us, to return perhaps when whatever it will be—suffering, national disaster, maybe even (if nothing else will serve) military defeat—will have taught us to prize truth and pay any price, accept any sacrifice (oh yes, we are brave and tough too; we just intend to put off having to be as long as possible) to regain and hold it again as we should never have let it go: on its own compromiseless terms of taste and responsibility. Truth—that long clean clear simple undeviable unchallengeable straight and shining line, on one side of which black is black and on the other white is white, has now become an angle, a point of view having nothing to do with truth nor even with fact, but depending solely on where you are standing when you look at it. Or rather—better—where you can contrive to have him standing whom you are trying to fool or obfuscate when he looks at it.

Across the board in fact, a parlay, a daily triple: truth and freedom and liberty. The American sky which was once the topless empyrean of freedom, the American air which was once the living breath of liberty, are now become one vast down-crowding pressure to abolish them both, by destroying man's individuality as a man by (in that turn) destroying the last vestige of privacy without which man cannot be an individual. Our very architecture itself has warned us. Time was when you could see neither from inside nor from outside through the walls of our houses. Time is when you can see from inside out though still not from outside in through the walls.

Time will be when you can do both. Then privacy will indeed be gone; he who is individual enough to want it even to change his shirt or bathe in, will be cursed by one universal American voice as subversive to the American way of life and the American flag.

If (by that time) walls themselves, opaque or not, can still stand before that furious blast, that force, that power rearing like a thunder-clap into the American zenith, multiple-faced yet mutually conjunctived, bellowing the words and phrases which we have long since emasculated of any significance or meaning other than as tools, implements, for the further harassment of the private individual human spirit, by their furious and immunised high priests: 'Security'. 'Subversion'. 'Anti-Communism'. 'Christianity'. 'Prosperity'. 'The American Way'. 'The Flag'.

With odds at balance (plus a little fast footwork now and then of course) one individual can defend himself from another individual's liberty. But when powerful federations and organizations and amalgamations like publishing corporations and religious sects and political parties and legislative committees can absolve even one of their working units of the restrictions of moral responsibility by means of such catch-phrases as 'Freedom' and 'Salvation' and 'Security' and 'Democracy', beneath which blanket absolution the individual salaried practitioners are themselves freed of individual responsibility and restraint, then let us beware. Then even people like Doctor Oppenheimer and Colonel Lindbergh and me (the weekly magazine staff-writer too if he really was compelled to choose between good taste and starvation) will have to confederate in our turn to preserve that privacy in which alone the artist and scientist and humanitarian can function.

Or to preserve life itself, breathing; not just artists and scientists and humanitarians, but the parents by law or biology of doctors of osteopathy too. I am thinking of course of the Cleveland doctor convicted recently of the brutal slaying of his wife, three of whose parents—his wife's father and his own father and mother—with one exception did not even outlive that trial regarding which the Press itself, which kept the sorry business on most of the nation's front pages up to the very end, is now on record as declaring that it was overcovered far beyond its value and importance. I am thinking of the three victims. Not the convicted man: he will doubtless live a long time yet; but of the three parents, two of whom died—one of them anyway—because, to quote the Press itself 'he was wearied of life', and the third one, the mother, by her own hand, as though she had said *I can bear no more of this*. Perhaps they died solely because of the crime, though one wonders why the coincidence of their deaths was not with the commission of the murder but with the publicity of the trial. And if it was not solely because of the tragedy itself that one of the victims was, quote, 'wearied of life' and another obviously said *I can bear no more*—if they had more than that one reason to relinquish and (one) even repudiate life, and the man was guilty as the jury said he was, just what medieval witch-hunt did that power called Freedom of the Press, which in any civilised culture must be accepted as that dedicated paladin through whose inflexible rectitude truth shall prevail and justice and mercy be done, condone and abet that the criminal's very progenitors be eliminated from the earth in expiation of his crime? And if he was innocent as he said he was, what crime did that champion of the weak and the oppressed itself participate in?

Or (to repeat) not the artist. America has not yet found any place for him who deals only in things of the human spirit except to use his notoriety to sell soap or cigarettes or fountain pens or to advertise automobiles and cruises and resort hotels, or (if he can be taught to contort fast enough to meet the standards) in radio or moving pictures where he can produce enough income tax to be worth attention. But the scientist and the humanitarian, yes: the humanitarian in science and the scientist in the humanity of man, who might yet save that civilization which the professionals at saving it—the publishers who condone their own battening on man's lust and folly, the politicians who condone their own trafficking in his stupidity and greed, and the churchmen who condone their own trading on his fear and superstition—seem to be proving that they cant.

[*Harper's,* July 1955; the text printed here has been taken from Faulkner's typescript.]

⌘ ⌘ ⌘

Impressions of Japan

THE ENGINES are long since throttled back; the overcast sinks slowly upward with no semblance whatever of speed until suddenly you see the aircraft's shadow scudding the cottony hillocks; and now speed has returned again, aircraft and shadow now rushing toward one another as toward one mutual headlong destruction.

To break through the overcast and fling that shadow once more down, upon an island. It looks like land, like any other air-found landfall, yet you know it is an island, almost as if you saw both sea-bound flanks of it at the same instant, like a transparent slide; an island more miraculously found in the waste of water than Wake or Guam even, since here is a civilization, an ordered and ancient homogeny of the human race.

*   *   *

It is visible and audible, spoken and written too: a communication between man and man because humans speak it; you hear and see them. But to this one western ear and eye it means nothing because it resembles nothing which that western eye remembers; there is nothing to measure it against, nothing for memory and habit to say, 'Why, this looks like the word for house or home or happiness;' not even just cryptic but acrostic too, as though the splashed symbols of the characters held not mere communication but something urgent and important beyond just information, promising toward some ultimate wisdom or knowledge containing the secret of man's salvation. But then no more, because there is nothing for western memory to measure it against: so not the mind to listen but only the ear to hear that chirrup and skitter of syllables like the cries of birds in the mouths of children, like music in the mouths of women and young girls.

*   *   *

The faces: Van Gogh and Manet would have loved them: that of the pilgrim with staff and pack and dusty with walking, mounting the stairs toward the Temple in the early sunlight; the Temple lay-brother or perhaps servant, his gown tucked about his thighs, squatting in the gate of the compound before beginning, or perhaps having already set it into motion, the day; that of the old woman vending peanuts beneath the gate for tourists to feed the pigeons with: a face worn with living and re-membering, as though not one life had been long enough but rather every separate breath had been needed to etch into it all those fine and myriad lines; a face durable and now even a comfort to her, as if it had by now blotted up whatever had ever ached or sorrowed behind it, leaving it free now of the anguishes and the griefs and the enduring: here is one anyway who never read Faulkner and neither knows nor cares why he came to Japan nor gives one single damn what he thinks of Ernest Hemingway.

*   *   *

He is much too busy to have time to bother about whether he is happy or not, quite dirty, perhaps five years old, pastless and apparently immune even from parents, playing in the gutter with the stub of a ciga-rette.

*   *   *

The bowl of mountains containing the lake is as full of hard rapid air as the mouth of a wind-tunnel; for some time now we have been thinking that maybe it is already too late to take a reef in the mainsail: yet there it is. It is only a skiff yet to the western eye it is as invincibly and irrevocably alien as a Chinese junk, driven by a battered U.S. made outboard engine and containing a woman in a kimono beneath an open paper parasol such as would have excited no comment in a sunny reach of the English Thames, as fragile and invulnerable in the center of that hard blue bowl of wind as a butterfly in the eye of a typhoon.

*   *   *

The geisha's mass of blue-black lacquered hair encloses the painted face like a helmet, surmounts, crowns the slender body's ordered and ritual posturing like a grenadier's bearskin busby, too heavy in appearance for that slender throat to bear, the painted fixed expressionless face immobile and immune also above the studied posturing: yet behind that painted and lifeless mask is something quick and alive and elfin: or more than elfin: puckish: or more than puckish even: sardonic and quizzical, a gift for comedy, and more: for burlesque and caricature: for a sly and vicious revenge on the race of men.

*   *   *

Kimono. It covers her from throat to ankles; with a gesture as feminine as the placing of a flower or as female as the cradling of a child, the hands themselves can be concealed into the sleeves until there remains one unbroken chalice-shape of modesty proclaiming her femininity where nudity would merely parade her mammalian femaleness. A modesty which flaunts its own immodestness like the crimson rose tossed by no more than one white flick of hand, from the balcony window—

modesty, than which there is nothing more immodest and which therefore is a woman's dearest possession; she should defend it with her life.

* * *

Loyalty. In her western clothes, blouse and skirt, she is merely one more dumpy and nondescript young woman though in kimono at the deft balanced rapid tripping glide she too comes into her own share of that national heritage of feminine magic. Though she has more than that; she partakes of her share of that other quality which women have in this land which was not given them by what they have on: loyalty, constancy, fidelity, not for, but at least one hopes not without, reward. She does not speak my language nor I hers, yet in two days she knows my countryman's habit of waking soon after first light so that each morning when I open my eyes a coffee tray is already on the balcony table; she knows I like a fresh room to breakfast in when I return from walking, and it is so: the room done for the day and the table set and the morning paper ready; she asks without words why I have no clothes to be laundered today, and without words asks permission to sew the buttons and darn the socks; she calls me wise man and teacher, who am neither, when speaking of me to others; she is proud to have me for her client and, I hope, pleased that I try to deserve that pride and match with courtesy that loyalty. There is a lot of loose loyalty in this land. Even a little of it is too valuable to be ignored. I would wish that all of it were deserved or at least appreciated as I have tried to do.

* * *

This is the same rice paddy which I know back home in Arkansas and Mississippi and Louisiana, where it replaces now and then the cotton. This one is merely a little smaller and a little more fiercely cultivated, right up to the single row of beans which line the very edge of the irrigation canals, the work here done by hand where in my country machines do it since we have more machines than we have people; nature is the same: only the economy is different.

And the names are the same names too: Jonathan and Winesap and Delicious; the heavy August foliage is blue-gray with the same spray which we use. But there the resemblance ceases: every single apple enclosed in its twist of paper until that whole tree to this western eye becomes significant and festive and ceremonial like the symbolical tree of the western rite of Christmas. Only it is more significant here: where in the West there is one small often artificial tree to a family, wrested from the living dirt to be decked in ritual tinsel and then to die as though the tree were not the protagonist of a rite but the victim of a sacrifice, here not one tree to a family but every tree of all is dressed and decked to proclaim and salute older gods than Christ: Demeter and Ceres.

*   *   *

Briefer and faster now, toward the journey's nearing end: goldenrod, as evocative of dust and autumn and hay fever as ever in Mississippi, against a tall bamboo fence.

The scenery is beautiful but the faces are better still.

The swift supple narrow grace with which the young girl bows and in that same one flowing motion recovers, tougher through very tenderness than the rigid culture which bent her as is the willow bough itself to the hard gust which can never do more than sway it.

The tools they use evoke the ones Noah must have built his ark with, yet the framework of the house seems to rise and stand without nails in the fitted joints nor even the need for nails, as if here were a magic, an art in the simple building of man's habitations which our western ancestors seemed to have lost somewhere when they moved.

And always the water, the sound, the plash and drip of it, as if here were a people making constant oblation to water as some peoples do to what they call their luck.

So kind the people that with three words the guest can go anywhere and live: Gohan: Sake: Arrigato. And one more word:

Tomorrow now the aircraft lightens, a moment more and the wheels will wrench free of the ground, already dragging its shadow back toward the overcast before the wheels are even tucked up, into the overcast and then through it, the land, the island gone now which memory will always know though eye no longer remembers. Sayonara.

[Press release by the United States Embassy in Tokyo, 1955; collected in *Faulkner at Nagano*, ed. Robert A. Jelliffe, Tokyo, 1956, from which the text printed here has been taken, with corrections from an incomplete Faulkner typescript.]

❈ ❈ ❈

To the Youth of Japan

A HUNDRED YEARS ago, my country, the United States, was not one economy and culture, but two of them, so opposed to each other that ninety-five years ago they went to war against each other to test which one should prevail. My side, the South, lost that war, the battles of which were fought not on neutral ground in the waste of the ocean, but in our own homes, our gardens, our farms, as if Okinawa and Guadalcanal had been not islands in the distant Pacific but the precincts of Honshu and Hokkaido. Our land, our homes were invaded by a conqueror who remained after we were defeated; we were not only devastated by the battles which we lost, the conqueror spent the next ten years after our defeat and surrender despoiling us of what little war had left. The victors in our war made no effort to rehabilitate and reestablish us in any community of men or of nations.

But all this is past; our country is one now. I believe our country is even stronger because of that old anguish since that very anguish taught us compassion for other peoples whom war has injured. I mention it only to explain and show that Americans from my part of America at least can understand the feeling of the Japanese young people of today that the future offers him nothing but hopelessness, with nothing anymore to hold to or believe in. Because the young people of my country during those ten years must have said in their turn: "What shall we do now? Where shall we look for future? Who can tell us what do to, how to hope and believe?"

I would like to think that there was someone there at that time too, to speak to them out of what little of experience and knowledge a few more years might have added to what he had, to reassure them that man is tough, that nothing, nothing—war, grief, hopelessness, despair—can last as long as man himself can last; that man himself will prevail over all his anguishes, provided he will make the effort to; make the effort to believe in man and in hope—to seek not for a mere crutch to lean on, but to stand erect on his own feet by believing in hope and in his own toughness and endurance.

I believe that is the only reason for art—for the music, the poetry, the painting—which man has produced and is still ready to dedicate himself to. That art is the strongest and most durable force man has invented or discovered with which to record the history of his invincible durability and courage beneath disaster, and to postulate the validity of his hope.

I believe it is war and disaster which remind man most that he needs a record of his endurance and toughness. I think that that is why after our own disaster there rose in my country, the South, a resurgence of good writing, writing of a good enough quality that people in other lands began to talk of a "regional" Southern literature even until I, a countryman, have become one of the first names in our literature which the Japanese people want to talk to and listen to.

I believe that something very like that will happen here in Japan within the next few years—that out of your disaster and despair will come a group of Japanese writers whom all the world will want to listen to, who will speak not a Japanese truth but a universal truth.

Because man's hope is in man's freedom. The basis of the universal truth which the writer speaks is freedom in which to hope and believe, since only in liberty can hope exist—liberty and freedom not given man as a free gift but as a right and a responsibility to be earned if he deserves it, is worthy of it, is willing to work for it by means of courage and sacrifice, and then to defend it always.

And that Freedom must be complete freedom for all men; we must choose now not between color and color nor between kind and kind nor between ideology and ideology. We must choose simply between being slave and being free. Because the day is past now when we can choose a little of each. We cannot choose a freedom established on a hierarchy of freedom, on a caste system of degree of equality like military rank. We think of the world today as being a helpless battleground in which two mighty forces face each other in the form of two irreconcilable ideologies. I do not believe they are two ideologies. I believe that only one of them is an ideology because the other is simply a human belief that no government shall exist immune to the check of the consent of the governed; that only one of them is a political state or ideology, because the other one is simply a mutual state of man mutually believing in mutual liberty, in which politics is merely one more of the clumsy methods to make and hold good that condition in which all man shall be free. A clumsy method, until we have found something better, as most of the mechanics of social democracy creak and rattle. But until we do find a better, democracy will do, since man is stronger and tougher and more enduring than even his mistakes and blundering.

[*To the Youth of Japan,* Tokyo, 1955 (a pamphlet published by the U. S. Information Service); collected in *Faulkner at Nagano,* ed. Robert A. Jelliffe, Tokyo, 1956.]

✻ ✻ ✻

Letter to
a Northern Editor[*]

MY FAMILY has lived for generations in one same small section of north Mississippi. My great-grandfather held slaves and went to Virginia in command of a Mississippi infantry regiment in 1861. I state this simply as credentials for the sincerity and factualness of what I will try to say.

From the beginning of this present phase of the race problem in the South, I have been on record as opposing the forces in my native country which would keep the condition out of which this present evil and trouble has grown. Now I must go on record as opposing the forces outside the South which would use legal or police compulsion to eradicate that evil overnight. I was against compulsory segregation. I am just as strongly against compulsory integration. Firstly of course from principle. Secondly because I dont believe it will work.

There are more Southerners than I who believe as I do and have taken the same stand I have taken, at the same price of contumely and insult and threat from other Southerners which we foresaw and were willing to accept because we believed we were helping our native land which we love to accept a new condition which it must accept whether it wants to or not. That is, by still

---

* Faulkner's title; originally published as "A Letter to the North."

being Southerners, yet not being a part of the general majority Southern point of view; by being present yet detached, committed and attainted neither by Citizens' Council nor NAACP; by being in the middle, being in position to say to any incipient irrevocability: 'Wait, wait now, stop and consider first.'

But where will we go, if that middle becomes untenable? if we have to vacate it in order to keep from being trampled? Apart from the legal aspect, apart even from the simple incontrovertible immorality of discrimination by race, there was another simply human quantity which drew us to the Negro's side: the simple human instinct to champion the underdog. But if we, the (comparative) handful of Southerners I have tried to postulate, are compelled by the simple threat of being trampled if we dont get out of the way, to vacate that middle where we could have worked to help the Negro improve his condition—compelled to move for the reason that no middle any longer exists—we will have to make a new choice. And this time the underdog will not be the Negro since he, the Negro, will now be a segment of the topdog, and so the underdog will be that white embattled minority who are our blood and kin. These non-Southern forces will now say, 'Go then. We dont want you because we wont need you again.' My reply to that is, 'Are you sure you wont?'

So I would say to the NAACP and all the organizations who would compel immediate and unconditional integration: 'Go slow now. Stop now for a time, a moment. You have the power now; you can afford to withhold for a moment the use of it as a force. You have done a good job, you have jolted your opponent off-balance and he is now vulnerable. But stop there for a moment; dont give him the advantage of a chance to cloud the issue by that purely automatic sentimental appeal to that same universal human instinct for automatic sympathy for the underdog simply because he is under.'

And I would say this too. The rest of the United States knows next to nothing about the South. The present idea and picture which they hold of a people decadent and even obsolete through inbreeding and illiteracy— the inbreeding a result of the illiteracy and the isolation so that there is nothing else to do at night—as to be a kind of species of juvenile delinquents with a folklore of blood and violence, yet who, like juvenile delinquents, can be controlled by firmness once they are brought to believe that the police mean business, is as baseless and illusory as that one a generation ago of (oh yes, we subscribed to it too) columned porticoes and magnolias. The rest of the United States assumes that this condition in the South is so simple and so uncomplex that it can be changed tomorrow by the simple will of the national majority backed by legal edict. In fact, the North does not even recognise what it has seen in its own newspapers. I have at hand an editorial from the *New York Times* of February 10th on the rioting at the University of Alabama because of the admission as a student of Miss Lucy, a Negro. The editorial said: 'This is the first time that force and violence have become a part of the question.' That is not correct. To all Southerners, no matter which side of the question of racial equality they supported, the first implication, and—to the Southerner— even promise, of force and violence was the Supreme Court decision itself. After that, by any standards at all and following as inevitably as night and day, was the case of the three white teen-agers, members of a field trip group from a Mississippi high school (and, as teen-agers do, probably wearing the bright parti-colored blazers or jackets blazoned across the back with the name of the school) who were stabbed in passing on a Washington street by Negroes they had never seen before and who apparently had never seen them before either; and that of the Till boy and the two Mississippi juries which freed the defendants from both charges; and of the Mississippi garage attendant killed by a white man because, according to the white man, the Negro filled the tank of the white man's car full of gasoline when all the white man wanted was two dollars' worth.

This problem is far beyond a mere legal one. It is even far beyond the moral one it is and still was a hundred years ago in 1860, when many Southerners, including Robert Lee, recognised it as a moral one at the very instant when they in their turn elected to champion the underdog because that underdog was blood and kin and home. The Northerner is not even aware yet of what that war really proved. He assumes that it merely proved to the Southerner that he was wrong. It didn't do that because the Southerner already knew he was wrong and accepted that gambit even when he knew it was the fatal one. What that war should have done, but failed to do, was to prove to the North that the South will go to any length, even that fatal and already doomed one, before it will accept alteration of its racial condition by mere force of law or economic threat.

Since I went on record as being opposed to compulsory racial inequality, I have received many letters. A few of them approved. But most of them were in opposition. And a few of these were from southern Negroes, the only difference being that they were polite and courteous instead of being threats and insults, saying in effect: 'Please, Mr Faulkner, stop talking and be quiet. You are a good man and you think you are helping us.

But you are not helping us. You are doing us harm. You are playing into the hands of the NAACP so that they are using you to make trouble for our race that we dont want. Please hush, you look after your white folks' trouble and let us take care of ours.' This one in particular was a long one, from a woman who was writing for and in the name of the pastor and the entire congregation of her church. It went on to say that the Till boy got exactly what he asked for, coming down there with his Chicago ideas, and that all his mother wanted was to make money out of the role of her bereavement. Which sounds exactly like the white people in the South who justified and even defended the crime by declining to find that it was one.

We have had many violent inexcusable personal crimes of race against race in the South, but since 1919 the major examples of communal race tension have been more prevalent in the North, like the Negro family who were refused acceptance in the white residential district in Chicago, and the Korean-American who suffered for the same reason in Anaheim, Calif. Maybe it is because our solidarity is not racial, but instead is the majority white segregationist plus the Negro minority like my correspondent above, who prefer peace to equality. But suppose the line of demarcation should become one of race: the white minority like myself compelled to join the white segregation majority no matter how much we oppose the principle of inequality; the Negro minority who want peace compelled to join the Negro majority who advocate force, no matter how much that minority wanted only peace?

So the Northerner, the liberal, does not know the South. He cant know it from his distance. He assumes that he is dealing with a simple legal theory and a simple moral idea. He is not. He is dealing with a fact: the fact of an emotional condition of such fierce unanimity as to scorn the fact that it is a minority and which will go to any length and against any odds at this moment to justify and, if necessary, defend that condition and its right to it.

So I would say to all the organizations and groups which would force integration on the South by legal process: 'Stop now for a moment. You have shown the Southerner what you can do and what you will do if necessary; give him a space in which to get his breath and assimilate that knowledge; to look about and see that (1) Nobody is going to force integration on him from the outside; (2) That he himself faces an obsolescence in his own land which only he can cure; a moral condition which not only must be cured but a physical condition which has got to be cured if he, the white Southerner, is to have any peace, is not to be faced with another legal process or maneuver every year, year after year, for the rest of his life.'

[*Life,* March 5, 1956; the text printed here has been taken from Faulkner's typescript, with corrections he made or accepted before the article was first published.]

❈ ❈ ❈

On Fear:
Deep South in Labor: Mississippi[*]

(The American Dream: What
Happened to It?)

IMMEDIATELY after the Supreme Court decision abolishing segregation in schools, the talk began in Mississippi of ways and means to increase taxes to raise the standard of the Negro schools to match the white ones. I wrote the following letter to the open forum page of our most widely-read Memphis paper:

We Mississippians already know that our present schools are not good enough. Our young men and women themselves prove that to us every year by the fact that, when the best of them want the best of education which they are entitled to and competent for, not only in the humanities but in the professions and crafts—law and medicine and engineering—too, they must go out of the state to get it. And quite often, too often, they dont come back.

So our present schools are not even good enough for white people; our present State reservoir of education is not of high enough quality to assuage the thirst

---

* Faulkner's title; originally published as "On Fear: The South in Labor."

of even our white young men and women. In which case, how can it possibly assuage the thirst and need of the Negro, who obviously is thirstier, needs it worse, else the Federal Government would not have had to pass a law compelling Mississippi (among others of course) to make the best of our education available to him.

That is, our present schools are not even good enough for white people. So what do we do? make them good enough, improve them to the best possible? No. We beat the bushes, rake and scrape to raise additional taxes to establish another system at best only equal to that one which is already not good enough, which therefore wont be good enough for Negroes either; we will have two identical systems neither of which are good enough for anybody.

A few days after my letter was printed in the paper, I received by post the carbon copy of a letter addressed to the same forum page of the Memphis paper. It read as follows: 'When Weeping Willie Faulkner splashes his tears about the inadequacy of Mississippi schools . . . we question his gumption in these respects' etc. From there it went on to cite certain facts of which all Southerners are justly proud: that the seed-stock of education in our land was preserved through the evil times following the Civil War when our land was a defeated and occupied country, by dedicated teachers who got little in return for their dedication. Then, after a brief sneer at the quality of my writing and the profit motive which was the obvious reason why I was a writer, he closed by saying: 'I suggest that Weeping Willie dry his tears and work up a little thirst for knowledge about the basic economy of his state.'

Later, after this letter was printed in the Memphis paper in its turn, I received from the writer of it a letter addressed to him by a correspondent in another small Mississippi town, consisting in general of a sneer at the Nobel Prize which was awarded me, and commending the Weeping Willie writer for his promptness in taking to task anyone traitorous enough to hold education more important than the color of the educatee's skin. Attached to it was the Weeping Willie writer's reply. It said in effect: 'In my opinion Faulkner is the most capable commentator on Southern facts of life to date. . . . If we could insult him into acquiring an insight into the basic economy of our region, he could (sic) do us a hell of a lot of good in our fight against integration.'

My answer was that I didn't believe that insult is a very sound method of teaching anybody anything, of persuading anyone to think or act as the insulter believes they should. I repeated that what we needed in Mississippi was the best possible schools, to make the best possible use of the men and women we produced, regardless of what color they were. And even if we could not have a school system which would do that, at least let us have one which would make no distinction among pupils except that of simple ability, since our principal and perhaps desperate need in America today was that all Americans at least should be on the side of America; that if all Americans were on the same side, we would not need to fear that other nations and ideologies would doubt us when we talked of human freedom.

But this is beside the point. The point is, what is behind this. The tragedy is not the impasse, but what is behind the impasse—the impasse of the two apparently irreconcilable facts which we are faced with in the South: the one being the decree of our national government that there be absolute equality in education among all citizens, the other being the white people in the South who say that white and Negro pupils shall never sit in the same classroom. Only apparently irreconcilable, because they must be reconciled since the only alternative to change is death. In fact, there are people in the South, Southerners born, who not only believe they can be reconciled but who love our land—not love white people specifically nor love Negroes specifically, but our land, our country: our climate and geography, the qualities in our people, white and Negro too, for honesty and fairness, the splendors in our traditions, the glories in our past—enough to try to reconcile them, even at the cost of displeasing both sides: the contempt of the Northern radicals who believe we dont do enough, the contumely and threats of our own Southern reactionaries who are convinced that anything we do is already too much.

The tragedy is, the reason behind the fact, the fear behind the fact that some of the white people in the South—people who otherwise are rational, cultured, gentle, generous and kindly—will—must—fight against every inch which the Negro gains in social betterment; the fear behind the desperation which could drive rational and successful men (my correspondent, the Weeping Willie one, is a banker, perhaps president of a—perhaps the—bank in another small Mississippi town like my own) to grasp at such straws for weapons as contumely and threat and insult to change the views or anyway the voice which dares to suggest that betterment of the Negro's condition does not necessarily presage the doom of the white race. Nor is the tragedy the fear so much as the tawdry quality of the fear—fear not of the Negro as an individual Negro nor even as a race, but as

an economic class or stratum or factor, since what the
Negro threatens is not the Southern white man's social
system but the Southern white man's economic system—
that economic system which the white man knows and
dares not admit to himself is established on an obsolescence—the artificial inequality of man—and so is itself already obsolete and hence doomed. He knows that only
three hundred years ago the Negro's naked grandfather
was eating rotten elephant or hippo meat in an African
rain-forest, yet in only three hundred years the Negro
produced Dr Ralph Bunche and George Washington
Carver and Booker T. Washington. The white man
knows that only ninety years ago not one percent of the
Negro race could own a deed to land, let alone read that
deed; yet in only ninety years, although his only contact
with a county courthouse is the window through which
he pays the taxes for which he has no representation, he
can own his land and farm it with inferior stock and
worn-out tools and gear—equipment which any white
man would starve with—and raise children and feed and
clothe them and send them to what schools are available
and even now and then send them North where they can
have equal scholastic opportunity, and end his life holding his head up because he owes no man, with even
enough over to pay for his coffin and funeral. That's
what the white man in the South is afraid of: that the
Negro, who has done so much with no chance, might do
so much more with an equal one that he might take the
white man's economy away from him, the Negro now
the banker or the merchant or the planter and the white
man the share-cropper or the tenant. That's why the Negro can gain our country's highest decoration for valor
beyond all call of duty for saving or defending or preserving white lives on foreign battle-fields yet the South-

ern white man dares not let that Negro's children learn their abc's in the same classroom with the children of the white lives he saved or defended.

*   *   *

Now the Supreme Court has defined exactly what it meant by what it said: that by 'equality' it meant, simply, equality, without qualifying or conditional adjectives: not 'separate but equal' nor 'equally separate', but simply, equal; and now the Mississippi voices are talking of something which does not even exist anymore.

In the first half of the nineteenth century, before slavery was abolished by law in the United States, Thomas Jefferson and Abraham Lincoln both held that the Negro was not yet competent for equality.

That was more than ninety years ago now, and nobody can say whether their opinions would be different now or not.

But assume that they would not have changed their belief, and that that opinion is right. Assume that the Negro is still not competent for equality, which is something which neither he nor the white man knows until we try it.

But we do know that, with the support of the Federal Government, the Negro is going to gain the right to try and see if he is fit or not for equality. And if the Southern white man cannot trust him with something as mild as equality, what is the Southern white man going to do when he has power—the power of his own fifteen millions of unanimity backed by the Federal Government—when the only check on that power will be that Federal Government which is already the Negro's ally?

In 1849, Senator John C. Calhoun made his address in favor of secession if the Wilmot Proviso was ever adopted. On Oct. 12th of that year, Senator Jefferson

Davis wrote a public letter to the South, saying: 'The generation which avoids its responsibility on this subject sows the wind and leaves the whirlwind as a harvest to its children. Let us get together and build manufactures, enter upon industrial pursuits, and prepare for our own self-sustenance.'

At that time the Constitution guaranteed the Negro as property along with all other property, and Senator Calhoun and Senator Davis had the then undisputed validity of States' Rights to back their position. Now the Constitution guarantees the Negro equal right to equality, and the states' rights which the Mississippi voices are talking about do not exist anymore. We—Mississippi— sold our states' rights back to the Federal Government when we accepted the first cotton price-support subsidy twenty years ago. Our economy is not agricultural any longer. Our economy is the Federal Government. We no longer farm in Mississippi cotton-fields. We farm now in Washington corridors and Congressional committee-rooms.

We—the South—didn't heed Senator Davis's words then. But we had better do it now. If we are to watch our native land wrecked and ruined twice in less than a hundred years over the Negro question, let us be sure this time that we know where we are going afterward.

*   *   *

There are many voices in Mississippi. There is that of one of our United States senators, who, although he is not speaking for the United States Senate and what he advocates does not quite match the oath he took when he entered into his high office several years ago, at least has made no attempt to hide his identity and his condition. And there is the voice of one of our circuit judges, who, although he is not now speaking from the Bench and

what he advocates also stands a little awry to his oath
that before the law all men are equal and the weak shall
be succored and defended, makes no attempt either to
conceal his identity and condition. And there are the
voices of the ordinary citizens who, although they do not
claim to speak specifically for the white Citizens' Coun-
cils and the NAACP, do not try to hide their sentiments
and their convictions; not to mention those of the
schoolmen—teachers and professors and pupils—though,
since most Mississippi schools are State-owned or -sup-
ported, they dont always dare to sign their names to the
open letters.

There are all the voices in fact, except one. That one
voice which would adumbrate them all to silence, being
the superior of all since it is the living articulation of the
glory and the sovereignty of God and the hope and aspiration of man. The Church, which is the strongest unified force in our Southern life since all Southerners are
not white and are not democrats, but all Southerners are
religious and all religions serve the same single God, no
matter by what name He is called. Where is that voice
now, the only reference to which I have seen was in an
open forum letter to our Memphis paper which said that
to his (the writer's) knowledge, none of the people who
begged leave to doubt that one segment of the human
race was forever doomed to be inferior to all the other
segments just because the Old Testament five thousand
years ago said it was, were communicants of any church.

Where is that voice now, which should have pro-
pounded perhaps two but certainly one of these still-
unanswered questions?

1. The Constitution of the U.S. says: Before the
   law, there shall be no artificial inequality—race

creed or money—among citizens of the United States.

2. Morality says: Do unto others as you would have others do unto you.

3. Christianity says: I am the only distinction among men since whosoever believeth in Me, shall never die.

Where is this voice now, in our time of trouble and indecision? Is it trying by its silence to tell us that it has no validity and wants none outside the sanctuary behind its symbolical spire?

* * *

If the facts as stated in the *Look* magazine account of the Till affair are correct, this remains: two adults, armed, in the dark, kidnap a fourteen-year-old boy and take him away to frighten him. Instead of which, the fourteen-year-old boy not only refuses to be frightened, but, unarmed, alone, in the dark, so frightens the two armed adults that they must destroy him.

What are we Mississippians afraid of? Why do we have so low an opinion of ourselves that we are afraid of people who by all our standards are our inferiors?—economically: i.e., they have so much less than we have that they must work for us not on their terms but on ours; educationally: i.e., their schools are so much worse than ours that the Federal Government has to threaten to intervene to give them equal conditions; politically: i.e., they have no recourse in law for protection from nor restitution for injustice and violence.

Why do we have so low an opinion of our blood and traditions as to fear that, as soon as the Negro enters our house by the front door, he will propose marriage to our daughter and she will immediately accept him?

Our ancestors were not afraid like this—our grand-fathers who fought at First and Second Manassas and Sharpsburg and Shiloh and Franklin and Chickamauga and Chancellorsville and the Wilderness; let alone those who survived that and had the additional and even greater courage and endurance to resist and survive Reconstruction, and so preserved to us something of our present heritage. Why are we, descendants of that blood and inheritors of that courage, afraid? What are we afraid of? What has happened to us in only a hundred years?

* * *

For the sake of argument, let us agree that all white Southerners (all white Americans maybe) curse the day when the first Briton or Yankee sailed the first shipload of manacled Negroes across the Middle Passage and auctioned them into American slavery. Because that doesn't matter now. To live anywhere in the world today and be against equality because of race or color, is like living in Alaska and being against snow. We have already got snow. And as with the Alaskan, merely to live in armistice with it is not enough. Like the Alaskan, we had better use it.

Suddenly about five years ago and with no warning to myself, I adopted the habit of travel. Since then I have seen (a little of some, a little more of others) the Far and Middle East, North Africa, Europe and Scandinavia. The countries I saw were not communist (then) of course, but they were more: they were not even communist-inclined, where it seemed to me they should have been. And I wondered why. Then suddenly I said to myself with a kind of amazement: It's because of America. These people still believe in the American dream; they do not know yet that something happened to it. They believe in us and are willing to trust and follow us not because of our material power: Russia has that: but because of the idea of individual human freedom and liberty and equality on which our nation was founded, which our founding fathers postulated the word 'America' to mean.

And, five years later, the countries which are still free of communism are still free simply because of that: that belief in individual liberty and equality and freedom which is the one idea powerful enough to stalemate the idea of communism. And we can thank our gods for that since we have no other weapon to fight communism with; in diplomacy we are children to communist diplomats, and production in a free country can always suffer because under monolithic government all production can go to the aggrandisement of the State. But then, we dont need anything more since that simple belief of man that he can be free is the strongest force on earth and all we need to do is use it.

Because it makes a glib and simple picture, we like to think of the world situation today as a precarious and explosive balance of two irreconcilable ideologies confronting each other: which precarious balance, once it totters, will drag the whole universe into the abyss along with it. That's not so. Only one of the opposed forces is an ideology. The other one is that simple fact of Man: that simple belief of individual man that he can and should and will be free. And if we who are still free want to continue so, all of us who are still free had better confederate and confederate fast with all others who still have a choice to be free—confederate not as black people nor white people nor blue or pink or green people, but as people who still are free, with all other people who are still free; confederate together and stick together too, if we want a world or even a part of a world in which individual man can be free, to continue to endure.

And we had better take in with us as many as we can get of the nonwhite peoples of the earth who are not completely free yet but who want and intend to be, before that other force which is opposed to individual freedom, befools and gets them. Time was when the nonwhite man was content to—anyway, did—accept his instinct for freedom as an unrealisable dream. But not anymore; the white man himself taught him different with that phase of his—the white man's—own culture which took the form of colonial expansion and exploitation based and morally condoned on the premise of inequality not because of individual incompetence but of mass race or color. As a result of which, in only ten years we have watched the nonwhite peoples expel, by bloody violence when necessary, the white man from all the portions of the Middle East and Asia which he once dominated, into which vacuum has already begun to move that other and inimical power which people who believe in freedom are at war with—that power which says to the nonwhite man: 'We dont offer you freedom because there is no such thing as freedom; your white overlords whom you have just thrown out have already proved that to you. But we offer you equality, at least equality in slavedom; if you are to be slaves, at least you can be slaves to your own color and race and religion.'

We, the western white man who does believe that there exists an individual freedom above and beyond this mere equality of slavedom, must teach the nonwhite peoples this while there is yet a little time left. We, America, who are the strongest national force opposing communism and monolithicism, must teach all other peoples, white and nonwhite, slave or (for a little while yet) still free. We, America, have the best opportunity to do this because we can begin here, at home; we will not need to send costly freedom task-forces into alien and inimical nonwhite places already convinced that there is no such thing as freedom and liberty and equality and peace for nonwhite people too, or we would practise it at home. Because our nonwhite minority is already on our side; we dont need to sell the Negro on America and freedom because he is already sold; even when ignorant from inferior or no education, even despite the record of his history of inequality, he still believes in our concepts of freedom and democracy.

That is what America has done for them in only three hundred years. Not done *to* them: done *for* them because to our shame we have made little effort so far to teach them to be Americans, let alone to use their capacities and capabilities to make us a stronger and more unified America;—the people who only three hundred years ago lived beside one of the largest bodies of inland water on earth and never thought of sail, who yearly had to move by whole villages and tribes from famine and pestilence and enemies without once thinking of wheel, yet in three hundred years have become skilled artisans and craftsmen capable of holding their own in a culture of technocracy; the people who only three hundred years ago were eating the carrion in the tropical jungles yet in only three hundred years have produced the Phi Beta Kappas and the Doctor Bunches and the Carvers and the Booker Washingtons and the poets and musicians; who have yet to produce a Fuchs or Rosenberg or Gold or Burgess or McLean or Hiss, and where for every Robeson there are a thousand white ones.

The Bunches and Washingtons and Carvers and the musicians and the poets who were not just good men and women but good teachers too, teaching him—the Negro—by precept and example what a lot of our white people have not learned yet: that to gain equality, one must deserve it, and to deserve equality, one must understand what it is: that there is no such thing as equality *per se,* but only equality *to:* equal right and opportunity to make the best one can of one's life within one's capacity and capability, without fear of injustice or oppression or violence. If we had given him this equality ninety or fifty or even ten years ago, there would have been no Supreme Court ruling about segregation in 1954.

But we didn't. We dared not; it is our southern white man's shame that in our present economy the Negro must not have economic equality; our double shame that we fear that giving him more social equality will jeopardise his present economic status; our triple shame that even then, to justify our stand, we must becloud the issue with the bugaboo of miscegenation; what a commentary that the one remaining place on earth where the white man can flee and have his uncorrupted blood protected and defended by law, is in Africa—Africa: the source and origin of the threat whose present presence in America will have driven the white man to flee it.

Soon now all of us—not just Southerners nor even just Americans, but all people who are still free and want to remain so—are going to have to make a choice, lest the next (and last) confrontation we face will be, not communists against anti-communists, but simply the remaining handful of white people against the massed myriads of all the people on earth who are not white. We will have to choose not between color nor race nor religion nor between East and West either, but simply between being slaves and being free. And we will have to choose completely and for good; the time is already past now when we can choose a little of each, a little of both. We can choose a state of slavedom, and if we are powerful enough to be among the top two or three or ten, we can have a certain amount of license—until someone more powerful rises and has us machine-gunned against a cellar wall. But we cannot choose freedom established on a hierarchy of degrees of freedom, on a caste system of equality like military rank. We must be free not because we claim freedom, but because we practise it; our freedom must be buttressed by a homogeny equally and unchallengeably free, no matter what color they are, so that all the other inimical forces everywhere—systems political or religious or racial or national—will not just respect us because we practise freedom, they will fear us because we do.

[*Harper's,* June 1956; the text printed here has been taken from Faulkner's revised typescript.]

❈ ❈ ❈

A Letter to the Leaders in the Negro Race*

RECENTLY I was quoted in several magazines with the statement that 'I . . . between the United States and Mississippi . . . would choose Mississippi . . . even (at the price or if it meant) shooting down Negroes in the street.' Each time I saw this statement, I corrected it by letter, to this effect: That is a statement which no sober man would make nor any sane man believe, for the reason that it is not only foolish, but dangerous, since the moment for that choice and that subsequent act will never arise, but even to suggest it would only further inflame the few (I believe) people in the United States who might still believe such a moment could occur.

I quote the following from a piece of mine printed in *Life,* March 5th last, entitled "A Letter to the North," this part of the "Letter" addressed specifically to the NAACP and the other organizations working actively for the abolishment of segregation: 'Go slow now. Stop now for a time, a moment. You have the power now; you can afford to withhold for a moment the use of it as a force. You have done a good job, you have jolted your opponent off-balance and he is now vulnerable. But stop there for a moment; dont give him the advantage of a chance to cloud the issue by that purely automatic sym-

* Faulkner's title; originally published as "If I Were a Negro."

pathy for the underdog simply because he is under . . .
You have shown the Southerner what you can do and
what you will do if necessary; give him a space in which
to get his breath and assimilate that knowledge; to look
about and see that (1) Nobody is going to force integration on him from the outside; (2) That he himself faces
an obsolescence in his own land which only he can cure;
a moral condition which not only must be cured but a
physical condition which has got to be cured if he, the
white Southerner, is to have any peace, is not to be faced
with another legal process or maneuver every year, year
after year, for the rest of his life.'

By 'Go slow, pause for a moment', I meant, 'Be flexible'. When I wrote the letter and then used every means
I knew to get it printed in time, Autherine Lucy had
just been compelled to withdraw temporarily from the
University of Alabama by a local violence already of
dangerous proportions. I believed that when the judge
validated her claim to be re-admitted, which he would
have to do, that the forces supporting her would send
her back for re-admission, and that when that happened
she would probably lose her life. That didn't happen. I
want to believe that the forces supporting Miss Lucy
were wise enough themselves not to send her back—not
merely wise enough to save her life, but wise enough to
foresee that even her martyrdom would in the long run
be less effective than the simple, prolonged, endless nui-
sance-value of her threat, which was what I meant by
'. . . a physical condition which has got to be cured if
he, the white Southerner, is to have any peace, is not to
be faced with another (sic) Miss Lucy every year . . .
for the rest of his life.'

Not the individual Negro to abandon or lower one jot
his hope and will for equality, but his leaders and organ-

izations to be always flexible and adaptable to circumstance and locality in their methods of gaining it. If I were a Negro in America today, that is the course I would advise the leaders of my race to follow: to send every day to the white school to which he was entitled by his ability and capacity to go, a student of my race, fresh and cleanly dressed, courteous, without threat or violence, to seek admission; when he was refused I would forget about him as an individual, but tomorrow I would send another one, still fresh and clean and courteous, to be refused in his turn, until at last the white man himself must recognise that there will be no peace for him until he himself has solved the dilemma.

This was Gandhi's way. If I were a Negro, I would advise our elders and leaders to make this our undeviating and inflexible course—a course of inflexible and unviolent flexibility directed against not just the schools but against all the public institutions from which we are interdict, as is being done against the Montgomery, Alabama, bus lines. But always with flexibility: inflexible and undeviable only in hope and will but flexible always to adapt to time and place and circumstance. I would be a member of NAACP, since nothing else in our U.S. culture has yet held out to my race that much of hope. But I would remain only under conditions: That it recognise the most serious quantity in our problem which, so far as I know, it has not publicly recognised yet; That it make that same flexibility the watchword of its methods. I would say to others of my race that we must never curb our hopes and demands for equal rights, but merely to curb with flexibility our methods of demanding them. I would say to other members of my race that I do not know how long 'slow' will take, but if you will grant me to mean by 'going slow', being flexible, I do not believe that anything else save 'going slow' will advance our hopes. I would say to my race, The watchword of our flexibility must be decency, quietness, courtesy, dignity; if violence and unreason come, it must not be from us. I would say that all the Negroes in Montgomery should support the bus-line boycott, but never that all of them *must,* since by that *must,* we will descend to the same methods which those opposing us are using to oppress us, and our victory will be worth nothing until it is willed and not compelled. I would say that our race must adjust itself psychologically, not to an indefinite continuation of a segregated society, but rather to a continuation as long as necessary of that inflexible unflagging flexibility which in the end will make the white man himself sick and tired of fighting it.

It is easy enough to say glibly, 'If I were a Negro, I would do this or that.' But a white man can only imagine himself for the moment a Negro; he cannot be that man of another race and griefs and problems. So there are some questions he can put to himself but cannot answer, for instance: Q. Would you lower your sights on your life's goals and reduce your aspirations for reasons of realism? A. No. I would impose flexibility on the methods. Q. Would this apply to your children? A. I would teach them both the aspirations and the flexibility. But here is hope, since life itself is hope in simply being alive since living is change and change must be either advancement or death. Q. How would you conduct yourself so as to avoid controversy and hostility and make friends for your people instead of enemies? A. By decency, dignity, moral and social responsibility. Q. How would you pray to God for human justice and racial salvation? A. I dont believe man prays to God for human justice and racial salvation. I believe he affirms to God that immortal individual human dignity which has always outlasted injustice and before which families and clans and tribes talking of themselves as a race of men and not the race of Man, rise and pass and vanish like so much dust. He merely affirms his own belief in the grace and dignity and immortality of individual man, as Dostoievsky's Ivan did when he repudiated any heaven whose order was founded on the anguished cry of one single child. Q. Surrounded by antagonistic white people, would you find it hard not to hate them? A. I would repeat to myself Booker T. Washington's words when he said: 'I will let no man, no matter what his color, ever make me hate him.'

So if I were a Negro, I would say to my people: 'Let us be always unflaggingly and inflexibly flexible. But always decently, quietly, courteously, with dignity and without violence. And above all, with patience. The white man has devoted three hundred years to teaching us to be patient; that is one thing at least in which we are his superiors. Let us turn it into a weapon against him. Let us use this patience not as a passive quality, but as an active weapon. But always, let us practise cleanliness and decency and courtesy and dignity in our contacts with him. He has already taught us to be more patient and courteous with him than he is with us; let us be his superior in the others too.'

But above all, I would say this to the leaders of our race: 'We must learn to deserve equality so that we can hold and keep it after we get it. We must learn responsibility, the responsibility of equality. We must learn that there is no such thing as a 'right' without any ties to it, since anything given to one free for nothing is worth exactly that: nothing. We must learn that our inalienable right to equality, to freedom and liberty and the pursuit of happiness, means exactly what our founding fathers meant by it: the right to *opportunity* to be free and equal, provided one is worthy of it, will work to gain it and then work to keep it. And not only the right to that opportunity, but the willingness and the capacity to accept the responsibility of that opportunity—the responsibilities of physical cleanliness and of moral rectitude, of a conscience capable of choosing between right and wrong and a will capable of obeying it, of reliability toward other men, the pride of independence of charity or relief.

'The white man has not taught us that. He taught us only patience and courtesy. He did not even see that we had the environment in which we could teach ourselves cleanliness and independence and rectitude and reliability. So we must teach ourselves that. Our leaders must teach us that. We as a race must lift ourselves by our own bootstraps to where we are competent for the responsibilities of equality, so that we can hold on to it when we get it. Our tragedy is that these virtues of responsibility are the white man's virtues of which he boasts, yet we, the Negro, must be his superior in them. Our hope is that, having beaten him in patience and courtesy, we can probably beat him in these others too.'

[*Ebony,* September 1956; the text printed here has been taken from Faulkner's typescript.]

⌘ ⌘ ⌘

Albert Camus

CAMUS said that the only true function of man, born into an absurd world, is to live, be aware of one's life, one's revolt, one's freedom. He said that if the only solution to the human dilemma is death, then we are on the wrong road. The right track is the one that leads to life, to the sunlight. One cannot unceasingly suffer from the cold.

So he did revolt. He did refuse to suffer from the unceasing cold. He did refuse to follow a track which led only to death. The track he followed was the only possible one which could not lead only to death. The track he followed led into the sunlight in being that one devoted to making with our frail powers and our absurd material, something which had not existed in life until we made it.

He said, 'I do not like to believe that death opens upon another life. To me, it is a door that shuts.' That is, he tried to believe that. But he failed. Despite himself, as all artists are, he spent that life searching himself and demanding of himself answers which only God could know; when he became the Nobel laureate of his year, I wired him 'On salut l'âme qui constamment se cherche et se demande'; why did he not quit then, if he did not want to believe in God?

At the very instant he struck the tree, he was still searching and demanding of himself; I do not believe that in that bright instant he found them. I do not believe they are to be found. I believe they are only to be searched for, constantly, always by some fragile member of the human absurdity. Of which there are never many, but always somewhere at least one, and one will always be enough.

People will say He was too young; he did not have time to finish. But it is not *How long,* it is not *How much;* it is, simply *What.* When the door shut for him, he had already written on this side of it that which every artist who also carries through life with him that one same foreknowledge and hatred of death, is hoping to do: *I was here.* He was doing that, and perhaps in that bright second he even knew he had succeeded. What more could he want?

[*Transatlantic Review,* Spring 1961; the text printed here has been taken from Faulkner's typescript. This previously appeared in *Nouvelle Revue Française,* March 1960, in French.]

❋ ❋ ❋

T W O

Speeches

Funeral Sermon for Mammy Caroline Barr

DELIVERED AT OXFORD, MISSISSIPPI
FEBRUARY 4, 1940

Caroline has known me all my life. It was my privilege to see her out of hers. After my father's death, to Mammy I came to represent the head of that family to which she had given a half century of fidelity and devotion. But the relationship between us never became that of master and servant. She still remained one of my earliest recollections, not only as a person, but as a fount of authority over my conduct and of security for my physical welfare, and of active and constant affection and love. She was an active and constant precept for decent behavior. From her I learned to tell the truth, to refrain from waste, to be considerate of the weak and respectful to age. I saw fidelity to a family which was not hers, devotion and love for people she had not borne.

She was born in bondage and with a dark skin and most of her early maturity was passed in a dark and tragic time for the land of her birth. She went through vicissitudes which she had not caused; she assumed cares and griefs which were not even her cares and griefs. She was paid wages for this, but pay is still just money. And she never received very much of that, so that she never laid up anything of this world's goods. Yet she accepted that too without cavil or calculation or complaint, so that by that very failure she earned the gratitude and affection of the family she had conferred the fidelity and devotion upon, and gained the grief and regret of the aliens who loved and lost her.

She was born and lived and served, and died and now is mourned; if there is a heaven, she has gone there.

[The Falkner and Faulkner families' beloved servant, Mammy Caroline Barr, died January 31, 1940. On February 4 William Faulkner delivered her funeral sermon, as she had requested, in the parlor at Rowanoak. On February 5 it was published in the Memphis *Commercial Appeal*. (See pp. 275 for this text.)

On February 7 Faulkner wrote Robert K. Haas at Random House, thanking him for a "note and clipping." (See *Selected Letters of William Faulkner,* ed. Joseph Blotner, New York, 1977, p. 118.) Obviously the clipping is not the *Commercial Appeal* text of the funeral sermon, published only two days earlier, but presumably a wire service announcement of the death and funeral sermon. In his letter Faulkner told Haas, "This is what I said, and when I got it on paper afterward, it turned out to be pretty good prose." And he ended the letter with the text of the sermon printed here, shortened and much revised from the *Commercial Appeal* version.]

Address upon Receiving the Nobel Prize for Literature

STOCKHOLM, DECEMBER 10, 1950

I feel that this award was not made to me as a man, but to my work—a life's work in the agony and sweat of the human spirit, not for glory and least of all for profit, but to create out of the materials of the human spirit something which did not exist before. So this award is only mine in trust. It will not be difficult to find a dedication for the money part of it commensurate with the purpose and significance of its origin. But I would like to do the same with the acclaim too, by using this moment as a pinnacle from which I might be listened to by the young men and women already dedicated to the same anguish and travail, among whom is already that one who will some day stand here where I am standing.

Our tragedy today is a general and universal physical fear so long sustained by now that we can even bear it. There are no longer problems of the spirit. There is only the question: When will I be blown up? Because of this, the young man or woman writing today has forgotten the problems of the human heart in conflict with itself which alone can make good writing because only that is worth writing about, worth the agony and the sweat.

He must learn them again. He must teach himself that the basest of all things is to be afraid; and, teaching himself that, forget it forever, leaving no room in his workshop for anything but the old verities and truths of the heart, the old universal truths lacking which any story is ephemeral and doomed—love and honor and pity and pride and compassion and sacrifice. Until he does so, he labors under a curse. He writes not of love but of lust, of defeats in which nobody loses anything of value, of victories without hope and, worst of all, without pity or compassion. His griefs grieve on no universal bones, leaving no scars. He writes not of the heart but of the glands.

Until he relearns these things, he will write as though he stood among and watched the end of man. I decline to accept the end of man. It is easy enough to say that man is immortal simply because he will endure: that when the last ding-dong of doom has clanged and faded from the last worthless rock hanging tideless in the last red and dying evening, that even then there will still be one more sound: that of his puny inexhaustible voice, still talking. I refuse to accept this. I believe that man will not merely endure: he will prevail. He is immortal, not because he alone among creatures has an inexhaustible voice, but because he has a soul, a spirit capable of compassion and sacrifice and endurance. The poet's, the writer's, duty is to write about these things. It is his privilege to help man endure by lifting his heart, by reminding him of the courage and honor and hope and pride and compassion and pity and sacrifice which have been the glory of his past. The poet's voice need not merely be the record of man, it can be one of the props, the pillars to help him endure and prevail.

[The text printed here has been taken from Faulkner's original typescript of the version which was first printed in the *New York Herald Tribune Book Review,* January 14, 1951. This version was slightly revised from that which he delivered in Stockholm, and which was published in American newspapers at the time.]

Address to the Graduating Class
University High School

OXFORD, MISSISSIPPI, MAY 28, 1951

Years ago, before any of you were born, a wise Frenchman said, 'If youth knew; if age could.' We all know
what he meant: that when you are young, you have the
power to do anything, but you don't know what to do.
Then, when you have got old and experience and observation have taught you answers, you are tired, frightened; you don't care, you want to be left alone as long as
you yourself are safe; you no longer have the capacity or
the will to grieve over any wrongs but your own.

So you young men and women in this room tonight,
and in thousands of other rooms like this one about the
earth today, have the power to change the world, rid it
forever of war and injustice and suffering, provided you
know how, know what to do. And so according to the old
Frenchman, since you can't know what to do because
you are young, then anyone standing here with a head
full of white hair, should be able to tell you.

But maybe this one is not as old and wise as his white
hairs pretend or claim. Because he can't give you a glib
answer or pattern either. But he can tell you this, because he believes this. What threatens us today is fear.
Not the atom bomb, nor even fear of it, because if the

bomb fell on Oxford tonight, all it could do would be to kill us, which is nothing, since in doing that, it will have robbed itself of its only power over us: which is fear of it, the being afraid of it. Our danger is not that. Our danger is the forces in the world today which are trying to use man's fear to rob him of his individuality, his soul, trying to reduce him to an unthinking mass by fear and bribery—giving him free food which he has not earned, easy and valueless money which he has not worked for;— the economies or ideologies or political systems, communist or socialist or democratic, whatever they wish to call themselves, the tyrants and the politicians, American or European or Asiatic, whatever they call themselves, who would reduce man to one obedient mass for their own aggrandisement and power, or because they themselves are baffled and afraid, afraid of, or incapable of, believing in man's capacity for courage and endurance and sacrifice.

That is what we must resist, if we are to change the world for man's peace and security. It is not men in the mass who can and will save Man. It is Man himself, created in the image of God so that he shall have the power and the will to choose right from wrong, and so be able to save himself because he is worth saving;—Man, the individual, men and women, who will refuse always to be tricked or frightened or bribed into surrendering, not just the right but the duty too, to choose between justice and injustice, courage and cowardice, sacrifice and greed, pity and self;—who will believe always not only in the right of man to be free of injustice and rapacity and deception, but the duty and responsibility of man to see that justice and truth and pity and compassion are done.

So, never be afraid. Never be afraid to raise your voice for honesty and truth and compassion, against injustice and lying and greed. If you, not just you in this room tonight, but in all the thousands of other rooms like this one about the world today and tomorrow and next week, will do this, not as a class or classes, but as individuals, men and women, you will change the earth. In one generation all the Napoleons and Hitlers and Caesars and Mussolinis and Stalins and all the other tyrants who want power and aggrandisement, and the simple politicians and time-servers who themselves are merely baffled or ignorant or afraid, who have used, or are using, or hope to use, man's fear and greed for man's enslavement, will have vanished from the face of it.

[*Oxford Eagle*, May 31, 1951; printed there entirely in italics.]

Address upon Being Made
an Officer of the Legion of Honor

NEW ORLEANS, OCTOBER 26, 1951

Un artiste doit recevoir avec humilite ce dignite conferré a lui par cette payes la quelle a ete toujours la mere universelle des artists.

Un Americain doit cherir avec la tendresse toujours chacque souvenir de cette pays la quelle a ete toujours la soeur d'Amerique.

Un homme libre doit guarder avec l'espérance et l'orgeuil aussi l'accolade de cette pays la quelle etait la mere de la liberte de l'homme et de l'esprit humaine.

[In November 1951 Faulkner gave a manuscript of this address to his editor, Saxe Commins. It was reproduced as an illustration in the *Princeton University Library Chronicle*, XVIII (Spring 1957), from which the text printed here has been taken, entirely without correction.]

Address to the Delta Council

CLEVELAND, MISSISSIPPI, MAY 15, 1952

When the invitation to be here today first reached me, it
came from Mr. Billy Wynn. It contained one of the nic-
est compliments anyone ever received. Mr. Wynn said,
"We not only want to honor this particular fellow-Mis-
sissippian, we want him to honor us."

You can't beat that. To reverse a metaphor, that is a
sword with not only two edges, but with both edges on
the same side; the receiver is accoladed twice with one
stroke: He is honored again in honoring them who
proffered the original honor. Which is exactly the sort of
gesture which we Southerners like to believe that only
another Southerner could have thought of, invented.
And, sure enough, it happens so often as to convince us
that we were right.

He also gave me the Council's permission to speak on
any subject I liked. That subject won't be writing or
farming either. In my fan mail during the past year,
there was a correspondence with another Mississippi
gentleman, who takes a very dim view of my writing
ability and my ideas both. He is a Deltan, he may be
here today, and can ratify this. In one of his last letters,
having reviewed again his opinion of a Mississippian
who could debase and defile his native state and people
as I have done, he said he not only didn't believe I could

write, he didn't even believe I knew anything about farming, either. I answered that it wasn't me who made the claims about my degree as a writer, and so I would agree with him on that one; and after fifteen years of trying to cope not only with the Lord but with the federal government too to make something grow at a profit out of the ground, I was willing to agree with him on both of them.

So I shan't talk about either writing or farming. I have another subject. And, having thought about it, maybe I don't know very much about this one either, for the reason that none of us seem to know much about it any more, that all of us may have forgotten one of the primary things on which this country was founded.

Years ago, our fathers founded this country, this nation, on the premise of the rights of man. As they expressed it, "the inalienable right of man to life, liberty, and the pursuit of happiness." In those days, they knew what those words meant, not only the ones who expressed them, but the ones who heard and believed and accepted and subscribed to them. Because until that time, men did not always have those rights. At least, until that time, no nation had ever been founded on the idea that those rights were possible, let alone inalienable. So not only the ones who said the words, but the ones who merely heard them, knew what they meant. Which was this: "Life and liberty in which to pursue happiness. Life free and secure from oppression and tyranny, in which all men would have the liberty to pursue happiness." And both of them knew what they meant by "pursue." They did not mean just to chase happiness, but to work for it. And they both knew what they meant by "happiness" too: not just pleasure, idleness, but peace, dignity, independence and self-respect; that man's inalienable right was, the peace and freedom in which, by his own efforts and sweat, he could gain dignity and independence, owing nothing to any man.

So we knew what the words meant then, because we didn't have these things. And, since we didn't have them, we knew their worth. We knew that they were worth suffering and enduring and, if necessary, even dying to gain and preserve. We were willing to accept even the risk of death for them, since even if we lost them ourselves in relinquishing life to preserve them, we would still be able to bequeath them intact and inalienable to our children.

Which is exactly what we did, in those old days. We left our homes, the land and graves of our fathers and all familiar things. We voluntarily gave up, turned our backs on, a security which we already had and which we could have continued to have, as long as we were willing to pay the price for it, which price was our freedom and liberty of thought and independence of action and the right of responsibility. That is, by remaining in the old world, we could have been not only secure, but even free of the need to be responsible. Instead, we chose the freedom, the liberty, the independence and the inalienable right to responsibility; almost without charts, in frail wooden ships with nothing but sails and our desire and will to be free to move them, we crossed an ocean which did not even match the charts we did have; we conquered a wilderness in order to establish a place, not to be secure in because we did not want that, we had just repudiated that, just crossed three thousand miles of dark and unknown sea to get away from that; but a place to be free in, to be independent in, to be responsible in.

And we did it. Even while we were still battling the

wilderness with one hand, with the other we fended and beat off the power which would have followed us even into the wilderness we had conquered, to compel and hold us to the old way. But we did it. We founded a land, and founded in it not just our right to be free and independent and responsible, but the inalienable duty of man to be free and independent and responsible.

That's what I am talking about: responsibility. Not just the right, but the duty of man to be responsible, the necessity of man to be responsible if he wishes to remain free; not just responsible to and for his fellow man, but to himself; the duty of a man, the individual, each individual, every individual, to be responsible for the consequences of his own acts, to pay his own score, owing nothing to any man.

We knew it once, had it once. Because why? Because we wanted it above all else, we fought for it, endured, suffered, died when necessary, but gained it, established it, to endure for us and then to be bequeathed to our children.

Only, something happened to us. The children inherited. A new generation came along, a new era, a new age, a new century. The times were easier; the life and future of our nation as a nation no longer hung in balance; another generation, and we no longer had enemies, not because we were strong in our youth and vigor, but because the old tired rest of earth recognized that here was a nation founded on the principle of individual man's responsibility as individual man.

But we still remembered responsibility, even though, with easier times, we didn't need to keep the responsibility quite so active, or at least not so constantly so. Besides, it was not only our heritage, it was too recent yet for us to forget it, the graves were still green of them who had bequeathed it to us, and even of them who had died in order that it might be bequeathed. So we still remembered it, even if a good deal of the remembering was just lip-service.

Then more generations; we covered at last the whole face of the western earth; the whole sky of the western hemisphere was one loud American affirmation, one vast Yes; we were the whole world's golden envy; never had the amazed sun itself seen such a land of opportunity, in which all a man needed were two legs to move to a new place on, and two hands to grasp and hold with, in order to amass to himself enough material substance to last him the rest of his days and, who knew? even something over for his and his wife's children. And still he paid lip-service to the old words "freedom" and "liberty" and "independence;" the sky still rang and ululated with the thunderous affirmation, the golden Yes. Because the words in the old premise were still true yet, for the reason that he still believed they were true. Because he did not realize yet that when he said "security," he meant security for himself, for the rest of his days, with perhaps a little over for his children: not for the children and the children's children of all men who believed in liberty and freedom and independence, as the old fathers in the old strong, dangerous times had meant it.

Because somewhere, at some moment, something had happened to him, to us, to all the descendants of the old tough, durable, uncompromising men, so that now, in 1952, when we talk of security, we don't even mean for the rest of our own lives, let alone that of our and our wife's children, but only for so long as we ourselves can hold our individual place on a public relief roll or at a bureaucratic or political or any other organization's gravy-trough. Because somewhere, at some point, we had lost or forgot or voluntarily rid ourselves of that one other thing, lacking which, freedom and liberty and independence cannot even exist.

That thing is the responsibility, not only the desire and the will to be responsible, but the remembrance from the old fathers of the need to be responsible. Either we lost it, forgot it, or we deliberately discarded it. Either we decided that freedom was not worth the responsibility of being free, or we forgot that, to be free, a man must assume and maintain and defend his right to be responsible for his freedom. Maybe we were even robbed of responsibility, since for years now the very air itself—radio, newspapers, pamphlets, tracts, the voices of politicians—has been loud with talk about the rights of man,—not the duties and obligations and responsibilities of man, but only the "rights" of man; so loud and so constant that apparently we have come to accept the sounds at their own evaluation, and to believe too that man has nothing else but rights:—not the rights to independence and freedom in which to work and endure in his own sweat in order to earn for himself what the old ancestors meant by happiness and the pursuit of it, but only the chance to swap his freedom and independence for the privilege of being free of the responsibilities of independence; the right not to earn, but to be given, until at last, by simple compound usage, we have made respectable and even elevated to a national system, that which the old tough fathers would have scorned and condemned: charity.

In any case, we no longer have responsibility. And if we were robbed of it by such as this which now seems to have taken over responsibility, it was because we were vulnerable to that kind of ravishment; if we simply lost or forgot responsibility, then we too are to be scorned.

But if we deliberately discarded it, then we have condemned ourselves, because I believe that in time, maybe not too long a time, we will discover that, as was said about one of Napoleon's acts, what we have committed is worse than a crime: it was a mistake.

Two hundred years ago, the Irish statesman, John Curran, said, "God hath vouchsafed man liberty only on condition of eternal vigilance; which condition if he break it, servitude is the consequence of his crime and the punishment of his guilt." That was only two hundred years ago, because our own old New England and Virginia and Carolina fathers knew that three hundred years ago, which was why they came here and founded this country. And I decline to believe that we, their descendants, have really forgotten it. I prefer to believe rather that it is because the enemy of our freedom now has changed his shirt, his coat, his face. He no longer threatens us from across an international boundary, let alone across an ocean. He faces us now from beneath the eagle-perched domes of our capitols and from behind the alphabetical splatters on the doors of welfare and other bureaus of economic or industrial regimentation, dressed not in martial brass but in the habiliments of what the enemy himself has taught us to call peace and progress, a civilization and plenty where we never before had it as good, let alone better; his artillery is a debased and respectless currency which has emasculated the initiative for independence by robbing initiative of the only mutual scale it knew to measure independence by.

The economists and sociologists say that the reason for this condition is, too many people. I don't know about that, myself, since in my opinion I am even a worse sociologist and economist than my Delta fan considers me a writer or a farmer. But even if I were a sociologist or economist, I would decline to believe this. Because to believe this, that man's crime against his freedom is that there are too many of him, is to believe that man's sufferance on the face of the earth is threatened, not by his environment, but by himself: that he cannot hope to cope with his environment and its evils, because he cannot even cope with his own mass. Which is exactly what those who misuse and betray the mass of him for their own aggrandisement and power and tenure of office, believe: that man is incapable of responsibility and freedom, of fidelity and endurance and courage, that he not only cannot choose good from evil, he cannot even distinguish it, let alone practice the choice. And to believe that, you have already written off the hope of man, as they who have reft him of his inalienable right to be responsible, have done, and you might as well quit now and let man stew on in peace in his own recordless and oblivious juice, to his deserved and ungrieved doom.

I, for one, decline to believe this. I decline to believe that the only true heirs of Boone and Franklin and George and Booker T. Washington and Lincoln and Jefferson and Adams and John Henry and Paul Bunyan and Johnny Appleseed and Lee and Crockett and Hale and Helen Keller, are the ones denying and protesting in the newspaper headlines over mink coats and oil tankers and federal indictments for corruption in public office. I believe that the true heirs of the old tough durable fathers are still capable of responsibility and self-respect, if only they can remember them again. What we need is not fewer people, but more room between them, where those who would stand on their own feet, could, and those who won't, might have to. Then the welfare, the relief, the compensation, instead of being nationally sponsored cash prizes for idleness and ineptitude, could

go where the old independent uncompromising fathers
themselves would have intended it and blessed it: to
those who still cannot, until the day when even the last
of them except the sick and the old, would also be among
them who not only can, but will.

[*Delta Democrat-Times,* May 18, 1952; one correction has
been made from the pamphlet printing of the speech published by the Delta Council, May 1952.]

Address to the Graduating Class
Pine Manor Junior College

WELLESLEY, MASSACHUSETTS, JUNE 8, 1953

What's wrong with this world is, it's not finished yet. It is not completed to that point where man can put his final signature to the job and say, "It is finished. We made it, and it works."

Because only man can complete it. Not God, but man. It is man's high destiny and proof of his immortality too, that his is the choice between ending the world, effacing it from the long annal of time and space, and completing it. This is not only his right, but his privilege too. Like the phoenix it rises from the ashes of its own failure with each generation, until it is your turn now in your flash and flick of time and space which we call today, in this and in all the stations in time and space today and yesterday and tomorrow, where a handful of aged people like me, who should know but no longer can, are facing young people like you who can do, if they only knew where and how, to perform this duty, accept this privilege, bear this right.

In the beginning, God created the earth. He created it completely furnished for man. Then He created man completely equipped to cope with the earth, by means of free will and the capacity for decision and the ability to learn by making mistakes and learning from them because he had a memory with which to remember and so learn from his errors, and so in time make his own peaceful destiny of the earth. It was not an experiment. God didn't merely believe in man, He knew man. He knew that man was competent for a soul because he was capable of saving that soul and, with it, himself. He knew that man was capable of starting from scratch and coping with the earth and with himself both; capable of teaching himself to be civilized, to live with his fellow man in amity, without anguish to himself or causing anguish and grief to others, and of appreciating the value of security and peace and freedom, since our dreams at night, the very slow evolution of our bodies themselves, remind us constantly of the time when we did not have them. He did not mean freedom from fear, because man does not have the right to be free of fear. We are not so weak and timorous as to need to be free of fear; we need only use our capacity to not be afraid of it and so relegate fear to its proper perspective. He meant security and peace in which to not be afraid, freedom in which to decree and then establish security and peace. And He demanded of man only that we work to deserve and gain these things—liberty, freedom of the body and spirit both, security for the weak and helpless, and peace for all—because these were the most valuable things He could set within our capacity and reach.

During all this time, the angels (with one exception; God had probably had trouble with this one before) merely looked on and watched—the serene and blameless seraphim, that white and shining congeries who, with the exception of that one whose arrogance and pride God had already had to curb, were content merely to bask for eternity in the reflected glory of the miracle of man, content merely to watch, uninvolved and not even caring, while man ran his worthless and unregretted course toward and at last into that twilight where he would be no more. Because they were white, immaculate, negative, without past, without thought or grief or regrets or hopes, except that one—the splendid dark incorrigible one, who possessed the arrogance and pride to demand with, and the temerity to object with, and the ambition to substitute with—not only to decline to accept a condition just because it was a fact, but to want to substitute another condition in its place.

But this one's opinion of man was even worse than that of the negative and shining ones. This one not only believed that man was incapable of anything but baseness, this one believed that baseness had been inculcated in man to be used for base personal aggrandizement by them of a higher and more ruthless baseness. So God used the dark spirit too. He did not merely cast it shrieking out of the universe, as He could have done. Instead, He used it. He already presaw the long roster of the ambition's ruthless avatars—Genghis and Caesar and William and Hitler and Barca and Stalin and Bonaparte and Huey Long. But He used more—not only the ambition and the ruthlessness and the arrogance to show man what to revolt against, but also the temerity to revolt and the will to change what one does not like. Because He presaw the long roster of the other avatars of that rebellious and uncompromising pride also, the long roster of names longer and more enduring than those of the tyrants and oppressors. They are the long annal of the men and women who have anguished over man's condition and who have held up to us not only the mirror of our follies and greeds and lusts and fears, but have reminded us constantly of the tremendous shape of our godhead too—the godhead and immortality which we cannot repudiate even if we dared, since we cannot rid ourselves of it but only it can rid itself of us—the philosophers and artists, the articulate and grieving who have reminded us always of our capacity for honor and courage and compassion and pity and sacrifice.

But they can only remind us that we are capable of revolt and change. They do not need, we do not need anyone to tell us what we must revolt against and efface from the earth if we are to live in peace and security on it, because we already know that. They can only remind us that man can revolt and change by telling, showing, reminding us how, not lead us, since to be led, we must surrender our free will and our capacity and right to make decisions out of our own personal soul. If we are to be led into peace and security by some individual gauleiter or gang of them, like a drove of sheep through a gate in a fence, it will merely be from one enclosure to another, through another fence with another closable gate in it, and all history has shown us that this will be the gauleiter's enclosure and fence and his hand which closes and locks the gate, and *that* kind of peace and security will be exactly the sort of peace and security which a flock of sheep deserve.

So He used that split part of the dark proud one's character to remind us of our heritage of free will and decision; He used the poets and philosophers to remind us, out of our own recorded anguish, of our capacity for courage and endurance. But it is we ourselves who must employ them. This time it is you, here, in this room and in all the others like it about the world at this time and occasion in your lives. It is us, we, not as groups or classes but as individuals, simple men and women individually free and capable of freedom and decision, who must decide, affirm simply and firmly and forever never to be led like sheep into peace and security, but ourselves, us, simple men and women simply and mutually confederated for a time, a purpose, an end, for the simple reason that reason and heart have both shown us that we want the same thing and must have it and intend to have it.

To do it ourselves, as individuals, not because we have to merely in order to survive, but because we wish to, will to out of our heritage of free will and decision, the possession of which has given us the right to say how we shall live, and the long proof of our recorded immortality to remind us that we have the courage to elect that right and that course.

The answer is very simple. I don't mean easy, but simple. It is so simple in fact that one's first reaction is something like this: "If that's all it takes, what you will get for it can't be very valuable, very enduring." There is an anecdote about Tolstoy, I think it was, who said in the middle of a discussion on this subject: "All right, I'll start being good tomorrow—if you will too." Which was wit, and had, as wit often does, truth in it—a profound truth in fact to all of them who are incapable of belief in man. But not to them who can and do believe in man. To them, it is only wit, the despairing repudiation of man by a man exhausted into despair by his own anguish over man's condition. These do not say, *The answer is simple, but how difficult,* instead these say, *The answer is not easy, but very simple.* We do not need, the end does not even require, that we dedicate ourselves from this moment on to be Joans of Arc with trumpets and banners and battle-dust toward an end which we will not even see since it will merely be a setting for the monument of martyrdom. It can be done within, concomitant with, the normal life which everyone wants and every-

one should have. In fact, that normal life which everyone wants and deserves and can have—provided of course
we work for it, are willing to make a reasonable amount
of sacrifice commensurate with how much it is worth
and how much we want and deserve it—can be dedicated
to this end and be much more efficacious than all the
loud voices and the cries and the banners and trumpets
and dust.

Because it begins at home. We all know what "home"
means. Home is not necessarily a place fixed in geography. It can be moved, provided the old proven values
which made it home and lacking which it cannot be
home, are taken along too. It does not necessarily mean
or demand physical ease, least of all, never in fact, physical security for the spirit, for love and fidelity to have
peace and security in which to love and be faithful, for
the devotion and sacrifice. Home means not just today,
but tomorrow and tomorrow, and then again tomorrow
and tomorrow. It means someone to offer the love and
fidelity and respect to who is worthy of it, someone to
be compatible with, whose dreams and hopes are your
dreams and hopes, who wants and will work and sacrifice
also that the thing which the two of you have together
shall last forever; someone whom you not only love but
like too, which is more, since it must outlast what when
we are young we mean by love because without the liking and the respect, the love itself will not last.

Home is not merely four walls—a house, a yard on a
particular street, with a number on the gate. It can be a
rented room or an apartment—any four walls which
house a marriage or a career or both the marriage and
career at once. But it must be all the rooms or apartments; all the houses on that street and all the streets in
that association of streets until they become a whole, an

integer, of people who have the same aspirations and hopes and problems and duties. Perhaps that collection, association, integer, is set in the little spot of geography which produced us in the image of, to be the inheritors of, its problems and dreams. But this is not necessary either; it can be anywhere, so long as we accept it as home; we can even move it, providing and demanding only that we are willing to accept the new problems and duties and aspirations with which we have replaced the old ones which we left behind us, will accept the hopes and aspirations of the people already there, who had established that place as an integer worthy of being served, and are willing to accept our hopes and aspirations in return for their duties and problems. Because the duties and problems were already ours; we merely changed their designations; we cannot shed obligations by moving, because if it is home we want, we do not want to escape them. They are in fact still the same ones, performed and solved for the same reason and result: the same peace and security in which love and devotion can be love and devotion without fear of violence and outrage and change.

If we accept this to mean "home," we do not need to look further than home to find where to start to work, to begin to change, to begin to rid ourselves of the fears and pressures which are making simple existence more and more uncertain and without dignity or peace or security, and which, to those who are incapable of believing in man, will in the end rid man of his problems by ridding him of himself. Let us do what is within our power. It will not be easy, of course: just simple. Let us think first of, work first toward, saving the integer, association, collection which we call home. In fact, we must break ourselves of thinking in the terms foisted on us by

the split-offs of that old dark spirit's ambition and ruthlessness: the empty clanging terms of "nation" and "fa-
therland" or "race" or "color" or "creed." We need look
no further than home; we need only work for what we
want and deserve here. Home—the house or even the
rented room so long as it includes all the houses and
rented rooms in which hope and aspire the same hopes
and aspirations—the street, then all the streets where
dwell that voluntary association of people, simple men
and women mutually confederated by identical hopes
and aspirations and problems and duties and needs, to
that point where they can say, "These simple things—security and freedom and peace—are not only possible, not
only can and must be, but they shall be." Home: not
where *I* live or *it* lives, but where *we* live: a thousand
then tens of thousands of little integers scattered and
fixed firmer and more impregnable and more solid than
rocks or citadels about the earth, so that the ruthless and
ambitious split-offs of the ancient dark spirit shall look
at the one and say, "There is nothing for us here," then
look further, at the rest of them fixed and founded like
fortresses about the whole inhabited earth, and say,
"There is nothing for us any more anywhere. Man—
simple unfrightened invincible men and women—has
beaten us." Then man can put that final signature to his
job and say, "We finished it, and it works."

[*Atlantic Monthly,* August 1953]

✵ ✵ ✵

Address upon Receiving the National Book Award for Fiction

NEW YORK, JANUARY 25, 1955

By artist I mean of course everyone who has tried to create something which was not here before him, with no other tools and material than the uncommerciable ones of the human spirit; who has tried to carve, no matter how crudely, on the wall of that final oblivion beyond which he will have to pass, in the tongue of the human spirit, 'Kilroy was here.'

That is primarily, and I think in its essence, all that we ever really tried to do. And I believe we will all agree that we failed. That what we made never quite matched and never will match the shape, the dream of perfection which we inherited and which drove us and will continue to drive us, even after each failure, until anguish frees us and the hand falls still at last.

Maybe it's just as well that we are doomed to fail, since, as long as we do fail and the hand continues to hold blood, we will try again; where, if we ever did attain the dream, match the shape, scale that ultimate peak of perfection, nothing would remain but to jump off the other side of it into suicide. Which would not only deprive us of our American right to existence, not only inalienable but harmless too, since by our standards, in our culture, the pursuit of art is a peaceful hobby like breeding Dalmations, it would leave refuse in the form of, at best indigence and at worst downright crime resulting from unexhausted energy, to be scavenged and removed and disposed of. While this way, constantly and steadily occupied by, obsessed with, immersed in trying to do the impossible, faced always with the failure which we decline to recognize and accept, we stay out of trouble, keep out of the way of the practical and busy people who carry the burden of America.

So all are happy—the giants of industry and commerce, and the manipulators for profit or power of the mass emotions called government, who carry the tremendous load of geopolitical solvency, the two of which conjoined are America; and the harmless breeders of the spotted dogs (unharmed too, protected, immune in the inalienable right to exhibit our dogs to one another for acclaim, and even to the public too; defended in our right to collect from them at the rate of five or ten dollars for the special signed editions, and even at the rate of thousands to special fanciers named Picasso or Matisse).

Then something like this happens—like this, here, this afternoon; not just once and not even just once a year. Then that anguished breeder discovers that not only his fellow breeders, who must support their mutual vocation in a sort of mutual desperate defensive confederation, but other people, people whom he had considered outsiders, also hold that what he is doing is valid. And not only scattered individuals who hold his doings valid, but enough of them to confederate in their turn, for no mutual benefit of profit or defense but simply because they also believe it is not only valid but important that man should write on that wall 'Man was here also A.D. 1953 or '54 or '55', and so go on record like this this afternoon.

To tell not the individual artist but the world, the time itself, that what he did is valid. That even failure is worth while and admirable, provided only that the failure is splendid enough, the dream splendid enough, unattainable enough yet forever valuable enough, since it was of perfection.

So when this happens to him (or to one of his fellows; it doesn't matter which one, since all share the validation of the mutual devotion) the thought occurs that perhaps one of the things wrong with our country is success. That there is too much success in it. Success is too easy. In our country a young man can gain it with no more than a little industry. He can gain it so quickly and easily that he has not had time to learn the humility to handle it with, or even to discover, realise, that he will need humility.

Perhaps what we need is a dedicated handful of pioneer-martyrs who, between success and humility, are capable of choosing the second one.

[*New York Times Book Review,* February 6, 1955; the text printed here has been taken from Faulkner's original typescript.]

Address to the Southern Historical Association

For the moment and for the sake of the argument, let's say that, a white Southerner and maybe even any white American, I too curse the day when the first Negro was brought against his will to this country and sold into slavery. Because that doesn't matter now. To live anywhere in the world of A.D. 1955 and be against equality because of race or color, is like living in Alaska and being against snow.

Inside the last two years I have seen (a little of some, a good deal of others) Japan, the Philippines, Siam, India, Egypt, Italy, West Germany, England and Iceland. Of these countries, the only one I would say definitely will not be communist ten years from now, is England. And if these other countries do not remain free, then England will no longer endure as a free nation. And if all the rest of the world becomes communist, it will be the end of America too as we know it; we will be strangled into extinction by simple economic blockade since there will be no one anywhere anymore to sell our products to; we are already seeing that now in the problem of our cotton.

And the only reason all these countries are not communist already, is America, not just because of our material power, but because of the idea of individual human freedom and liberty and equality on which our nation was founded, and which our founding fathers postulated the name of America to mean. These countries are still free of communism simply because of that—that belief in individual liberty and equality and freedom—that one belief powerful enough to stalemate the idea of communism. We have no other weapon to fight communism with but this, since in diplomacy we are children to communist diplomats, and in production we will always lag behind them since under monolithic government all production can go to the aggrandizement of the State. But then, we don't need anything else, since that idea— that simple belief of man that he can be free—is the strongest force on earth; all we need to do is, use it.

Because it is glib and simple, we like to think of the world situation today as a precarious and explosive balance of two irreconcilable ideologies confronting each other; which precarious balance, once it totters, will drag the whole world into the abyss along with it. That's not so. Only one of the forces is an ideology, an idea. Because the second force is the simple fact of Man: the simple belief of individual man that he can and should and will be free. And if we who so far are still free, want to continue to be free, all of us who are still free had better confederate, and confederate fast, with all others who still have a choice to be free—confederate not as black people nor white people nor pink nor blue nor green people, but as people who still are free with all other people who still are free; confederate together and stick together too, if we want a world or even a part of a world in which individual man can be free, to continue to endure.

And we had better take in with us as many as we can get of the nonwhite peoples of the earth who are not completely free yet but who want to be and intend to be, before that other force which is opposed to individual freedom, befools and gets them. Time was when the nonwhite was content to—anyway, did—accept his instinct for freedom as an unrealizable dream. But not any more; the white man himself taught him different with that phase of his—the white man's—own culture which took the form of colonial expansion and exploitation based and morally condoned on the premise of inequality not because of individual incompetence, but of mass race or color. As a result of which, in only ten years, we have watched the nonwhite peoples expel, by bloody violence when necessary, the white man from all of the middle east and Asia which he once dominated. And into that vacuum has already begun to move that other and inimical power which people who believe in freedom are at war with—that power which says to the nonwhite man: "We don't offer you freedom because there is no such thing as freedom; your white overlords whom you just threw out have already proved that to you. But we offer you equality: at least equality in slavedom; if you are to be slaves, at least you can be slaves to your own color and race and religion."

We, the western white man who does believe that there exists an individual freedom above and beyond this mere equality of slavedom, must teach the nonwhite peoples this while there is yet a little time left. We, America, who are the strongest force opposing communism and monolithicism, must teach all other peoples, white and nonwhite, slave or (for a little while yet) still free. We, America, have the best chance to do this because we can do it here, at home, without needing to send costly freedom expeditions into alien and inimical places already convinced that there is no such thing as freedom and liberty and equality and peace for all people, or we would practice it at home.

The best chance and the easiest job, because our non-white minority is already on our side; we don't need to sell them on America and freedom because they are already sold; even when ignorant from inferior or no education, even despite the record and history of inequality, they still believe in our concepts of freedom and democracy.

That is what America has done for them in only three hundred years. Not *to* them: *for* them, because to our shame we have made little effort so far to teach them to be Americans, let alone to use their capacities to make of ourselves a stronger and more unified America:—the people who only three hundred years ago were eating rotten elephant and hippo meat in African rain-forests, who lived beside one of the biggest bodies of inland water on earth and never thought of a sail, who yearly had to move by whole villages and tribes from famine and pestilence and human enemies without once thinking of a wheel, yet in only three hundred years in America produced Ralph Bunche and George Washington Carver and Booker T. Washington, who have yet to produce a Fuchs or Rosenberg or Gold or Greenglass or Burgess or McLean or Hiss, and for every prominent communist or fellow-traveler like Robeson, there are a thousand white ones.

I am not convinced that the Negro wants integration in the sense that some of us claim to fear he does. I believe he is American enough to repudiate and deny by simple American instinct any stricture or regulation forbidding us to do something which in our opinion would be harmless if we did it, and which we probably would not want to do anyway. I think that what he wants is equality, and I believe that he too knows there is no such thing as equality *per se,* but only equality *to:* equal right and opportunity to make the best one can of one's life within one's capacity and capability, without fear of injustice or oppression or threat of violence. If we had given him this equal right to opportunity ninety or fifty or even ten years ago, there would have been no Supreme Court decision about how we run our schools.

It is our white man's shame that in our present southern economy, the Negro must not have economic equality; our double shame that we fear that giving him more social equality will jeopardize his present economic status; our triple shame that even then, to justify ourselves, we must becloud the issue with the purity of white blood; what a commentary that the one remaining place on earth where the white man can flee and have his blood protected and defended by law, is Africa—Africa: the source and origin of the people whose presence in America will have driven the white man to flee from defilement.

Soon now all of us—not just Southerners nor even just Americans, but all people who are still free and want to remain so—are going to have to make a choice. We will have to choose not between color nor race nor religion nor between East and West either, but simply between being slaves and being free. And we will have to choose completely and for good; the time is already past now when we can choose a little of each, a little of both. We can choose a state of slavedom, and if we are powerful enough to be among the top two or three or ten, we can have a certain amount of license—until someone more powerful rises and has us machine-gunned against a cellar wall. But we cannot choose freedom established on a hierarchy of degrees of freedom, on a caste system of equality like military rank. We must be free not because we claim freedom, but because we practice it; our freedom must be buttressed by a homogeny equally and unchallengeably free, no matter what color they are, so that all the other inimical forces everywhere—systems political or religious or racial or national—will not just respect us because we practice freedom, they will fear us because we do.

The question is no longer of white against black. It is no longer whether or not white blood shall remain pure, it is whether or not white people shall remain free.

We accept insult and contumely and the risk of violence because we will not sit quietly by and see our native land, the South, not just Mississippi but all the South, wreck and ruin itself twice in less than a hundred years, over the Negro question.

We speak now against the day when our Southern people who will resist to the last these inevitable changes in social relations, will, when they have been forced to accept what they at one time might have accepted with dignity and goodwill, will say, "Why didn't someone tell us this before? Tell us this in time?"

[Memphis *Commercial Appeal,* November 11, 1955; the text printed here is that of the revised and expanded version first published in the pamphlet *Three Views of the Segregation Decisions,* Atlanta, Southern Regional Council, 1956.]

Address upon Receiving the
Silver Medal of the Athens Academy

I accept this medal not alone as an American nor as a writer but as one chosen by the Greek Academy to represent the principle that man shall be free.

The human spirit does not obey physical laws. When the sun of Pericles cast the shadow of civilized man around the earth, that shadow curved until it touched America. So when someone like me comes to Greece he is walking the shadow back to the source of the light which cast the shadow. When the American comes to this country he has come back to something that was familiar. He has come home. He has come back to the cradle of civilized man. I am proud that the Greek people have considered me worthy to receive this medal. It will be my duty to return to my country and tell my people that the qualities in the Greek race—toughness, bravery, independence and pride—are too valuable to lose. It is the duty of all men to see that they do not vanish from the earth.

[Press release issued by the United States Information Service in Athens at the time of the address. Faulkner received help in writing this speech from Duncan Emrich, cultural affairs officer of the American embassy. See Joseph Blotner, *Faulkner: A Biography,* New York, 1984, p. 637.]

Address to the American Academy of Arts and Letters in Presenting the Gold Medal for Fiction to John Dos Passos

NEW YORK, MAY 22, 1957

The artist, the writer, must never have any doubts about where he intends to go; the aim, the dream, must be that high to be worth that destination and the anguish of the effort to reach it. But he must have humility regarding his competence to get there, about his methods, his craft and his craftsmanship in it.

So the fact that the artist has no more actual place in the American culture of today than he has in the American economy of today, no place at all in the warp and woof, the thews and sinews, the mosaic of the American dream as it exists today, is perhaps a good thing for him since it teaches him humility in advance, gets him into the habit of humility well ahead whether he would or no; in which case, none of us has been better trained in humility than this man whom the Academy is honoring today. Which proves also that that man, that artist, who can accept the humility, will, must, in time, sooner or later, work through the humility and the oblivion into that moment when he and the value of his life's work will be recognized and honored at least by his fellow craftsmen, as John Dos Passos and his life's work are at this moment.

It is my honor to share in his by having been chosen to hand this medal to him. No man deserves it more, and few have waited longer for it.

[*Proceedings of the American Academy of Arts and Letters and the National Institute of Arts and Letters,* second series, New York, 1958; the text printed here has been taken from a copy of Faulkner's typescript. According to Malcolm Cowley, Faulkner's actual address was abbreviated, and recorded. What he said was, "Oratory can't add anything to John Dos Passos' stature, and if I know anything about writers, he may be grateful for a little less of it. So I'll say, mine is the honor to partake of his in handing this medal to him. No man deserves it more." See Malcolm Cowley, *The Faulkner-Cowley File,* New York, 1966, pp. 146–7.]

Address to the Raven, Jefferson, and ODK Societies of the University of Virginia

CHARLOTTESVILLE, FEBRUARY 20, 1958

A Word to Virginians

A hundred years ago Abraham Lincoln said, "This nation cannot endure half slave and half free." If he were alive today he would amend it: "This nation cannot endure containing a minority as large as ten percent held second class in citizenship by the accident of physical appearance." As a lesser man might put it, this nor any country or community of people can no more get along in peace with ten percent of its population arbitrarily unassimilated than a town of five thousand people can get along in peace with five hundred unbridled horses loose in the streets, or say a community of five thousand cats with five hundred unassimilated dogs among them, or vice versa. For peaceful coexistence, all must be one thing: either all first class citizens, or all second class citizens; either all people or all horses; either all cats or all dogs.

Perhaps the Negro is not yet capable of more than second class citizenship. His tragedy may be that so far he is competent for equality only in the ratio of his white blood. But even if that is so, the problem of the second class citizens still remains. It would not solve the problem even if the Negro were himself content to remain only a second class citizen even though relieved of his first class responsibilities by his classification. The fact would still remain that we are a nation established on the fact that we are only ninety percent unified in power. With only ninety percent of unanimity, we would face (and hope to survive in it) an inimical world unified against us even if only in inimicality. We cannot be even ninety percent unified against that inimical world which outnumbers us, because too much of even that ninety percent of power is spent and consumed by the physical problem of the ten percent of irresponsibles.

It is easy enough for the North to blame on us, the South, the fact that this problem is still unsolved. If I were a northerner, that's what I would do: tell myself that one hundred years ago, we, both of us, North and South, had put it to the test, and had solved it. That it is not us, the North, but you, the South, who have refused to accept that verdict. Nor will it help us any to remind the North that, by ratio of Negro to white in population, there is probably more of inequality and injustice there than with us.

Instead, we should accept that gambit. Let us say to the North: All right, it is our problem, and we will solve it. For the sake of argument, let us agree that as yet the Negro is incapable of equality for the reason that he could not hold and keep it even if it were forced on him with bayonets; that once the bayonets were removed, the first smart and ruthless man black or white who came along would take it away from him, because he, the Negro, is not yet capable of, or refuses to accept, the responsibilities of equality.

So we, the white man, must take him in hand and teach him that responsibility; this will not be the first time nor the last time in the long record of man's history that moral principle has been identical with and even inextricable from practical common sense. Let us teach him that, in order to be free and equal, he must first be worthy of it, and then forever afterward work to hold and keep and defend it. He must learn to cease forever more thinking like a Negro and acting like a Negro. This will not be easy for him. His burden will be that, because of his race and color, it will not suffice for him to think and act like just any white man: he must think and act like the best among white men. Because where the white man, because of his race and color, can practise morality and rectitude just on Sunday and let the rest of the week go hang, the Negro can never let up nor deviate.

That is our job here in the South. It is possible that the white race and the Negro race can never really like and trust each other; this for the reason that the white man can never really know the Negro, because the white man has forced the Negro to be always a Negro rather than another human being in their dealings, and therefore the Negro cannot afford, does not dare, to be open with the white man and let the white man know what he, the Negro, thinks. But I do know that we in the South, having grown up with and lived among Negroes for generations, are capable in individual cases of liking and trusting individual Negroes, which the North can never do because the northerner only fears him.

So we alone can teach the Negro the responsibility of

personal morality and rectitude—either by taking him into our white schools, or giving him white teachers in his own schools until we have taught the teachers of his own race to teach and train him in these hard and un-pleasant habits. Whether or not he ever learns his a-b-c's or what to do with common fractions, wont matter. What he must learn are the hard things—self-restraint, honesty, dependability, purity; to act not even as well as just any white man, but to act as well as the best of white men. If we dont, we will spend the rest of our lives dodg-ing among the five hundred unbridled horses; we will look forward each year to another Clinton or Little Rock not only further and further to wreck what we have so far created of peaceful relations between the two races, but to be international monuments and milestones to our ridicule and shame.

And the place for this to begin is Virginia, the mother of all the rest of us of the South. Compared to you, my country—Mississippi, Alabama, Arkansas—is still fron-tier, still wilderness. Yet even in our wilderness we look back to that mother-stock as though it were not really so distant and so far removed. Even in our wilderness the old Virginia blood still runs and the old Virginia names —Byrd and Lee and Carter—still endure. There is no family in our wilderness but has that old aunt or grand-mother to tell the children as soon as they can hear and understand: Your blood is Virginia blood too; your great-great-great grandfather was born in Rockbridge or Fairfax or Prince George—Valley or Piedmont or Tide-water, right down to the nearest milestone, so that Vir-ginia is a living place to that child long before he ever heard (or cares) about New York or, for that matter, America.

So let it begin in Virginia, toward whom the rest of us

are already looking as the child looks toward the parent for a sign, a signal where to go and how to go. A hundred years ago the hot-heads of Mississippi and Georgia and South Carolina would not listen when the mother of us all tried to check our reckless and headlong course; we ignored you then, to all our grief, yours more than any since you bore more of the battles. But this time we will hear you. Let this be the voice of that wilderness, speaking not just to Mother Virginia but to the best of her children—sons found and chosen worthy to be trained to the old pattern in the University established by Mr Jefferson to be not just a dead monument to, but the enduring fountain of his principles of order within the human condition and the relationship of man with man—the messenger, the mouthpiece of all, saying to the mother of us all: Show us the way and lead us in it. I believe we will follow you.

[*University of Virginia Magazine,* Spring 1958; collected in *Faulkner in the University,* edited by Frederick L. Gwynn and Joseph L. Blotner, University of Virginia Press, 1959. The text printed here has been taken from Faulkner's typescript.]

⁂ ⁂ ⁂

Address to the English Club of the University of Virginia

CHARLOTTESVILLE, APRIL 24, 1958

A Word to Young Writers

Two years ago President Eisenhower conceived a plan based on an idea which is basically a sound one. This was that world conditions, the universal dilemma of mankind at this moment, are what they are simply because individual men and women of different races and tongues and conditions cannot discuss with one another these problems and dilemmas which are primarily theirs, but must attempt to do so only through the formal organizations of their antagonistic and seemingly irreconcilable governments.

That is, that individual people in all walks of life should be given opportunity to speak to their individual opposite numbers all over the earth—laborer to laborer, scientist to scientist, doctors and lawyers and merchants and bankers and artists to their opposite numbers everywhere.

There was nothing wrong with this idea. Certainly no artist—painter, musician, sculptor, architect, writer— would dispute it because this—trying to communicate man to man regardless of race or color or condition—is exactly what every artist has already spent all his life trying to do, and as long as he breathes will continue to do.

What doomed it in my opinion was symptomised by the phraseology of the President's own concept: laborer to laborer, artist to artist, banker to banker, tycoon to tycoon. What doomed it in my opinion was an evil inherent in our culture itself; an evil quality inherent in (and perhaps necessary though I for one do not believe this last) in the culture of any country capable of enduring and surviving through this period of history. This is the mystical belief, almost a religion, that individual man cannot speak to individual man because individual man can no longer exist. A belief that there is no place anymore where individual man can speak quietly to individual man of such simple things as honesty with oneself and responsibility toward others and protection for the weak and compassion and pity for all because such individual things as honesty and pity and responsibility and compassion no longer exist and man himself can hope to continue only by relinquishing and denying his individuality into a regimented group of his arbitrary factional kind, arrayed against an opposite opposed arbitrary factional regimented group, both filling the same air at the same time with the same double-barreled abstractions of 'peoples' democracy' and 'minority rights' and 'equal justice' and 'social welfare'—all the synonyms which take all the shame out of irresponsibility by not merely inviting but even compelling everyone to participate in it.

So in this case—I mean the President's People-to-People Committee—the artist too, who has already spent his life trying to communicate simply people to people the problems and passions of the human heart and how to survive them or anyway endure them, has in effect been asked by the President of his country to affirm that mythology which he has already devoted his life to denying: the mythology that one single individual man is nothing, and can have weight and substance only when organised into the anonymity of a group where he will have surrendered his individual soul for a number.

It would be sad enough if only at such moments as this—I mean, formal recognition by his country of the validity of his life's dedication—did the artist have to run full-tilt into what might be called almost a universal will to regimentation, a universal will to obliterate the humanity from man even to the extent of relieving him not only of moral responsibility but even of physical pain and mortality by effacing him individually into any, it does not matter which as long as he has vanished into one of them, nationally-recognised economic group by profession or trade or occupation or income-tax bracket or, if nothing else offers, finance-company list. His tragedy is that today he must even combat this pressure, waste some part of his puny but (if he is an artist) precious individual strength against this universal will to efface his individual humanity, in order to be an artist. Which comes at last to the idea I want to suggest, which is what seems to me to be the one dilemma in which all young writers today participate.

I think that perhaps all writers, while they are 'hot,' working at top speed to try to get said all they feel the terrific urgency to say, dont read the writers younger, after, themselves, perhaps for the same reason which the sprinter or the distance-runner has: he does not have time to be interested in who is behind him or even up with him, but only in who is in front. That was true in my own case anyway, so there was a gap of about twenty-five years during which I had almost no acquaintance whatever with contemporary literature.

So, when a short time ago I did begin to read the writing being done now, I brought to it not only ignorance but a kind of innocence, freshness, what you might call a point of view and an interest virgin of preconceptions. Anyway, I got from the first story an impression which has repeated itself so consistently since, that I shall offer it as a generalisation. This is, that the young writer of today is compelled by the present state of our culture which I tried to describe, to function in a kind of vacuum of the human race. His characters do not function, live, breathe, struggle, in that moil and seethe of simple humanity as did those of our predecessors who were the masters from whom we learned our craft: Dickens, Fielding, Thackeray, Conrad, Twain, Smollett, Hawthorne, Melville, James; their names are legion whose created characters were not just weaned but even spawned into a moil and seethe of simple human beings whose very existence was an affirmation of an incurable and indomitable optimism—men and women like themselves, understandable and comprehensible even when antipathetical, even in the very moment while they were murdering or robbing or betraying you, since theirs too were the same simple human lusts and hopes and fears uncomplicated by regimentation or group compulsion— a moil and seethe of humanity into which they could venture not only unappalled and welcome but with pleasure too and with no threat of harm since the worst that could happen to them would be a head bumped by what was only another human head, an elbow or a knee skinned but that too was only another human knee or elbow which did the skinning—a moil and seethe of mankind which accepted and believed in and functioned according, not to angles, but to moral principles; where truth was not where you were standing when you looked at it but was an unalterable quality or thing which could and would knock your brains out if you did not accept it or at least respect it.

While today the young writer's characters must function not in individuality but in isolation, not to pursue in myriad company the anguishes and hopes of all human hearts in a world of a few simple comprehensible truths and moral principles, but to exist alone inside a vacuum of facts which he did not choose and cannot cope with and cannot escape from like a fly inside an inverted tumbler.

Let me repeat: I have not read all the work of this present generation of writing; I have not had time yet. So I must speak only of the ones I do know. I am thinking now of what I rate the best one: Salinger's *Catcher in the Rye,* perhaps because this one expresses so completely what I have tried to say: a youth, father to what will, must someday be a man, more intelligent than some and more sensitive than most, who (he would not even have called it by instinct because he did not know he possessed it) because God perhaps had put it there, loved man and wished to be a part of mankind, humanity, who tried to join the human race and failed. To me, his tragedy was not that he was, as he perhaps thought, not tough enough or brave enough or deserving enough to be accepted into humanity. His tragedy was that when he attempted to enter the human race, there was no human race there. There was nothing for him to do save buzz, frantic and inviolate, inside the glass walls of his tumbler until he either gave up or was himself by himself, by his own frantic buzzing, destroyed. One thinks of course immediately of Huck Finn, another youth already father to what will some day soon now be a man. But in Huck's case all he had to combat was his small size, which time would cure for him; in time he would be as big as any man he had to cope with; and even as it was, all the adult world could do to harm him was skin his nose a little; humanity, the human race, would and was accepting him already; all he needed to do was just to grow up in it.

That is the young writer's dilemma as I see it. Not just his, but all our problems, is to save mankind from being desouled as the stallion or boar or bull is gelded; to save the individual from anonymity before it is too late and humanity has vanished from the animal called man. And who better to save man's humanity than the writer, the poet, the artist, since who should fear the loss of it more since the humanity of man is the artist's life blood.

[*Faulkner in the University,* edited by Frederick L. Gwynn and Joseph L. Blotner, University of Virginia Press, 1959. The text has been corrected from Faulkner's typescript.]

Address to the
U. S. National Commission for
UNESCO

DENVER, COLORADO, OCTOBER 2, 1959

It is not the part, nor is there any need for any of us Americans, South, Middle or North, to welcome one another to our country, anymore than to welcome each other into the humanity of man. The fact that we are here at this moment, have come all our various distances, at trouble and sacrifice and expense, to be here at this moment is proof that we have served our apprenticeship to the human spirit and are now full and veteran members in the humanity of man.

That is, we have gathered here from our arduous distances because we believe that "I, Me" is more important than any government or language. We are descendants of people who in the old hemisphere believed that to be possible, and burst the old bonds into a new hemisphere where that belief could be tested. There are times, too many times, when we have failed in that dream. But out of every failure there arises always a new handfull who decline to be convinced by failure, who believe still that the human problems can be solved. As we have met here today, not in the name of races or ideologies, but of humanity, the spirit of man, to try again. We will fail again perhaps, but at least we have learned that that failure will not be important either. That failure will not even have laurels to rest on, since out of that failure also will rise its handfull, still irreconcilable and undismayed.

Mr. Khrushchev says that Communism, the police state, will bury the free ones. He is a smart gentleman, he knows that this is nonsense since freedom, man's dim concept of and belief in the human spirit is the cause of all his troubles in his own country. But if he means that Communism will bury capitalism, he is correct. That funeral will occur about ten minutes after the police bury gambling. Because simple man, the human race, will bury both of them. That will be when we have expended the last grain, dram and iota of our natural resources. But man himself will not be in that grave. The last sound on the worthless earth will be two human beings trying to launch a homemade space ship and already quarreling about where they are going next.

[*Unesco News* press release, October 2, 1959. Faulkner received help in writing this speech from Foreign Service Officer Abram Minell. See Joseph Blotner, *Faulkner: A Biography,* New York, 1984, p. 674.]

Address to the American Academy of Arts and Letters upon Acceptance of the Gold Medal for Fiction

NEW YORK, MAY 24, 1962

Miss Welty, Mr. President, Members of the Academy, Ladies and Gentlemen: This award has, to me, a double value. It is not only a comforting recognition of some considerable years of reasonably hard and arduous, anyway consistently dedicated, work. It also recognizes and affirms, and so preserves, a quantity in our American legend and dream well worth preserving.

I mean a quantity in our past: that past which was a happier time in the sense that we were innocent of many of the strains and anguishes and fears which these atomic days have compelled on us. This award evokes the faded airs and dimming rotogravures which record that vanished splendor still inherent in the names of Saint Louis and Leipzig, the quantity which they celebrated and signified recorded still today in the labels of wine bottles and ointment jars.

I think that those gold medals, royal and unique above the myriad spawn of their progeny which were the shining ribbons fluttering and flashing among the booths and stalls of forgotten county fairs in recognition and accolade of a piece of tatting or an apple pie, did much more than record a victory. They affirmed the premise that there are no degrees of best; that one man's best is the equal of any other best, no matter how asunder in time or space or comparison, and should be honored as such.

We should keep that quantity, more than ever now, when roads get shorter and easier between aim and gain and goals become less demanding and more easily attained, and there is less and less space between elbows and more and more pressure on the individual to relinquish into one faceless serration like a mouthful of teeth, simply in order to find room to breathe. We should remember those times when the idea of an individuality of excellence compounded of resourcefulness and independence and uniqueness not only deserved a blue ribbon but got one. Let the past abolish the past when—and if—it can substitute something better; not us to abolish the past simply because it was.

[*Proceedings of the American Academy of Arts and Letters and the National Institute of Arts and Letters,* second series, New York, 1963. Joseph Blotner wrote a draft of this speech. See Blotner, *Faulkner: A Biography,* New York, 1984, p. 703.]

THREE

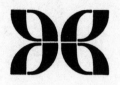

Introductions

Foreword

Sherwood Anderson & Other Famous Creoles

(NEW ORLEANS, 1926*)

FIRST, let me tell you something about our Quarter, the Vieux Carre. Do you know our quarter, with its narrow streets, its old wrought-iron balconies and its southern European atmosphere? An atmosphere of richness and soft laughter, you know. It has a kind of ease, a kind of awareness of the unimportance of things that outlanders like myself—I am not a native—were taught to believe important. So it is no wonder that as one walks about the quarter one sees artists here and there on the shady side of the street corners, sketching houses and balconies. I have counted as many as forty in a single afternoon, and though I did not know their names nor the value of their paintings, they were my brothers. And in this fellowship where no badges are worn and no sign of greeting is required, I passed them as they bent over their canvasses, and as I walked onward I mused on the richness of our American life that permits forty people to

---

* Originally this Foreword was printed entirely in italics. The book was a privately published collection of sketches, "Drawn by Wm. Spratling & Arranged by Wm. Faulkner."

spend day after day painting pictures in a single area comprised in six city blocks.

When this young man, Spratling, came to see me, I did not remember him. Perhaps I had passed him in the street. Perhaps he had been one of the painters at whose easel I had paused, to examine. Perhaps he knew me. Perhaps he had recognized me when I paused, perhaps he had been aware of the fellowship between us and had said to himself, 'I will talk to him about what I wish to do; I will talk my thought out to him. He will understand, for there is a fellowship between us.'

But when he came to call on me, I did not remember him at all. He wore a neat business suit and carried merely a portfolio under his arm, and I did not recognize him. And after he had told me his name and laid the portfolio on the corner of my desk and sat opposite me and began to expound his plan to me, I had a kind of a vision. I saw myself being let in for something. I saw myself incurring an obligation which I should later regret, and as we sat facing one another across my desk, I framed in my mind the words with which I should tell him No. Then he leaned forward and untied the portfolio and spread it open before me, and I understood. And I said to him, 'What you want me for is a wheelhorse, is it?' And when he smiled his quick shy smile, I knew that we should be friends.

We have one priceless universal trait, we Americans. That trait is our humor. What a pity it is that it is not more prevalent in our art. This characteristic alone, being national and indigenous, could, by concentrating our emotional forces inward upon themselves, do for us what England's insularity did for English art during the reign of Elizabeth. One trouble with us American artists is that we take our art and ourselves too seriously. And perhaps seeing ourselves in the eyes of our fellow artists, will enable those who have strayed to establish anew a sound contact with the fountainhead of our American life.

W. F.

Introduction

TO THE MODERN LIBRARY EDITION OF

Sanctuary

(NEW YORK, 1932)

THIS book was written three years ago. To me it is a cheap idea, because it was deliberately conceived to make money. I had been writing books for about five years, which got published and not bought. But that was all right. I was young then and hard-bellied. I had never lived among nor known people who wrote novels and stories and I suppose I did not know that people got money for them. I was not very much annoyed when publishers refused the mss. now and then. Because I was hard-gutted then. I could do a lot of things that could earn what little money I needed, thanks to my father's unfailing kindness which supplied me with bread at need despite the outrage to his principles at having been of a bum progenitive.

Then I began to get a little soft. I could still paint houses and do carpenter work, but I got soft. I began to think about making money by writing. I began to be concerned when magazine editors turned down short stories, concerned enough to tell them that they would buy these stories later anyway, and hence why not now. Meanwhile, with one novel completed and consistently refused for two years, I had just written my guts into

The Sound and the Fury though I was not aware until the book was published that I had done so, because I had done it for pleasure. I believed then that I would never be published again. I had stopped thinking of myself in publishing terms.

But when the third mss., *Sartoris*, was taken by a publisher and (he having refused *The Sound and the Fury*) it was taken by still another publisher, who warned me at the time that it would not sell, I began to think of myself again as a printed object. I began to think of books in terms of possible money. I decided I might just as well make some of it myself. I took a little time out, and speculated what a person in Mississippi would believe to be current trends, chose what I thought was the right answer and invented the most horrific tale I could imagine and wrote it in about three weeks and sent it to Smith, who had done *The Sound and the Fury* and who wrote me immediately, "Good God, I can't publish this. We'd both be in jail." So I told Faulkner, "You're damned. You'll have to work now and then for the rest of your life." That was in the summer of 1929. I got a job in the power plant, on the night shift, from 6 P.M. to 6 A.M., as a coal passer. I shoveled coal from the bunker into a wheelbarrow and wheeled it in and dumped it where the fireman could put it into the boiler. About 11 o'clock the people would be going to bed, and so it did not take so much steam. Then we could rest, the fireman and I. He would sit in a chair and doze. I had invented a table out of a wheelbarrow in the coal bunker, just beyond a wall from where a dynamo ran. It made a deep, constant humming noise. There was no more work to do until about 4 A.M., when we would have to clean the fires and get up steam again. On these nights, between 12 and 4, I wrote *As I Lay Dying* in six weeks, without changing a word. I sent it to Smith and wrote him that by it I would stand or fall.

I think I had forgotten about *Sanctuary,* just as you might forget about anything made for an immediate purpose, which did not come off. *As I Lay Dying* was published and I didn't remember the mss. of *Sanctuary* until Smith sent me the galleys. Then I saw that it was so terrible that there were but two things to do: tear it up or rewrite it. I thought again, "It might sell; maybe 10,000 of them will buy it." So I tore the galleys down and rewrote the book. It had been already set up once, so I had to pay for the privilege of rewriting it, trying to make out of it something which would not shame *The Sound and the Fury* and *As I Lay Dying* too much and I made a fair job and I hope you will buy it and tell your friends and I hope they will buy it too.

New York, 1932.   WILLIAM FAULKNER.

Foreword

TO

The Faulkner Reader

(NEW YORK, 1954)

MY GRANDFATHER had a moderate though reasonably diffuse and catholic library; I realize now that I got most of my early education in it. It was a little limited in its fiction content, since his taste was for simple straightforward romantic excitement like Scott or Dumas. But there was a heterogeneous scattering of other volumes, chosen apparently at random and by my grandmother, since the flyleaves bore her name and the dates in the 1880's and '90's of that time when even in a town as big as Memphis, Tennessee, ladies stopped in their carriages in the street in front of the stores and shops, and clerks and even proprietors came out to receive their commands—that time when women did most of the book-buying and the reading too, naming their children Byron and Clarissa and St. Elmo and Lothair after the romantic and tragic heroes and heroines and the even more romantic creators of them.

One of these books was by a Pole, Sienkiewicz—a story of the time of King John Sobieski, when the Poles, almost single-handed, kept the Turks from overrunning Central Europe. This one, like all books of that period, at least the ones my grandfather owned, had a preface, a foreword. I never read any of them; I was too eager to get on to what the people themselves were doing and anguishing and triumphing over. But I did read the foreword in this one, the first one I ever took time to read; I don't know why now. It went something like this:

This book was written at the expense of considerable effort, to uplift men's hearts, and I thought: *What a nice thing to have thought to say.* But no more than that. I didn't even think, *Maybe some day I will write a book too and what a shame I didn't think of that first so I could put it on the front page of mine.* Because I hadn't thought of writing books then. The future didn't extend that far. This was 1915 and '16; I had seen an aeroplane and my mind was filled with names: Ball, and Immelman and Boelcke, and Guynemer and Bishop, and I was waiting, biding, until I would be old enough or free enough or anyway could get to France and become glorious and beribboned too.

Then that had passed. It was 1923 and I wrote a book and discovered that my doom, fate, was to keep on writing books: not for any exterior or ulterior purpose: just writing the books for the sake of writing the books; obviously, since the publisher considered them worth the financial risk of being printed, someone would read them. But that was unimportant too as measured against the need to get them written, though naturally one hopes that who read them would find them true and honest and even perhaps moving. Because one was too busy writing the books during the time while the demon which drove him still considered him worthy of, deserving of, the anguish of being driven, while the blood and glands and flesh still remained strong and potent, the heart and the imagination still remained undulled to follies and lusts and heroisms of men and women; still writing the books because they had to be written after the blood and glands began to slow and cool a little and the heart began to tell him, *You don't know the answer either and you will never find it,* but still writing the books because the demon was still kind; only a little more severe and unpitying: until suddenly one day he saw that that old half-forgotten Pole had had the answer all the time.

To uplift man's heart; the same for all of us: for the ones who are trying to be artists, the ones who are trying to write simple entertainment, the ones who write to shock, and the ones who are simply escaping themselves and their own private anguishes.

Some of us don't know that this is what we are writing for. Some of us will know it and deny it, lest we be accused and self-convicted and condemned of sentimentality, which people nowadays for some reason are ashamed to be tainted with; some of us seem to have curious ideas of just where the heart is located, confusing it with other and baser glands and organs and activities. But we all write for this one purpose.

This does not mean that we are trying to change man, improve him, though this is the hope—maybe even the intention—of some of us. On the contrary, in its last analysis, this hope and desire to uplift man's heart is completely selfish, completely personal. He would lift up man's heart for his own benefit because in that way he can say No to death. He is saying No to death for himself by means of the hearts which he has hoped to uplift, or even by means of the mere base glands which he has disturbed to that extent where they can say No to death on their own account by knowing, realizing, having been told and believing it: *At least we are not vegetables because the hearts and glands capable of partaking in this excitement are not those of vegetables, and will, must, endure.*

So he who, from the isolation of cold impersonal print, can engender this excitement, himself partakes of the immortality which he has engendered. Some day he will be no more, which will not matter then, because isolated and itself invulnerable in the cold print remains that which is capable of engendering still the old deathless excitement in hearts and glands whose owners and custodians are generations from even the air he breathed and anguished in; if it was capable once, he knows that it will be capable and potent still long after there remains of him only a dead and fading name.

New York
November, 1953

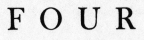

FOUR

Book Reviews

Review

OF

The Road Back

BY ERICH MARIA REMARQUE

THERE is a victory beyond defeat which the victorious know nothing of. A bourne, a shore of refuge beyond the lost battles, the bronze names and the lead tombs, guarded and indicated not by the triumphant and man-limbed goddess with palm and sword, but by some musing and motionless handmaiden of despair itself.

Man does not seem to be able to stand very much prosperity; least of all does a people, a nation. Defeat is good for him, for it. Victory is the rocket, the glare, the momentary apotheosis at right angles with time and so doomed: a bursting diffusion of sparks at the last, dying and dead, leaving a word perhaps, a name, a date, for the tedium of children in primary history. It is the defeat which, serving him against his belief and his desire, turns him back upon that alone which can sustain him: his fellows, his racial homogeneity; himself; the earth, the implacable soil, monument and tomb of sweat.

This is beyond the talking, the hard words, the excuses and the reasons; beyond the despair. Beyond that dreadful desire and need to justify the disaster and give it significance by clinging to it, explaining it, which is the proven best way to support the inescapable. Victory requires no explanation. It is in itself sufficient: the fine screen, the shield; immediate and final: it will be contemplated only by history. While the whole contemporary world watches the defeat and the undefeated who, because of that fact, survived.

That's where the need to talk, to explain it, comes from. That's why Remarque puts into the mouths of characters speeches which they would have been incapable of making. It's not that the speeches were not true. If the characters had heard them spoken by another, they would have been the first to say, "That is so. This is what I think, what I would have said if I had just thought of it first." But they could not have said the speeches themselves. And this method is not justified, unless a man is writing propaganda. It is a writer's privilege to put into the mouths of his characters better speech than they would have been capable of, but only for the purpose of permitting and helping the character to justify himself or what he believes himself to be, taking down his spiritual pants. But when the character must express moral ideas applicable to a race, a situation, he is better kept in that untimed and unsexed background of the choruses of Greek senators.

But perhaps this is a minor point. Perhaps it is a racial fault of the author, as the outcome of the War was due in part to a German racial fault: a belief that a mathematical calculation would be superior to the despair of cornered rats. Anyway, Remarque justifies himself: ". . . I try to console him. What I say does not convince him, but it gives me some relief. . . . It is always so with comfort."

It is a moving book. Because Remarque was moved by the writing of it. Granted that his intent is more than opportunism, it still remains to be seen if art can be made of authentic experience transferred to paper word for word, of a peculiar reaction to an actual condition, even though it be vicarious. To a writer, no matter how susceptible he be, personal experience is just what it is to the man in the street who buttonholes him because he is a writer, with the same belief, the same conviction of individual significance: "Listen. All you have to do is write it down as it happened. My life, what has happened to me. It will make a good book, but I am not a writer myself. So I will give it to you. If I were a writer myself, had the time to write it down myself. You won't have to change a word." That does not make a book. No matter how vivid it be, somewhere between the experience and the blank page and the pencil, it dies. Perhaps the words kill it.

Give Remarque the benefit of the doubt and call the book a reaction to despair. Victory has its despairs, too, since the victorious not only do not gain anything, but when the hurrah dies away at last, they do not even know what they were fighting for, what they hoped to gain, because what little percentage there was in the whole affair, the defeated got it. If Germany had been victorious, this book would not have been written. And if the United States had not got back its troops 50-percent intact, save for the casual cases of syphilis and high metropolitan life, it would not be bought (which I hope and trust that it will be) and read. And it won't be the American Legion either that will buy the 40,000 copies, even if there are forty thousand of them that keep their dues paid up.

It moves you, as watching a child making mud pies on the day of its mother's funeral moves you. Yet at the end there is still that sense of missing significance, the feeling that, like so much that emerges from a losing side in any contest, and particularly from Germany since 1918, it was created primarily for the Western trade, to sell among the heathen like colored glass. From beyond the sentimentality, the defeat and the talking, this fact at least has emerged: America has been conquered not by the German soldiers that died in French and Flemish trenches, but by the German soldiers that died in German books.

[*New Republic,* May 20, 1931]

Review

OF

Test Pilot

BY JIMMY COLLINS

I was disappointed in this book. But it was better than I expected. I mean, better as current literature. I had expected, hoped, that it would be a kind of new trend, a literature or blundering at self-expression, not of a man, but of this whole new business of speed just to be moving fast; a kind of embryo, instead of the revelation by himself of a man who was a pretty good guy probably and did it pretty well and had more to say than some I know and in a sense was just incidentally writing about flying.

For the book turned out to be a perfectly normal and pretty good collection of anecdotes out of the life and experience of a professional flyer. They are wide in range and of varying degrees of worth and interest, and one, an actual experience which reads like fiction, is excellent, concise, and ordered, and not only sustained but restrained. None of them is long and none overtold (his sense of restraint along with his gift for narrative were the author's best qualities), though I feel that some of them never warranted the telling to begin with, and most of them are tinged with a kind of sentimental journalese—that reportorial rapport which seems to know at once and by sheer instinct when any public figure enters town and where to find him—which shows especially in his nature descriptions. You are never arrested by a single description of night sky or night earth or sunset or moonlight or fog; you have seen it before a hundred times and it has been phrased just that way in ten thousand newspaper columns and magazines. But then, Collins was a newspaper writer. But even if he had not been, this could justly be excused him because of the sort of life a test pilot would have to lead: a life which would never dare solitude, whose even idleness must take place where people congregate, which would not dare retire into introspection where it might contemplate sheer language calmly or it would have to cease to be that of a test pilot. But he had undeniable narrative skill; he would doubtless have written whether he flew or not. In fact, the book itself indicates that he apparently wanted to write, or at least that he flew only to make money to support his family.

Collins is dead, killed in the crash of an aeroplane which he was testing for the Navy, it being the custom of the military not to permit its own pilots to test new aeroplanes. The last chapter in the book is entitled "I Am Dead", and consists of an obituary which Collins wrote himself. I don't mean to make any commentary on twentieth-century publishing methods, the crass come-on schemes of modern day publishing, for whose benefit by an almost incredible fortuity Collins wrote the document, dared to it, I believe jokingly, by a friend, and I believe jokingly complying, because the book states that the dive which killed him was the last of a series on the last aeroplane which he intended to test, having perhaps gradually built up an income through his writing: but this should have been a private document, shown you privately by the friend with whom he left it. You are sorry to read it in a book. It should not have been included. It should have been quoted from, at most, quoted not as the document which it is, but for a figure which it contains, the only figure or phrase in the book which suddenly arrests the mind with the fine shock of poetry:

> The cold but vibrant fuselage was the last thing to feel my warm and living flesh.

But there is still another reason why "I Am Dead" should not have been included. Because this time Collins overwrote himself, the only time in the book. Because, though he may have begun it jokingly, he did not continue, since no man is going to joke to himself about his own death. So this time he overwrote. But I suppose this may be forgiven him too, since though a man stops sentimentalizing about love probably the day he discovers that both he and his first sweetheart not only can desire and even take another but do, he probably never reaches that day when he no longer sentimentalizes over his own passing.

But this is not what I hold against the book. What I hold is that it is not what I had hoped for. I had hoped to find a kind of embryo, a still formless forerunner or symptom of a folklore of speed, the high speed of today which I believe stands a good deal nearer to the end of the limits which human beings and material were capable of when man first dug iron, than to the beginning of those limits as they stood ten or twelve years ago when man first began to go really fast. Not the limits for the machines, but for the men who fly them: the limit at which blood vessels will burst and entrails rupture in making any sort of turn that will keep you in the same county, not to speak of co-ordination and perception of distance and depth, even when they invent or discover some way to alter further the law of top speed ratio to landing speed than by wing flaps so that all the flights will not have to start and stop from one of the Great Lakes. The precision pilots of today even must have absolutely perfect co-ordination and depth perception, so perhaps, being perfect, these will function at any speed up to infinity. But they will still have to do something about a pilot's blood vessels and guts. Perhaps they will contrive to create a kind of species or race, as they used to create and nurture races of singers and eunuchs, like Mussolini's Agello who flies more than four hundred miles an hour. They will be neither stalled ox nor game chicken, but capons: children culled by rules or even by machines from each generation and cloistered and in a sense emasculated and trained to conduct the vehicles in which the rest of us will hurtle from place to place. They will have to be taken in infancy because the precision pilot of today begins to train in his teens and is through in his thirties. These would be a species and in time a race and in time they would produce a folklore.

But probably by then the rest of us could not decipher it, perhaps not even hear it since already we have objects which can outpace their own sound and so their very singers would travel in what to us would be a sound-proof vacuum.

But it was not of this folklore that I was thinking. That one would be years in the making. I had thought of one which might exist even now and of which I had hoped that this book might be the symptom, the first fumbling precursor. It would be a folklore not of the age of speed nor of the men who perform it, but of the speed itself, peopled not by anything human or even mortal but by the clever willful machines themselves carrying nothing that was born and will have to die or which can even suffer pain, moving without comprehensible purpose toward no discernible destination, producing a literature innocent of either love or hate and of course of pity or terror, and which would be the story of the final disappearance of life from the earth. I would watch them, the little puny mortals, vanishing against a vast and timeless void filled with the sound of incredible engines, within which furious meteors moving in no medium hurtled nowhere, neither pausing nor flagging, forever destroying themselves and one another.

[*American Mercury,* November 1935. See, also, p. 328–33.]

Review

OF

The Old Man and the Sea

BY ERNEST HEMINGWAY

HIS BEST. Time may show it to be the best single piece of any of us, I mean his and my contemporaries. This time, he discovered God, a Creator. Until now, his men and women had made themselves, shaped themselves out of their own clay; their victories and defeats were at the hands of each other, just to prove to themselves or one another how tough they could be. But this time, he wrote about pity: about something somewhere that made them all: the old man who had to catch the fish and then lose it, the fish that had to be caught and then lost, the sharks which had to rob the old man of his fish; made them all and loved them all and pitied them all. It's all right. Praise God that whatever made and loves and pities Hemingway and me kept him from touching it any further.

[*Shenandoah,* III (Autumn 1952)]

FIVE

Public Letters

It is a difficult question. I can name offhand several books which I should like to have written, if only for the privilege of rewriting parts of them. But I dare say there are any number of angels in heaven today (particularly recent American arrivals) who look down upon the world and muse with a little regret on how much neater they would have done the job than the Lord, in the fine heat of His creative fury, did.

I think that the book which I put down with the un-qualified thought "I wish I had written that" is *Moby Dick*. The Greek-like simplicity of it: a man of forceful character driven by his sombre nature and his bleak heritage, bent on his own destruction and dragging his immediate world down with him with a despotic and utter disregard of them as individuals; the fine point to which the various natures caught (and passive as though with a foreknowledge of unalterable doom) in the fatality of his blind course are swept—a sort of Golgotha of the heart become immutable as bronze in the sonority of its plunging ruin; all against the grave and tragic rhythm of the earth in its most timeless phase: the sea. And the symbol of their doom: a White Whale. There's a death for a man, now; none of your patient pasturage for little grazing beasts you can't even see with the naked eye. There's magic in the very word. A White Whale. White is a grand word, like a crash of massed trumpets; and le-

---

* Faulkner was one of a number of authors asked what book they would most like to have written.

viathan himself has a kind of placid blundering majesty in his name. And then put them together!!! A death for Achilles, and the divine maidens of Patmos to mourn him, to harp white-handed sorrow on their golden hair.

And yet, when I remember Moll Flanders and all her teeming and rich fecundity like a market-place where all that had survived up to that time must bide and pass; or when I recall *When We Were Very Young*, I can wish without any effort at all that I had thought of that before Mr. Milne did.

WILLIAM FAULKNER

[*Chicago Tribune*, July 16, 1927]

✶ ✶ ✶

TO THE PRESIDENT OF THE LEAGUE
OF AMERICAN WRITERS

I most sincerely wish to go on record as being unalterably opposed to Franco and fascism, to all violations of the legal government and outrages against the people of Republican Spain.

WILLIAM FAULKNER

[*Writers Take Sides: Letters about the War in Spain from 418 American Authors*, New York, 1938]

✶ ✶ ✶

TO THE EDITOR OF THE MEMPHIS
Commercial Appeal

I see by the papers that the G. O. C. Second Army has seen fit to discipline for cause a unit in his command: vide crying "yoo-hoo" at golfers and ladies in shorts. Since which, he has been taken to task by every blood-thirsty civilian, military and personnel expert past draft age in or out of Congress.

I agree with them, being safe from the draft, too, even if not yet in Congress, though probably also bloodthirsty enough to be. The punishment was out of all propor-tion to the offense. The man who would cry "yoo-hoo" at a girl in shorts is not going to do her any harm, in shorts or in anything else or even out of them; nor, un-less his attitude changed considerably, harm to anyone else.

The disciplining of such a man is not the affair of the Army commander. It should have been relegated to the proper staff G. O. I don't know what her title is, but surely the Nation which will take its generals to task over minor matters of discipline, which has foisted on its drafted troops the designation "selectee" with its femi-nine ending, will not have failed as grade and rank in-creases. Corporals, of course, can be hostesses, sergeants can be home room mothers, sergeants major can be ma-trons, if married; submatrons otherwise; regimental ser-geants major can even be madam chairman if desired. Onward from here, into commissioned rank, a gentle veil will be drawn, since no newspaper is going to print what one lady can call another.

The *Arkansas Legion Weekly* has invoked the names of Captain Flagg and the lady from Armentières. I agree with that, too. I would certainly like to hear what Flagg or Mademoiselle either would call a man in khaki who cried "yoo-hoo" at a girl in shorts.

General Lear was wrong, indubitably. He should be chastised by every naval and Army expert who ever bought or begged or earned a vote. His system (teaching troops that they are soldiers and not village comedians on a hayride) is out of date by 25 years, away back to '17 and '18, when it not only failed to teach American soldiers that they might possibly lose battles, it didn't even teach them to recognize such a word as "strategic retreat." Incidentally, I wonder how many of the men in that unit complained, beyond the normal and natural grousing which is every soldier's inalienable right and privilege and which his officers, right up to the general commanding, Lear himself, would defend to the death—nay, past death: to court-martial.

Oxford, Miss.   WILLIAM FAULKNER

[Memphis *Commercial Appeal,* July 12, 1941]

❉ ❉ ❉

"His Name Was Pete"

His name was Pete. He was just a dog, a fifteen-months-old pointer, still almost a puppy even though he had spent one hunting season learning to be the dog he would have been in another two or three if he had lived that long.

But he was just a dog. He expected little of the world

into which he came without past and nothing of immortality either:—food (he didn't care what nor how little just so it was given with affection—a touch of a hand, a voice he knew even if he could not understand and answer the words it spoke); the earth to run on; air to breathe, sun and rain in their seasons and the covied quail which were his heritage long before he knew the earth and felt the sun, whose scent he knew already from his staunch and faithful ancestry before he himself ever winded it. That was all he wanted. But that would have been enough to fill the eight or ten or twelve years of his natural life because twelve years are not very many and it doesn't take much to fill them.

Yet short as twelve years are, he should normally have outlived four of the kind of motorcars which killed him —cars capable of climbing hills too fast to avoid a grown pointer dog. But Pete didn't outlive the first of his four. He wasn't chasing it; he had learned not to do that before he was allowed on highways. He was standing on the road waiting for his little mistress on the horse to catch up, to squire her safely home. He shouldn't have been in the road. He paid no road tax, held no driver's license, didn't vote. Perhaps his trouble was that the motorcar which lived in the same yard he lived in had a horn and brakes on it and he thought they all did. To say he didn't see the car because the car was between him and the late afternoon sun is a bad excuse because that brings the question of vision into it and certainly no one unable with the sun at his back to see a grown pointer dog on a curveless two-lane highway would think of permitting himself to drive a car at all, let alone one without either horn or brakes because next time Pete might be a human child and killing human children with motorcars is against the law.

No, the driver was in a hurry: that was the reason. Perhaps he had several miles to go yet and was already late for supper. That was why he didn't have time to slow or stop or drive around Pete. And since he didn't have time to do that, naturally he didn't have time to stop afterward; besides Pete was only a dog flung broken and crying into a roadside ditch and anyway the car had passed him by then and the sun was at Pete's back now, so how could the driver be expected to hear his crying?

But Pete has forgiven him. In his year and a quarter of life he never had anything but kindness from human beings; he would gladly give the other six or eight or ten of it rather than make one late for supper.

[*Oxford Eagle,* August 15, 1946]

⌘ ⌘ ⌘

TO THE EDITOR OF THE *Oxford Eagle*

Bravo your piece about the preservation of the courthouse. I am afraid your cause is already lost though. We have gotten rid of the shade trees which once circled the courthouse yard and bordered the Square itself, along with the second floor galleries which once formed awnings for the sidewalk; all we have left now to distinguish an old southern town from any one of ten thousand towns built yesterday from Kansas to California are the Confederate monument, the courthouse and the jail. Let us tear them down too and put up something covered with neon and radio amplifiers.

Your cause is doomed. They will go the way of the old Cumberland church. It was here in 1861; it was the only building on or near the square still standing in 1865. It was tougher than war, tougher than the Yankee Brigadier Chalmers and his artillery and all his sappers with dynamite and crowbars and cans of kerosene. But it wasn't tougher than the ringing of a cash register bell. It had to go—obliterated, effaced, no trace left—so that a sprawling octopus covering the country from Portland, Maine to Oregon can dispense in cut-rate bargain lots, bananas and toilet paper.

They call this progress. But they don't say where it's going; also there are some of us who would like the chance to say whether or not we want the ride.

WILLIAM FAULKNER

[*Oxford Eagle*, March 13, 1947]

⌘ ⌘ ⌘

TO THE EDITOR OF THE MEMPHIS
Commercial Appeal*

All native Mississippians will join in commending Attala County. But along with the pride and the hope we had better feel concern and grief and shame too; not grief for the dead children, but concern and grief because what we did was not enough; it was in effect only a little better than nothing, not for justice nor even punishment, just as you don't mete out justice or punishment to the mad dog or the rattlesnake; grief and shame

* In March 1950 three white men were convicted of the killing of three Negro children in Attala County, Mississippi. Two received sentences to life imprisonment, the other a sentence of ten years.

because we have gone on record with the outland people who are so quick to show us our faults and tell us how to remedy them, as having put the price of murdering three children at the same as robbing three banks or stealing three automobiles.

And those of us who were born in Mississippi and have lived all our lives in it, who have continued to live in it forty and fifty and sixty years at some cost and sacrifice simply because we love Mississippi and its ways and customs and soil and people; who because of that love have been ready and willing at all times to defend our ways and habits and customs from attack by the outlanders who we believed did not understand them, we had better be afraid too,—afraid that we have been wrong; that what we had loved and defended not only didn't want the defense and the love, but was not worthy of the one and indefensible to the other.

Which fear, at least, it is to be hoped that the two members of the jury who saved the murderer, will not share.

It is to be hoped that whatever reasons they may have had for saving him, will be enough so that they can sleep at night free of nightmares about the ten or fifteen or so years from now when the murderer will be paroled or pardoned or freed again, and will of course murder another child, who it is to be hoped—and with grief and despair one says it—will this time at least be of his own color.

Oxford, Miss.   WILLIAM FAULKNER

[Memphis *Commercial Appeal*, March 26, 1950]

✖ ✖ ✖

TO THE EDITOR OF THE MEMPHIS
Commercial Appeal

I have just read Clayton Stevens' letter in your Sunday issue, re my letter about the Turner trial.

The stand I took and the protest I made was against any drunken man, I don't care what color he is, murdering three children or even only one child. I don't care what color they are or it is.

It seems to me that the ones who injected race issues into this tragedy, were whoever permitted or created a situation furnishing free-gratis-for-nothing to all our Northern critics, the opportunity to have made this same statement and protest, but with a hundred times the savagery and a thousand times the unfairness and ten thousand times less the understanding of our problems and grief for our mistakes—except that I, a native of our land and a sharer in our errors, just happened to be on the spot in time to say it first. This should be some satisfaction to a Southerner.

Oxford, Miss.   WILLIAM FAULKNER

[Memphis *Commercial Appeal,* April 9, 1950]

✳ ✳ ✳

TO THE SECRETARY OF THE AMERICAN
ACADEMY OF ARTS AND LETTERS

Oxford, Miss.
12 June 1950

The medal received, also the transcription of Mr. Mac-Leish. It's very fine indeed to have these concrete evidences—the gold and the voice—of the considered judgment of one's peers. A man works for a fairly simple—limited—range of things: money, women, glory; all nice to have, but glory's best, and the best of glory is from his peers, like the soldier who has the good opinion not of man but of other soldiers, themselves experts in it, who are themselves brave too.

Though it still seems to me impossible to evaluate a man's work. None of mine ever quite suited me, each time I wrote the last word I would think, if I could just do it over, I would do it better, maybe even right. But I was too busy; there was always another one. I would tell myself, maybe I'm too young or too busy to decide; when I reach fifty, I will be able to decide how good or not. Then one day I was fifty and I looked back at it, and I decided that it was all pretty good—and then in the same instant I realised that that was the worst of all since that meant only that a little nearer now was the moment, instant, night: dark: sleep: when I would put it all away forever that I anguished and sweated over, and it would never trouble me anymore.

WILLIAM FAULKNER

[*Proceedings of the American Academy of Arts and Letters and the National Institute of Arts and Letters*, second series, 1951]

"TO THE VOTERS OF OXFORD"

Correction to paid printed statement of Private Citizens H. E. Finger, Jr., John K. Johnson, and Frank Moody Purser.

1. 'Beer was voted out in 1944 because of its obnoxiousness.'

Beer was voted out in 1944 because too many voters who drank beer or didn't object to other people drinking it, were absent in Europe and Asia defending Oxford where voters who preferred home to war could vote on beer in 1944.

2. 'A bottle of 4 percent beer contains twice as much alcohol as a jigger of whiskey.'

A 12 ounce bottle of four percent beer contains forty-eight one hundreths of one ounce of alcohol. A jigger holds one and one-half ounces (see Dictionary). Whiskey ranges from 30 to 45 percent alcohol. A jigger of 30 percent whiskey contains forty-five one hundreths of one ounce of alcohol. A bottle of 4 percent beer doesn't contain twice as much alcohol as a jigger of whiskey. Unless the whiskey is less than 32 percent alcohol, the bottle of beer doesn't even contain as much.

3. 'Money spent for beer should be spent for food, clothing and other essential consumer goods.'

By this precedent, we will have to hold another election to vote on whether or not the florists, the picture shows, the radio shops and the pleasure car dealers will be permitted in Oxford.

4. 'Starkville and Water Valley voted beer out; why not Oxford?'

Since Starkville is the home of Mississippi State, and Mississippi State beat the University of Mississippi at football, maybe Oxford, which is the home of the University of Mississippi, is right in taking Starkville for a model. But why must we imitate Water Valley? Our high school team beat theirs, didn't it?

Yours for a freer Oxford, where publicans can be law abiding publicans six days a week, and Ministers of God can be Ministers of God all seven days in the week, as the Founder of their Ministry commanded them to when He ordered them to keep out of temporal politics in His own words: 'Render unto Caesar the things that are Caesar's and to God the things that are God's.'

WILLIAM FAULKNER
Private Citizen

[Broadside distributed in Oxford about September 1, 1950]

* * *

TO THE EDITOR OF THE *Oxford Eagle*

Oxford, Miss.
Sept. 8, 1950

I notice that your paper has listed me among the proponents of legal beer. I resent that. I am every inch as

much an enemy of liberty and enlightenment and progress as any voting or drinking dry either in Oxford.

Our town is already overcrowded. If we had legal beer
and liquor here where you could buy it for only half of
what we pay bootleggers, not to mention the play-
grounds—tennis courts and swimming pools—and the
high school gymnasiums and the public libraries which
we could have with the proceeds and profits from one
four-year term of county-owned and operated beer and
liquor stores, we would have such an influx of people,
businesses and industries with thirty and forty thousand
dollar payrolls, that we old inhabitants could hardly
move on the streets; our merchants couldn't sleep in the
afternoon for the clashing and jangling of cash registers,
and we older citizens couldn't even get into the stores to
read a free magazine or borrow the telephone.

No; let us stick to the old ways. Our teen-age children
have cars or their friends do; they can always drive up to
Tennessee or to Quitman County for beer or whiskey,
and us graybeards who don't like travel can telephone for
it, as we always have done. Of course, it costs twice as
much when it is delivered to your door, and you usually
drink too much of it, than if you had to get up and go to
town to get it, but better [that] than to break up the
long and happy marriage between dry voters and illicit
sellers, for which our fair state supplies one of the last
sanctuaries and strongholds.

In fact, my effort in the recent election was only secondarily concerned with beer. I was making a protest. I
object to anyone making a public statement which any
fourth grade child with a pencil and paper, can disprove.
I object more to a priest so insulting the intelligence of
his hearers as to assume that he can make any statement,
regardless of its falsity, and because of respect for his

cloth, not one of them will try or dare to check up on it. But most of all,—and those ministers of sects which are not autonomous, who have synods or boards of bishops or other bodies of authority and control over them, might give a thought to this—I object to ministers of God violating the canons and ethics of their sacred and holy avocation by using, either openly or underhand, the weight and power of their office to try to influence a civil election.

WILLIAM FAULKNER

[*Oxford Eagle,* September 14, 1950]

✵ ✵ ✵

TO THE EDITOR OF *Time*

Re Waugh on Hemingway [Waugh criticized the critics of Hemingway's new novel, *Across the River and into the Trees*] in *Time,* Oct. 30:

Good for Mr. Waugh. I would like to have said this myself, not the Waugh of course but the equivalent Faulkner. One reason I did not is, the man who wrote some of the pieces in *Men Without Women* and *The Sun Also Rises* and some of the African stuff (and some —most—of all the rest of it too for that matter) does not need defending, because the ones who throw the spit-balls didn't write the pieces in *Men Without Women* and *The Sun Also Rises* and the African pieces and the rest of it, and the ones who didn't write *Men Without Women* and *The Sun Also Rises* and the African pieces and the rest of it don't have anything to stand on while they throw the spitballs.

Neither does Mr. Waugh need this from me. But I hope he will accept me on his side.

Oxford, Miss.   WILLIAM FAULKNER

[*Time,* November 13, 1950]

※ ※ ※

STATEMENT TO THE PRESS ON THE
WILLIE MCGEE CASE*

I do not want Willie McGee to be executed, because it will make him a martyr and create a long lasting stink in my native state.

If the crime of which he is accused was not one of force and violence, and I do not think it was proved that, then the penalty in this state or in any other similar case should not be death.

I have nothing in common with the representatives of the Civil Rights Congress except we both say we want Willie McGee to live.

I believe these women who visited in Mississippi re-

* McGee, a Negro convicted of raping a white woman, was executed at Laurel, Mississippi, in May 1951, four months after the United States Supreme Court had refused, for the third time in two years, to review the conviction. Faulkner released this statement to the press on March 26 to correct misquotations which had appeared in newspapers after he had been interviewed the preceding week by women representatives of the Civil Rights Congress.

cently are being used; that their cause would be best helped with the execution of Willie.

I did tell them if they wanted to save Willie they should talk to the women in the kitchen and make their arguments there rather than to the men and the politicians.

[Memphis *Commercial Appeal,* March 27, 1951]

✗ ✗ ✗

TO THE EDITOR OF THE *New York Times*

New York, Dec. 22, 1954.

This is about the Italian airliner which undershot the runway and crashed at Idlewild after failing three times to hold the instrument glide-path which would have brought it down to the runway.

It is written on the idea (postulate, if you like) that the instrument or instruments—altimeter-cum-drift-indicator—failed or had failed, was already out of order or incorrect before the moment when the pilot committed irrevocably the aircraft to it.

It is written in grief. Not just for the sorrow of the bereaved ones of those who died in the crash, and for the airline, the public carrier which, in selling the tickets, promised or anyway implied security for the trip, but for the crew, the pilot himself who will be blamed for the crash and whose record and memory will be tarnished by it; who, along with his unaware passengers, was victim not even of the failed instruments but victim of that mystical, unquestioning, almost religious awe and veneration in which our culture has trained us to hold gadgets—any gadget, if it is only complex enough and cryptic enough and costs enough.

I imagine that even after the first failure to hold the glide-path, certainly after the second one, his instinct—the seat of his pants, call it what you will—after that much experience, that many hours in the air, told him that something was wrong. And his seniority as a four-engine over-water captain probably told him where the trouble was. But he dared not accept that knowledge and (this presumes that even after the second failure he still had enough fuel left to reach a field which he could see) act on it.

Possibly at some time during the four attempts to land, very likely at some one of the final rapid seconds before he had irrevocably committed the aircraft—that compounding of mass and weight by velocity—to the ground, his co-pilot (or flight engineer or whoever else might have been in the cockpit at the time) probably said to him: "Look. We're wrong. Get the flaps and gear up and let's get to hell out of here." But he dared not. He dared not so flout and affront, even with his own life too at stake, our cultural postulate of the infallibility of machines, instruments, gadgets—a Power more ruthless even than the old Hebrew concept of its God, since ours is not even jealous and vengeful, caring nothing about individuals.

He dared not commit that sacrilege. If he had, nothing would have remained to him save to open the cockpit hatch and (a Roman) cast himself onto the turning blades of one of the inboard air-screws. I grieve for him, for that moment's victims. We all had better grieve for all people beneath a culture which holds any mechanical superior to any man simply because the one, being mechanical, is infallible, while the other, being nothing but man, is not just subject to failure but doomed to it.

WILLIAM FAULKNER

[*New York Times,* December 26, 1954]

❇ ❇ ❇

TO THE EDITOR OF THE MEMPHIS
Commercial Appeal

Oxford, Miss.
10 Feb., 1955

I have just read with interest the 'Letter to the Editor' of Mr Wolstenholme, of Hohenwald, Tenn., in your issue of Sunday, the 6th, in which he suggests that the Negro inhabitants of Memphis slums could nail up their rat-holes if they were not too shiftless to do it; and that the white investigating groups would do much better to come to Lewis County, where they could find plenty of white people deserving of their offices.

Does this mean that, for every rat-hole Shelby County Negroes have, Lewis County white folks have two? Which cant be right, since white folks, not being Negroes, are not shiftless; and therefore, for every rat-hole which a Shelby or Lewis County, Tennessee, or a Lafayette County, Mississippi, Negro has, a Shelby or Lewis County, Tennessee, or Lafayette County, Mississippi, white man cant have any. Which wont hold water either, since, for the simple reason that there are more rats than people, there is some inevitable and inescapable point at which the white man, no matter how unshiftless, is going to have one rat-hole. So, at what point on the scale of the Negro's non-rat-holes does the white man gain one or earn one or anyway have one rat-hole? Is unshiftless twice as unshiftless as shiftless, giving the white man twice as many rat-holes as the Negro man, or does this get us into the old insoluble problem in amateur physics about how much is twice as cold as zero?

WILLIAM FAULKNER

[Memphis *Commercial Appeal,* February 20, 1955; typescript]

❈ ❈ ❈

TO THE EDITOR OF THE MEMPHIS
Commercial Appeal

We Mississippians already know that our present schools are not good enough. Our young men and women themselves prove that to us every year by the fact that, when the best of them want the best of education which they are entitled to and are competent for, not only in the humanities but in the professions and crafts —law and medicine and engineering—too, they have to go out of the State to get it. And quite often, too often, they dont come back.

So our present schools are not even good enough for white people; our present State reservoir of education is not of high enough quality to assuage the thirst of even our white young men and women. In which case, how can it possibly assuage the thirst and need of the Negro, who obviously is thirstier, needs it worse, else the Federal Government would not have had to pass a law compelling Mississippi (among others of course) to make the best of our education available to him.

That is, our present schools are not even good enough for white folks. So what do we do? make them good enough, improve them to the best possible? No. We beat the bushes, rake and scrape to raise additional taxes to establish another system at best only equal to that one which is already not good enough, which therefore wont be good enough for Negroes either; we will have two identical systems neither of which are good enough for anybody. The question is not how foolish can people get because apparently there is no limit to that. The question is, how foolish in simple dollars and cents, let alone in wasted men and women, can we afford to be?

Oxford, Miss.   WILLIAM FAULKNER

[Memphis *Commercial Appeal,* March 20, 1955; typescript]

✻ ✻ ✻

TO THE EDITOR OF THE *New York Times*

Oxford, Miss., March 18, 1955.

I wonder when we will learn that the day is long since past when even local acts of national policy, let alone ones with foreign implications, can be committed by people with no more equipment than a United States flag and a primer on international law.

I am thinking of the people responsible for and involved in the expulsion from the United States of the Metropolitan of the Russian Orthodox Church, the consequence of which was the expulsion from Russia of Father Bissonnette of the Roman Catholic Church in America. I am thinking of both the people who could have expelled the Russian Metropolitan without it once occurring to them apparently that they might have to explain it to anyone; and the people who could have even dreamed that they could explain it or justify it to Communists, who by their very ideology are compelled to be inflexible enemies of the so-called Christian religion whether they want to be or not.

I don't mean the members of the State Department. That is, the professional ones, the dedicated career ones, the young ones who had that vocation in youth and taught themselves (not the Government they represent taught them; we don't train our agents and representatives to deal with people, the simple, incorrigible, intractable, invincible human heart, but only with numbers and rates of exchange) enough of the humanity of man to be competent for their dedications. I know enough of them myself to know that they would have had more sense. Only they had no choice, no say, because from the day they drew their first Saturday's wages they were harassed and harried by their masters—people who had acquired that masterhood simply as an incidental prerequisite to their elections to other offices by popular vote, or as a reward for having employed their powers that still others might be elected or appointed to offices which those others wanted or needed or, anyway, thirsted for. I'm thinking about them.

I wonder, until the moment when the public press brought the word to their attention (and, I hope, alarm and fear too), just how many members of the Government and Congress could have defined the word "Metropolitan" in even a hundred times the standard ten seconds allowed by the giveaway icebox-or-electric washer quiz programs to answer the ones like, for instance, what day of what month is the Fourth of July?

WILLIAM FAULKNER

[*New York Times,* March 25, 1955]

* * *

TO THE EDITOR OF THE MEMPHIS *Commercial Appeal*

I have just read the letters of Mr Neill, Mr Martin and Mr Womack in your issue of March 27th, in reply to my letter in your issue of March 20th.

To Mr Martin, and Mr Womack's first question: Whatever the cost of our present statewide school system is, we will have to raise that much again to establish another system equal to it. Let us take some of that new funds and make our present schools, from kindergarden up through the humanities and sciences and professions, not just the best in America but the best that schools can be; then the schools themselves will take care of the candidates, white and Negro both, who had no business in them in the first place.

Then the rest of the new fund could establish or improve trade and craft schools for the ones whom the first system, the academic one, had already eliminated before they had had time to do much harm in the terms of their own wasted days and the overcrowded classrooms and harried underpaid teachers which result in a general leavening and lowering of educational standards; not to mention making the best use of the men and women we produce. What we need is more Americans on our side. If all Americans were on the same side, we wouldn't need to try to bribe foreign countries which dont always stay bought, to support us.

Though I agree that this only solves integration: not the impasse of the emotional conflict over it. But at least it observes one of the oldest and soundest maxims: If you cant beat 'em, join 'em.

To Mr Womack's last question: I have no degrees nor diplomas from any school. I am an old veteran sixthgrader. Maybe that's why I have so much respect for education that I seem unable to sit quiet and watch it held subordinate in importance to an emotional state concerning the color of human skin.

Oxford, Miss.   WILLIAM FAULKNER

[Memphis *Commercial Appeal,* April 3, 1955; typescript]

✖ ✖ ✖

TO THE EDITOR OF THE MEMPHIS
Commercial Appeal

I have read Mr. Murphy's letter in your issue of April 3. I also received one from Dr. Flinsch, Dean, School of Engineering, Mississippi State College, along the same line. If my letter stated or implied any facts which are incorrect, I retract and apologize.

My aim was not to injure our present school system, but to take advantage of whatever changes in it the future holds, to improve our schools from their present condition of being a sort of community or state-supported baby sitters, where the pupil is compelled by law or custom to spend so many hours of the day, with nobody but often-underpaid teachers to be concerned about how much he learns.

Instead of holding the educational standard down to the lowest common denominator of the class or grade group, let us raise it to that of the highest.

Let us give every would-be pupil and student the equality and right to education in the terms in which our forefathers used the words equality and freedom and right: not equal right to charity, but equal right to the opportunity to do what he is capable of doing, freedom to attain the highest of standards—provided he is capable of it; or if he is not competent or will not work, let us learn early, before he has done much harm, that he is in the wrong occupation.

If we are to have two school systems, let the second one be for pupils ineligible not because of color but because they either can't or won't do the work of the first one.

Oxford, Miss.   WILLIAM FAULKNER

[Memphis *Commercial Appeal,* April 10, 1955]

※ ※ ※

TO THE EDITOR OF THE MEMPHIS
Commercial Appeal

I would like to say 'Well done' to the writer of the letter signed 'Student' from Dorsey, Miss. in your issue of April 10th. Let us make a canvass of the young people of Mississippi who are attending our present schools and will attend the integrated ones if or when they come, for their opinion of it; they are certainly interested parties.

We in the South are faced by two apparently irreconcilable facts: one, that the National Government has decreed absolute equality in education among all races; the other, the people in the South who say that it shall never happen. These two facts must be reconciled. I believe there are many young people too in Mississippi who believe they can be, who love our State—not love white people specifically nor Negroes specifically, but our land: our climate and geography, the qualities in our people, white and Negro both, for honesty and tolerance and fair play, the splendors in our traditions and the glories in our past—enough to try to reconcile them, even at the risk which the young writer from Dorsey took despite the fact that he didn't sign his name. And what a commentary that is on us: that in Mississippi communal adult opinion can reach such a general emotional pitch that our young sons and daughters dare not, from probably a very justified physical fear, sign their names to an opinion adverse to it.

Oxford, Miss.   WILLIAM FAULKNER

[Memphis *Commercial Appeal,* April 17, 1955; typescript]

※ ※ ※

PRESS DISPATCH WRITTEN IN ROME, ITALY,
FOR THE UNITED PRESS,
ON THE
EMMETT TILL CASE

When will we learn that if one county in Mississippi is to survive it will be because all Mississippi survives? That if the state of Mississippi survives, it will be because all America survives? And if America is to survive, the whole white race must survive first?

Because, the whole white race is only one-fourth of the earth's population of white and brown and yellow and black. So, when will we learn that the white man can no longer afford, he simply does not dare, to commit acts which the other three-fourths of the human race can challenge him for, not because the acts are themselves criminal, but simply because the challengers and accusers of the acts are not white in pigment?

Not to speak of the other Aryan peoples who are already the Western world's enemies because of political ideologies. Have we, the white Americans who can commit or condone such acts, forgotten already how only 15 years ago, what only the Japanese—a mere eighty million inhabitants of an island already insolvent and bankrupt —did to us?

How then can we hope to survive the next Pearl Harbor, if there should be one, with not only all peoples who are not white, but all peoples with political ideologies different from ours arrayed against us—after we have taught them (as we are doing) that when we talk of freedom and liberty, we not only mean neither, we don't even mean security and justice and even the preservation of life for people whose pigmentation is not the same as ours.

And not just the black people in Boer South Africa, but the black people in America too.

Because if we Americans are to survive, it will have to be because we choose and elect and defend to be first of all Americans to present to the world one homogeneous and unbroken front, whether of white Americans or black ones or purple or blue or green.

Perhaps we will find out now whether we are to survive or not. Perhaps the purpose of this sorry and tragic error committed in my native Mississippi by two white adults on an afflicted Negro child is to prove to us whether or not we deserve to survive.

Because if we in America have reached that point in our desperate culture when we must murder children, no matter for what reason or what color, we don't deserve to survive, and probably won't.

[*New York Herald Tribune,* September 9, 1955]

✄ ✄ ✄

TO THE EDITOR OF *Life*

Since *Life* printed my "Letter to the North" I have received many replies from outside the South. Many of them criticized the reasoning *in* the letter, but so far none of them seem to have divined the reason *behind* the letter, the reason behind the urgency for the widest possible circulation of it, in time; which lends weight to a statement in the letter to the effect that the United States outside the South does not understand the South.

The reason behind the letter was the attempt of an individual to save the South and the whole United States too from the blot of Miss Autherine Lucy's death. She had just been suspended by the University of Alabama; a day had been set when a judge would pass on the validity of the suspension. I believed that when the judge abrogated the suspension, which he would have to do, the forces supporting her attempt to enter the university as a student would send her back to it. I believed that if they did so, she would possibly lose her life.

She was not sent back, so the letter was not needed for that purpose. I hope it will never be. But if a similar situation bearing the seed of a similar tragedy should arise again, maybe the letter will help to serve.

Oxford, Miss.   WILLIAM FAULKNER

[*Life,* March 26, 1956]

✳ ✳ ✳

TO THE EDITOR OF THE *Reporter*

From letters I have received, and from quotations from it I have seen in *Time* and *Newsweek,* I think that some parts of the interview with me which I gave to the London *Sunday Times* interviewer and which, after notifying me, he made available to you, are not correct; needless to say, I did not read the interview before it went to print, nor have I seen it yet as printed.

If I had seen it before it went to print, these statements, which are not correct, could never have been imputed to me. They are statements which no sober man would make, nor, it seems to me, any sane man believe.

The South is not armed to resist the United States that I know of, because the United States is neither going to force the South nor permit the South to resist or secede either.

The statement that I or anyone else would choose any one state against the whole remaining Union of States, down to the ultimate price of shooting other human beings in the streets, is not only foolish but dangerous. Foolish because no sane man is going to choose one state against the Union today. A hundred years ago, yes. But not in 1956. And dangerous because the idea can further inflame those few people in the South who might still believe such a situation possible.

Oxford, Mississippi   WILLIAM FAULKNER

[*Reporter,* April 19, 1956]

✻ ✻ ✻

TO THE EDITOR OF *Time*

In our troubled times over segregation, it is imperative that no man be saddled with opinions on the subject which he has never held and, for that reason, never expressed. In New York last month . . . I gave an interview to a representative of the London *Sunday Times,* who (with my agreement) passed it on to the *Reporter.* I did not see the interview before it went into print. If I had, quotations from it which have appeared in *Time* could never have been imputed to me, since they contain opinions which I have never held, and statements which no sober man would make and, it seems to me, no sane man believe. That statement that I or anyone else in his right mind would choose any one state against the whole remaining Union of States, down to the ultimate price of shooting other human beings in the streets, is not only foolish but dangerous. Foolish, because no sane man is going to make that choice today even if he had the chance. A hundred years ago, yes, but not in 1956. And dangerous, because the idea can further inflame those few people in the South who might still believe such a situation possible.

Oxford, Miss. WILLIAM FAULKNER

[*Time,* April 23, 1956]

⌘ ⌘ ⌘

TO THE EDITOR OF *Time*

There is much criticism and condemnation, by individuals and our press, of the recent action of England in Egypt. Whether the act was right or wrong, do we critics always remember that the reasons why England believed she had to do what she did, are not all inside the British Isles? If the act was wrong, do we condemners always remember that twice now Britain has held off the enemy and so given us time to realize at last that we could not buy our way through wars and would have to fight them? Could one reason for our criticism and condemnation be the fear that now even England can no longer afford us an opportunity not to have to fight?

Oxford, Miss.   WILLIAM FAULKNER

[*Time,* December 10, 1956]

✷ ✷ ✷

TO THE EDITOR OF THE *New York Times*

Oxford, Miss., Dec. 11, 1956.

If what France, Britain and Israel did in Egypt was a crime, to throw away the fruits of it will be worse: it will be a folly; and I do not believe that nations anywhere any more can afford follies. Crimes, yes; but not follies.

What this country needs right now is not a golf player

but a poker player. A good one—bold, courageous, with icewater in his veins, and I never knew a good one of any other kind. With the cards which the Israelis, British and French have just given him free, without his having to pay chips to draw them, he would probably settle not just the Middle East but the whole world too for the next fifty years.

WILLIAM FAULKNER

[*New York Times,* December 16, 1956]

✹ ✹ ✹

TO THE EDITOR OF *Time*

Our old foreign policy was like the house policy of the gambling casino: cover all bets, wager everybody he is wrong and depend on the constant and modest profit of the house odds inherent in the dice or deck or wheel. Our new one seems to be the house manager's asking his syndicate to let the bouncer carry a pistol.

Oxford, Miss.   WILLIAM FAULKNER

[*Time,* February 11, 1957]

✹ ✹ ✹

TO THE EDITOR OF THE MEMPHIS
Commercial Appeal

A few years ago the Supreme Court rendered an opinion which we white Southerners didn't like, and we resisted it.

As a result, last month Congress was offered a bill containing a good deal more danger to us all than the presence of Negro children in white schools or Negro votes in white ballot boxes—danger which apparently only an expert could see.

Congress would have passed the bill, except for the fact that the expert was on hand in time. So we escaped—that time.

We are still resisting that opinion. As long as we continue to hold the Negro second class in citizenship—that is, subject to taxation and military service, yet denied the political right to vote for, and the economic and educational competence to be represented among those who tax and draft him—Congress will continue to be offered bills containing these same or similar dangers, which only an expert can recognize; until some day the expert won't be there in time, and one of them will pass.

Oxford, Miss.   WILLIAM FAULKNER

[Memphis *Commercial Appeal,* September 15, 1957]

❈ ❈ ❈

TO THE EDITOR OF THE *New York Times**

The tragedy of Little Rock is that it has at last brought out into the light a fact which we knew was there but which, until it was dragged forcibly out of hiding, we could ignore by pretending it wasn't there. This is the fact that white people and Negroes do not like and trust each other, and perhaps never can.

But maybe this is not a tragedy after all. Now, by having this fact out where we will have to look at it and recognise it and accept it, maybe we can realise that it is not important for us to like and trust each other. That it is not even [of] prime importance for us to live, rub along somehow, in amity and peace together. That what is important and necessary and urgent (urgent: we are reaching the point now where we haven't time anymore) is that we federate together, show a common unified front not for dull peace and amity, but for survival as a people and a nation.

It may already be too late; as a nation and a people we may already be on the way down and out. But I do not believe it. I decline to believe that in crisis we cannot rally our national character to that same courage and toughness which the English people for instance did when as a nation they stood alone in Europe for the national principle that men shall and can be free. Ours will be a bigger task not because the threat is greater but because we will have to stand up not as one nation among a continent of nations nor even in a hemisphere of nations, but as the last people unified nationally for

---

* Written at the height of the high school integration crisis in Little Rock, Arkansas.

liberty in an inimical world which already outnumbers us.

Against that principle which by physical force compels man to relinquish his individuality into the monolithic mass of a state dedicated to the premise that the state alone shall prevail, we, because of the lucky accident of our geography, may have to represent that last community of unified people dedicated to that opposed premise that man can be free by the very act of voluntarily merging and relinquishing his liberty into the liberty of all individual men who want to be free. We, because of the good luck of our still unspent and yet unexhausted past, may have to be the rallying point for all men, no matter what color they are or what tongue they speak, willing to federate into a community dedicated to the proposition that a community of individual free men not merely must endure, but can endure.

Oxford, Miss.   W ILLIAM F AULKNER

[*New York Times,* October 13, 1957; typescript]

✻ ✻ ✻

[NOTICE]

Mrs. Faulkner and I wish to thank the Mayor, Alderman Sisk, City Engineer Lowe and the City Attorney's office for the removal of the commercial signboard at our front gate on Old Taylor Road.

W ILLIAM F AULKNER

[*Oxford Eagle,* September 24, 1959]

✻ ✻ ✻

"NOTICE"

The posted woods on my property inside the city limits of Oxford contain several tame squirrels. Any hunter who feels himself too lacking in woodcraft and marksmanship to approach a dangerous wild squirrel, might feel safe with these. These woods are a part of the pasture used by my horses and milk cow; also, the late arrival will find them already full of other hunters. He is kindly requested not to shoot either of these.

WILLIAM FAULKNER

[*Oxford Eagle,* October 15, 1959]

❈ ❈ ❈

TO THE EDITOR OF THE *New York Times*[*]

OXFORD, MISS.
AUG. 24, 1960

Regarding U-2 Pilot Powers: Now the Russians will parade him about the non-Western world for the next ten years like a monkey in a cage, as a living example of the sort of courage and fidelity and endurance on which the United States must now desperately depend. Or bet-

[*] Faulkner's letter was written five days after pilot Francis Gary Powers had been convicted in Moscow of espionage and sentenced to ten years' imprisonment. In 1962 he was set free and returned to the United States, where he was officially cleared of any charge of misconduct.

ter still, set him free at once in contemptuous implication that a nation so desperately reduced is not worth anyone's respect or fear, the agents of its desperation no longer dangerous enough to be worth the honor of martyrdom nor even the cost of feeding them.

William Faulkner

[*New York Times,* August 28, 1960]

SIX

Essays

Verse, Old and Nascent:
A Pilgrimage

At the age of sixteen, I discovered Swinburne. Or rather, Swinburne discovered me, springing from some tortured undergrowth of my adolescence, like a highwayman, making me his slave. My mental life at that period was so completely and smoothly veneered with surface insincerity—obviously necessary to me at that time, to support intact my personal integrity—that I can not tell to this day exactly to what depth he stirred me, just how deeply the foot-prints of his passage are left in my mind. It seems to me now that I found him nothing but a flexible vessel into which I might put my own vague emotional shapes without breaking them. It was years later that I found in him much more than bright and bitter sound, more than a satisfying tinsel of blood and death and gold and the inevitable sea. True, I dipped into Shelley and Keats—who doesn't, at that age?—but they did not move me.

I do not think it was assurance so much, merely complacence and a youthful morbidity, which counteracted them and left me cold. I was not interested in verse for verse's sake then. I read and employed verse, firstly, for the purpose of furthering various philanderings in which I was engaged, secondly, to complete a youthful gesture I was then making, of being "different" in a small town. Later, my interest in fornication waning, I turned inevitably to verse, finding therein an emotional counterpart far more satisfactory for two reasons: (1) No partner was required (2) It was so much simpler just to close a book, and take a walk. I do not mean by this that I ever found anything sexual in Swinburne: there is no sex in Swinburne. The mathematician, surely; and eroticism just as there is eroticism in form and color and movement wherever found. But not that tortured sex in—say—D. H. Lawrence.

It is a time-honored custom to read Omar to one's mistress as an accompaniment to consummation—a sort of stringèd obligato among the sighs. I found that verse could be employed not only to temporarily blind the spirit to the ungraceful posturings of the flesh, but also to speed onward the whole affair. Ah, women, with their hungry snatching little souls! With a man it is—quite often—art for art's sake; with a woman it is always art for the artist's sake.

Whatever it was that I found in Swinburne, it completely satisfied me and filled my inner life. I cannot understand now how I could have regarded the others with such dull complacency. Surely, if one be moved at all by Swinburne he must inevitably find in Swinburne's forerunners some kinship. Perhaps it is that Swinburne, having taken his heritage and elaborated it to the despair of any would-be poet, has coarsened it to tickle the dullest of palates as well as the most discriminating, as used water can be drunk by both hogs and gods.

Therefore, I believe I came as near as possible to approaching poetry with an unprejudiced mind. I was subject to the usual proselyting of an older person, but the strings were pulled so casually as scarcely to influence my point of view. I had no opinions at that time, the opinions

I later formed were all factitious and were discarded. I approached Poetry unawed, as if to say; "Now, let's see what you have." Having used verse, I would now allow verse to use me if it could.

When the co-ordinated chaos of the war was replaced by the unco-ordinated chaos of peace I took seriously to reading verse. With no background whatever I joined the pack belling loudly after contemporary poets. I could not always tell what it was all about but "This is the stuff," I told myself, believing, like so many, that if one cried loudly enough to be heard above the din, and so convinced others that one was "in the know," one would be automatically accoladed. I joined an emotional B.P.O.E.

The beauty—spiritual and physical—of the South lies in the fact that God has done so much for it and man so little. I have this for which to thank whatever gods may be: that having fixed my roots in this soil all contact, saving by the printed word, with contemporary poets is impossible.

That page is closed to me forever. I read Robinson and Frost with pleasure, and Aldington; Conrad Aiken's minor music still echoes in my heart; but beyond these, that period might have never been. I no longer try to read the others at all.

It was *A Shropshire Lad* which closed the period. I found a paper-bound copy in a bookshop and when I opened it I discovered there the secret after which the moderns course howling like curs on a cold trail in a dark wood, giving off, it is true, an occasional note clear with beauty, but curs just the same. Here was reason for being born into a fantastic world: discovering the splendor of fortitude, the beauty of being of the soil like a tree about which fools might howl and which winds of disillusion and death and despair might strip, leaving it bleak, without bitterness; beautiful in sadness.

From this point the road is obvious. Shakespeare I read, and Spenser, and the Elizabethans, and Shelley and Keats. I read "Thou still unravished bride of quietness" and found a still water withal strong and potent, quiet with its own strength, and satisfying as bread. That beautiful awareness, so sure of its own power that it is not necessary to create the illusion of force by frenzy and motion. Take the odes to a Nightingale, to a Grecian urn, "Music to hear," etc.; here is the spiritual beauty which the moderns strive vainly for with trickery, and yet beneath it one knows are entrails; masculinity.

Occasionally I see modern verse in magazines. In four years I have found but one cause for interest; a tendency among them to revert to formal rhymes and conventional forms again. Have they, too, seen the writing on the wall? Can one still hope? Or is this age, this decade, impossible for the creation of poetry? Is there nowhere among us a Keats in embryo, someone who will tune his lute to the beauty of the world? Life is not different from what it was when Shelley drove like a swallow southward from the unbearable English winter; living may be different, but not life. Time changes us, but Time's self does not change. Here is the same air, the same sunlight in which Shelley dreamed of golden men and women immortal in a silver world and in which young John Keats wrote "Endymion" trying to gain enough silver to marry Fannie Brawne and set up an apothecary's shop. Is not there among us someone who can write something beautiful and passionate and sad instead of saddening?

[*Double Dealer,* April 1925; reprinted in *William Faulkner: Early Prose and Poetry,* ed. Carvel Collins, Boston, 1962; the text printed here is based on Faulkner's typescript, which is dated "October, 1924" and was reproduced in *Mississippi Poems by William Faulkner,* Oxford, Mississippi, 1979.]

❄ ❄ ❄

On Criticism

WALT WHITMAN said, among bombast and muscle-bound platitudes, that to have great poets there must be great audiences too. If Walt Whitman realized this it should be universally obvious in this day of radio to inform us and the so-called high-brow magazines to correct our information; not to speak of the personal touch of the lecture platform. And yet, what have the periodicals and lecturers done to create either great audiences or great writers of us? Do these Sybils take the neophyte gently in hand and instruct him in the fundamentals of taste? They do not even try to inculcate in him a reverence for their mysteries, (thus robbing criticism of even its emotional value—and how else are you to control the herd, except through its emotions? Was there ever a logical mob?). Thus there is no tradition, no esprit de corps: All that is necessary for admission to the ranks of criticism is a typewriter.

They do not even try to mould his opinions for him. True, it is scarcely worth while moulding anyone's opinions for him, but it is pleasant pastime changing his opinion from one fallacy to another, for his soul's sake. The American critic, like the prestidigitator, tries to find just how much he can let the spectator see, and still get away with it—the superiority of the hand over the eye. He takes the piece under examination for an instrument upon which to run difficult arpeggios of cleverness. This

seems so sophomoric, so useless; like the cornetist per-
forming aural acrobatics while waiting for the band to as-
semble. With this difference: the cornetist gets tired after
a while, and stops. The amazing possibility here occurs
that the critic enjoys his own music. Do they, then enjoy
reading each other? One can as easily imagine barbers
shaving each other for fun.

The American critic blinds, not only his audience but
himself as well, to the prime essential. His trade becomes
mental gymnastics: he becomes a reincarnation of the
side-show spell-binder of happy memory, holding the
yokelry enravished, not with what he says, but how he says
it. Their minds fly shut before the eye-filling meretricity
of pyrotechnics. Who has not heard this conversation?

"Have you seen the last . . . (suit yourself)? Jones
Brown is good this time; he . . . uh, What is that book? a
novel, I think . . . on the end of my tongue . . . by some fellow. Anyway, Jones refers to him as an aesthetic boy scout.
It's good: you must read it."

"Yes, I will: Brown is always good, do you remember
what he said about someone: 'A parrot that couldn't fly
and had never learned to curse'?"

And yet, when you ask him the author's name, or the
book's, or what it is about, he cannot tell you! He either
has not read it, or has not only been unmoved by it
but has waited to read Brown to form an opinion. And
Brown has offered no opinion whatever. Perhaps Brown
himself has none.

How much better they do this sort of thing in England
than in America! Of course there are in America critics as
sane and tolerant and as soundly equipped, but with a
few exceptions they have no status: the magazines which
set the standard ignore them; or finding conditions unbearable, they ignore the magazines and live abroad. In a

recent number of *The Saturday Review* Mr. Gerald Gould, reviewing *The Hidden Player* by Alfred Noyes, says:

"People do not talk like that . . . It will not do to set down ordinary speech of ordinary people; that would generally be dull . . . To give the deadly detail is misleading." Here is the essential of criticism. So just and clear and complete: there is nothing more to be said. A criticism which not only the public, but the author as well, may read with profit. But what American critic would let it go at this? Who among our literary arbiters could miss this chance of referring to Mr. Noyes as "an aesthetic boy scout," or something else as sophomoric and irrelevant? And what reader could then pick up the book with an unbiased mind, without a faint unease of patronage and pity . . . not for the book, but for Mr. Noyes? One in a hundred. And what writer, with his own compulsions to suffer, with his own urge to disfigure paper harrying him like a gad-fly, could get any profit or nourishment from being referred to as an aesthetic boy scout? Not one.

Saneness, that is the word. Live and let live; criticise with taste for a criterion, and not tongue. The English review criticises the book, the American the author. The American critic foists upon the reading public a distorted buffoon within whose shadow the titles of sundry uncut volumes vaguely lurk. Surely, if there are two professions in which there should be no professional jealousy, they are prostitution and literature.

As it is, competition becomes cutthroat. The writer cannot begin to compete with the critic, he is too busy writing and also he is organically unfitted for the contest. And if he had time and were properly armed, it would be unfair. The critic, once he becomes a habit with his readers, is considered infallible by them; and his contact with them is direct enough to allow him always the last word.

And with the American the last word carries weight, is culminative. Probably because it gives him a chance to talk some himself.

[*Double Dealer,* January–February 1925; reprinted in *William Faulkner: Early Prose and Poetry,* ed. Carvel Collins, Boston, 1962. That text is printed here.]

❋ ❋ ❋

Sherwood Anderson

FOR SOME REASON people seem to be interested not in what Mr. Anderson has written, but from what source he derives. The greater number who speculate upon his origin say he derives from the Russians. If so, he has returned home, *The Triumph of the Egg* having been translated into Russian. A smaller number hold to the French theory. A cabinetmaker in New Orleans discovered that he resembles Zola, though how he arrived at this I can not see, unless it be that Zola also wrote books.

Like most speculation all this is interesting but bootless. Men grow from the soil, like corn and trees: I prefer to think of Mr. Anderson as a lusty corn field in his native Ohio. As he tells in his own story, his father not only seeded him physically, but planted also in him that belief, necessary to a writer, that his own emotions are important, and also planted in him the desire to tell them to someone.

Here are the green shoots, battling with earth for sustenance, threatened by the crows of starvation; and here was Mr. Anderson, helping around livery stables and race tracks, striping bicycles in a factory until the impulse to tell his story became too strong to be longer resisted.

Winesburg, Ohio

The simplicity of this title! And the stories are as simply done: short, he tells the story and stops. His very inexperience, his urgent need not to waste time or paper taught him one of the first attributes of genius. As a rule first books show more bravado than anything else, unless it be tediousness. But there is neither of these qualities in *Winesburg*. Mr. Anderson is tentative, self-effacing with his George Willards and Wash Williamses and banker White's daughters, as though he were thinking: "Who am I, to pry into the souls of these people who, like myself, sprang from this same soil to suffer the same sorrows as I?" The only indication of the writer's individuality which I find in *Winesburg* is his sympathy for them, a sympathy which, had the book been done as a full-length novel, would have become mawkish. Again the gods looked out for him. These people live and breathe: they are beautiful. There is the man who organized a baseball club, the man with the "speaking" hands, Elizabeth Willard, middle-aged, and the oldish doctor, between whom was a love that Cardinal Bembo might have dreamed. There is a Greek word for a love like theirs which Mr. Anderson probably had never heard. And behind all of them a ground of fecund earth and corn in the green spring and the slow, full hot summer and the rigorous masculine winter that hurts it not, but makes it stronger.

Marching Men

Just as there are lesser ears and good ears among the corn, so are there lesser books and good books in Mr. Anderson's list. *Marching Men* is disappointing after *Wines-*

burg. But then anything any other American was doing at that time would have been disappointing after *Winesburg*.

Windy McPherson's Son

After reading *A Story Teller's Story,* one can see where Windy McPherson came from. And a comparison, I think, gives a clear indication of how far Mr. Anderson has grown. There is in both *Marching Men* and *Windy McPherson's Son* a fundamental lack of humor, so much so that this lack of humor militates against him, but then growing corn has little time for humor.

Poor White

The corn still grows. The crows of starvation can no longer bother it nor tear its roots up. In this book he seems to get his fingers and toes again into the soil, as he did in *Winesburg*. Here again is the old refulgent earth and people who answer the compulsions of labor and food and sleep, whose passions are uncerebral. A young girl feeling the sweet frightening inevitability of adolescence, takes it as calmly as a tree takes its rising sap, and sees the spring that brought it become languorous and drowsy with summer, its work accomplished.

Many Marriages

Here, I think, is a bad ear, because it is not Mr. Anderson. I don't know where it came from, but I do know that it is not a logical development from *Winesburg* and *Poor White*. The man here is a factory owner, a bourgeois, a man who was "top dog" because he was naturally forced to run his factory with people who had no factories of their own. In his other books there are no "under dogs" because there are no "top dogs"—save circumstance, your true democracy being at the same time a monarchy. And he gets away from the land. When he does this he is lost. And again humor is completely lacking. A 40-year-old man who has led a sedentary life must look sort of funny naked, walking up and down a room and talking. What would he do with his hands? Did you ever see a man tramping back and forth and talking, without putting his hands in his pockets? However, this story won the *Dial* prize in its year, so I am possibly wrong.

This has been translated into Russian and has been dramatized and produced in New York.

Horses and Men

A collection of short stories, reminiscent of *Winesburg,* but more sophisticated. After reading this book you inevitably want to reread *Winesburg*. Which makes one wonder if after all the short story is not Mr. Anderson's medium. No sustained plot to bother you, nothing tedious; only the sharp episodic phases of people, the portraying of which Mr. Anderson's halting questioning manner is best at. "I'm a Fool," the best short story in America, to my thinking, is the tale of a lad's adolescent pride in his profession (horse racing) and his body, of his belief in a world beautiful and passionate created for the chosen to race horses on, of his youthful pagan desire to preen in his lady's eyes that brings him low at last. Here is a personal emotion that does strike the elemental chord in mankind.

Horses! What an evocative word in the history of man. Poets have used the horse as a symbol, kingdoms have been won by him; throughout history he has been a part of the kings of sports from the days when he thundered with quadrigae, to modern polo. His history and the history of man are intermingled beyond any unraveling; separate both are mortal, as one body they partake of the immortality of the gods. No other living thing holds the same place in the life of man as he does, not even the dog. One sometimes kicks a dog just for the sake of the kick.

Horses are a very part of the soil from which Mr. Anderson came. With horses his forefathers pioneered the land, with horses they wrung and tamed it for corn; bones and sweat of numberless men and horses have helped to make the land fecund. And why shouldn't he (the horse) receive his tithe of the grain he helped to make? Why shouldn't the best of his race know unfettered the arrogance and splendor of speed?

It is well. He, the chosen of his race, becomes, with the chosen of the race of man, again immortal upon a dirt track: let his duller brethren break ground for the duller among the race of man, let them draw the wagon to town and back in the late dusk, plodding under the stars. Not for him, gelded and reft of pride, to draw a creaking laden wagon into the barn, not for him to plod sedately before a buggy under the moon, between the fields of corn along the land.

In this book there are people, people that walk and live, and the ancient stout earth that takes his heartbreaking labor and gives grudgingly, mayhap, but gives an hundredfold.

A Story Teller's Story

Here Mr. Anderson, trying to do one thing, has really written two distinct books. The first half, which was evidently intended to portray his physical picture, is really a novel based upon one character—his father. I don't recall a character anywhere exactly like him—sort of a cross between the Baron Hulot and Gaudissart. The second half of the book in which he draws his mental portrait is quite different: it leaves me with a faint feeling that it should have been in a separate volume.

Here Mr. Anderson pries into his own mind, in the same tentative manner in which he did the factory owner's mind. Up to here he is never philosophical; he believes that he knows little about it all, and leaves the reader to draw his own conclusions. He does not even offer opinions.

But in this second half of the book he assumes at times an elephantine kind of humor about himself, not at all the keen humor with which he pictured his father's character. I think that this is due to the fact that Mr. Anderson is interested in his reactions to other people, and very little in himself. That is, he has not enough active ego to write successfully of himself. That is why George Moore is interesting only when he is telling about the women he has loved or the clever things he has said. Imagine George Moore trying to write *Horses and Men*! Imagine Mr. Anderson trying to write *Confessions of a Young Man*! But the corn is maturing: I think the first half of *A Story Teller's Story* is the best character delineation he has done; but taking the book as a whole I agree with Mr. Llewellyn Powys in the *Dial:* it is not his best contribution to American literature.

I do not mean to imply that Mr. Anderson has no sense

of humor. He has, he has always had. But only recently
has he got any of it into his stories, without deliberately
writing a story with a humorous intent. I wonder sometimes if this is not due to the fact that he didn't have
leisure to write until long after these people had come to
be in his mind; that he had cherished them until his perspective was slightly awry. Just as we cherish those whom
we love; we sometimes find them ridiculous, but never
humorous. The ridiculous indicates a sense of superiority, but to find something partaking of an eternal sardonic
humor in our cherished ones is slightly discomforting.

No one, however, can accuse him of lacking in humor
in the portrayal of the father in his last book. Which, I
think, indicates that he has not matured yet, despite his
accomplishments so far. He who conceived this man has
yet something that will appear in its own good time.

We were spending a week-end on a river boat, Anderson and I. I had not slept much and so I was out and
watching the sun rise, turning the muddy reaches of the
Mississippi even, temporarily to magic, when he joined
me, laughing.

"I had a funny dream last night. Let me tell you about
it," was his opening remark—not even a good morning.

"I dreamed that I couldn't sleep, that I was riding
around the country on a horse—had ridden for days. At
last I met a man, and I swapped him the horse for a
night's sleep. This was in the morning and he told me
where to bring the horse, and so when dark came I was
right on time, standing in front of his house, holding the
horse, ready to rush off to bed. But the fellow never
showed up—left me standing there all night, holding the
horse."

To blame this man on the Russians! Or anybody else.
One of his closest friends called him "the Phallic Check-

hov." He is American, and more than that, a middle westerner, of the soil: he is as typical of Ohio in his way as Harding was in his. A field of corn with a story to tell and a tongue to tell it with.

I can not understand our passion in America for giving our own productions some remote geographical significance. "Maryland" chicken! "Roman" dressing! The "Keats" of Omaha! Sherwood Anderson, the "American" Tolstoi! We seem to be cursed with a passion for geographical cliche.

Certainly no Russian could ever have dreamed about that horse.

[Dallas *Morning News,* April 26, 1925; reprinted in *Princeton University Library Chronicle,* Spring 1957; reprinted in *William Faulkner: New Orleans Sketches,* ed. Carvel Collins, New York, 1968. The text printed here incorporates several minor corrections of errors in the newspaper text and the standardization of book titles.]

Literature and War

Siegfried Sassoon moves one who has himself slogged up to Arras or its corresponding objective, who has trod duck-boards and heard and felt them sqush and suck in the mud, who has seen the casual dead rotting beneath dissolving Flemish skies, who has smelt that dreadful smell of war—a combination of uneaten and evacuated food and slept-in mud and soiled and sweatty clothing—, who has spent four whiskey-less days cursing the General Staff. (One does not curse God in war: certainly anyone who can possibly be anywhere else, is there.)

And Henri Barbusse moves one who has lain on a dissolving hill-side soaked through and through by rain until the very particles of earth rise floating to the top of the atmosphere, and air and earth are a single medium in which one tries vainly to stand and which it would seem that even gun fire cannot penetrate.

And one can be moved by Rupert Brooke if he has done neither of these, if war be to him the Guards division eternally paraded, while the glorious dead can both fill saddles and coffins at the same time, in a region wherein men do not need food nor crave tobacco. And where there is no rain.

But it remains for R. H. Mottram to use the late war to a successful literary end, just as the Civil War needed its Stephen Crane to clear it of Negro Sergeants lying drunk in the guest rooms of the great house, and to cut off its languishing dusky curls.

Business as usual. What a grand slogan! Who has accused the Anglo-Saxon of being forever sentimental over war? Mankind's emotional gamut is like his auricular gamut: there are some things which he cannot feel, as there are sounds he cannot hear. And war, taken as a whole, is one of these things.

[*Mississippi Quarterly,* Summer 1973, ed. Michael Millgate. That text, based on Faulkner's typescript, probably written early in 1925, is printed here. The books to which Faulkner refers are: Sassoon, *The War Poems,* London, 1919; Barbusse, *Le Feu,* 1916, translated as *Under Fire: The Story of a Squad,* London, 1917; and Mottram, *The Spanish Farm,* London, 1924.]

❉ ❉ ❉

And Now What's To Do

His great-grandfather came into the country afoot from the Tennessee mountains, where he had killed a man, worked and saved and bought a little land, won a little more at cards and dice, and died at the point of a pistol while trying to legislate himself into a little more; his grandfather was a deaf, upright man in white linen, who wasted his inherited substance in politics. He had a law practice still, but he sat most of the day in the courthouse yard, a brooding, thwarted old man too deaf to take part in conversation and whom the veriest child could beat at checkers. His father loved horses better than books or learning; he owned a livery stable, and here the boy grew up, impregnated with the violent ammoniac odor of horses. At ten he could stand on a box and harness a horse and put it between runabout shafts almost as quickly as a grown man, darting beneath its belly like a cricket to buckle the straps, cursing it in his shrill cricket voice; by the time he was twelve he had acquired from the negro hostlers an uncanny skill with a pair of dice.

Each Christmas eve his father carried a hamper full of whisky in pint bottles to the stable and stood with it in the office door, against the firelight, while the negroes gathered and rolled their eyes and clicked their gleaming teeth in the barn cavern, filled with snorts and stampings of contentment. The boy, become adolescent, helped to drink this; old ladies smelled his breath at times and tried

to save his soul. Then he was sixteen and he began to ac-
quire a sort of inferiority complex regarding his father's
business. He had gone through grammar school and one
year in high school with girls and boys (on rainy days, in
a hack furnished by his father he drove about the neighborhood and gathered up all it would hold free of
charge) whose fathers were lawyers and doctors and
merchants—all genteel professions, with starched col-
lars. He had been unselfconscious then, accepting all
means of earning bread as incidental to following whatever occupation a man preferred. But not now. All this
was changed by his changing body. Before and during
puberty he learned about women from the negro
hostlers and the white night-man, by listening to their
talk. Now, on the street, he looked after the same girls he
had once taken to school in his father's hack, watching
their forming legs, imagining their blossoming thighs,
with a feeling of defiant inferiority. There was a giant in
him, but the giant was muscle-bound. The boys, the doctors' and merchants' and lawyers' sons, loafed on the corners before the drug stores. None of them could make a
pair of dice behave as he could.

An automobile came to town. The horses watched it
with swirling proud eyes and tossing snorts of alarm. The
war came, a sound afar off heard. He was eighteen, he
had not been in school since three years; the moth-eaten
hack rusted quietly among the jimson weeds in the stable
yard. He no longer smelled of ammonia, for he could
now win twenty or thirty dollars any Sunday in the crap
game in the wooded park near the railway station; and on
the drug store corner where the girls passed in soft
troops, touching one another with their hands and with
their arms you could not tell him from a lawyer's or a
merchant's or a doctor's son. The girls didn't, with their

ripening thighs and their mouths that keep you awake at night with unnameable things—shame of lost integrity, manhood's pride, desire like a drug. The body is tarnished, soiled in its pride, now. But what is it for, anyway?

A girl got in trouble, and he clung to boxcar ladders or lay in empty gondolas while railjoints clicked under the cold stars. Frost had not yet fallen upon the cotton, but it had touched the gum-lined Kentucky roads and the broad grazing lands, and lay upon the shocked corn of Ohio farm land beneath the moon. He lay on his back in an Ohio hay stack. The warm dry hay was about his legs. It had soaked a summer's sun, and it held him suspended in dry and sibilant warmth where he moved unsleeping, cradling his head, thinking of home. Girls were all right, but there were so many girls everywhere. So many of them a man had to get through with in the world, politely. It meant tactfully. Nothing to girls. Dividing legs dividing receptive. He had known all about it before, but the reality was like reading a story and then seeing it in the movies, with music and all. Soft things. Secretive, but like traps. Like going after something you wanted, and getting into a nest of spider webs. You got the thing, then you had to pick the webs off, and every time you touched one, it stuck to you. Even after you didn't want the thing anymore, the webs clung to you. Until after a while you remembered the way the webs itched and you wanted the thing again, just thinking of how the webs itched. No. Quicksand. That was it. Wade through once, then go on. But a man wont. He wants to go all the way through, somehow; break out on the other side. Everything incomplete somehow. Having to back off, with webs clinging to you. "Christ, you have to tell them so much. You cant think of it fast enough. And they never forget when you do and when you dont. What do they want, anyway?"

Across the moon a V of geese slid, their lonely cries
drifted in the light of chill and haughty stars across the
shocked corn and the supine delivered earth, lonely and
sad and wild. Winter: season of sin and death. The geese
were going south, but his direction was steadily north. In
an Ohio town one night, in a saloon, he got to know a
man who was travelling from county seat to county seat
with a pacing horse, making the county fairs. The man
was cunning in a cravatless collar, lachrymosely panegyric
of the pacing of the horse; and together they drifted
south again and again his garments became impregnated
with ammonia. Horses smelled good again, rankly ammoniac, with their ears like frost-touched vine leaves.

[*Mississippi Quarterly,* Summer 1973, based on Faulkner's
apparently unfinished manuscript, probably written in
the spring or early summer of 1925. That text is printed
here.

An unusual feature of the piece is its very clear auto-
biographical content. Faulkner may possibly have intended it to be a short story, and not everything in it
should be taken literally, but in the part he completed he
drew upon his own life to a greater extent than he did in
any piece of fiction he ever wrote. Not until a quarter of
a century later, in the part-fictional essay "Mississippi,"
did he again so clearly center a piece of writing upon his
own experiences.]

❈ ❈ ❈

The Composition, Editing, and Cutting of Flags in the Dust*

One day about two years ago I was speculating idly upon time and death when the thought occurred to me that doubtless as my flesh acquiesced more and more to the standardised compulsions of breath, there would come a day on which the palate of my soul would no longer react to the simple bread-and-salt of the world as I had found it in the finding years, just as after a while the physical palate remains apathetic until teased by truffles. And so I began casting about.

---

* In March 1934 Faulkner mailed from Oxford to his agent Morton Goldman in New York an untitled two-page manuscript describing the writing of his third novel, *Flags in the Dust* (though the title does not appear in the piece), its rejection by his publisher, and its subsequent editing and cutting by another hand. (That person was his friend and future agent Ben Wasson, also not named.) The manuscript is obviously early and was sent to his agent not for publication, for the handwriting is difficult to read, but presumably in the hope that it might be sold to a collector. (Faulkner was having serious financial difficulties at this time.) And it is possible that he was willing to dispose of the manuscript because he had already made a typescript from it, which is now not thought to have survived.

The piece was first transcribed and published by Joseph Blotner in the *Yale University Library Gazette*, January 1973, as "William Faulkner's Essay on the Composition of *Sartoris*." The piece was subsequently edited by George Hayhoe and this editor, and a clear text, with textual notes, appeared as an appendix to Hayhoe's 1979 University of South Carolina doctoral dissertation, "A Critical and Textual Study of William Faulkner's *Flags in the Dust*," which this

All that I really desired was a touchstone simply; a simple word or gesture, but having been these two years previously under the curse of words, having known twice before the agony of ink, nothing served but that I try by main strength to recreate between the covers of a book the world I was already preparing to lose and regret, feeling, with the morbidity of the young, that I was not only on the verge of decrepitude, but that growing old was to be an experience peculiar to myself alone out of all the teeming world, and desiring, if not the capture of that world and the fixing of it as you'd preserve a branch or a leaf, to indicate the lost forest, at least to keep the evocative skeleton of the dessicated leaf.

So I began to write, without much purpose, until I realised that to make it truely evocative it must be personal, in order to not only preserve my own interest in the writing, but to preserve my belief in the savor of the bread-and-salt. So I put people in it, since what can be more personal than reproduction, in its two senses, the aesthetic and the mammalian. In its one sense, really, since the aesthetic is still the female principle, the desire to

---

editor directed. That clear text, with further emendations, is printed here.

It is difficult to tell exactly when the piece was written. Faulkner states that this was two years after he began *Flags* which, if true, would place it in the late fall of 1928 or early in 1929. But it may well date from as much as a year later.

What was Faulkner's purpose in writing it? Perhaps it is a draft of a memorandum for the publisher of *Sartoris*—or for Wasson. Certainly his care in describing his reactions to the rejection and subsequent editing and cutting of his novel suggests that he intended to make some use of it, perhaps even publish it in some form. Hayhoe thinks it may have been written as an introduction for a later edition or reissue of *Sartoris*. But Faulkner would not have thought that so severe a criticism of the novel could have been a part of its republication, and he may have written it only for his own benefit.

feel the bones spreading and parting with something alive begotten of the ego and conceived by the protesting unleashing of flesh. So I got some people, some I invented, others I created out of tales I learned of nigger cooks and stable boys of all ages between one-armed Joby, eighteen, who taught me to write my name in red ink on the linen duster he wore for some reason we have both forgotten, to old Louvinia who remembered when the stars "fell" and who called my grandfather and my father by their Christian names until she died, in the long drowsy afternoons. Created I say, because they are composed partly from what they were in actual life and partly from what they should have been and were not: thus I improved on God, who, dramatic though He be, has no sense, no feeling for theatre.

And neither had I, for the first publisher to whom I submitted six hundred odd pages of mss. refused it on the ground that it was chaotic, without head or tail. I was shocked; my first emotion was blind protest, then I became objective for an instant, like a parent who is told that its child is a thief or an idiot or a leper; for a dreadful moment I contemplated it with consternation and despair, then like the parent I hid my own eyes in the fury of denial. I clung stubbornly to my illusion; I showed the mss. to a number of friends, who told me the same general thing—that the book lacked any form whatever; at last one of them took it to another publisher, who proposed to edit it enough to see just what was there.

In the meantime I had refused to have anything to do with it. I prefaced this by arguing hotly with the person designated to edit the mss. on all occasions that he was clumsy enough to be run to earth. I said, "A cabbage has grown, matured. You look at that cabbage; it is not symmetrical; you say, I will trim this cabbage off and make it art; I will make it resemble a peacock or a pagoda or three doughnuts. Very good, I say: you do that, then the cabbage will be dead."

"Then we'll make some kraut out of it," he said. "The same amount of sour kraut will feed twice as many people as cabbage." A day or so later he came to me and showed me the mss. "The trouble is," he said, "is that you had about six books in here. You were trying to write them all at once." He showed me what he meant, what he had done, and I realised for the first time that I had done better than I knew and the long work I had had to create opened before me and I felt myself surrounded by the limbo in which the shady visions, the host which stretched half formed, waiting each with its portion of that verisimilitude which is to bind into a whole the world which for some reason I believe should not pass utterly out of the memory of man, and I contemplated those shady but ingenious shapes by reason of whose labor I might reaffirm the impulses of my own ego in this actual world without stability, with a lot of humbleness, and I speculated on time and death and wondered if I had invented the world to which I should give life or if it had invented me, giving me an illusion of quickness.

❆ ❆ ❆

Mac Grider's Son*

About twice a year Charlie Hayes and I do a little barracks or airport fishing. In the winter it will be at the stove in Mr. Holmes' office, but in the summer almost any shade, even that of an airplane wing, will do. It is mostly in Canada or about the Great Lakes, though during the past two years we have got as far south as Reelfoot Lake or even Arkansas; sometimes I suppose we really believe that we are going to do it.

So (it was Saturday a week ago; my brother was getting our airplane gassed at Municipal Airport to go down home and I went over to Mrs. Caya's to get some chewing gum), when I went in the door and saw Hayes and another man at the counter, I immediately tied on a fly and began to strip off some line. Hayes and the other man

---

* Title supplied by editor. *War Birds: Diary of an Unknown Aviator* (New York, 1926), written by Elliott White Springs, is a part-fictional, part-autobiographical, account of the life and death of an American pilot in the Royal Flying Corps and Royal Air Force in World War I. Springs took a little of his material from the diary of his friend John McGavock Grider, who was killed in June 1918. *War Birds* was originally published anonymously, but in 1927 Springs added a Foreword in which he implied that the book was the actual diary of a dead friend, which he had edited. It was soon understood, widely if erroneously, that the unknown aviator and author of the diary was John McGavock Grider. Faulkner knew the book and apparently shared the general misapprehension about its authorship.

were not eating. They both wore goggles, so I knew that he was a student even before I saw that Hayes had a pencil and paper and was drawing a diagram of an aerofoil.

"This is Mister So-and-So," Hayes said: that's the way I hear names, being completely lacking in that presence of mind which catches names at once. Or maybe I was already making a false cast, reaching into my pocket for the nickel for the gum and Hayes and I already leaving Chicago for the North Michigan lakes, when the other man offered me a cigaret. I realized then that I had taken out a match box along with the nickel, and suddenly I thought, remembered, or maybe just registered: Grider? Grider?

"Mac Grider's son, George," Hayes said. Then I looked at the other for the first time, remembering him as I had glanced at him from the back as I came in: a man in the same sense in which they speak of each other as men in colleges, because even from the back that's what he looked like. Like he might be on the sophomore boxing team; big in the shoulders but not especially big anywhere else, in an open shirt and a pair of summer pants, with a young face good between the eyes and a mouth and chin more delicate than you might expect.

"Oh," I said. Then Hayes and I were well up toward Sault Ste. Marie, and, since the weather chart said that it would be cooler tomorrow, we had killed a moose or two. Then my brother called me; we all went out together, I slowing until Grider came up.

"How's flying?" I said.

"Fine," he said. "I've been at it about a week."

"A week," I said.

"Yes, I'm not so hot. I like it, though."

That was Saturday. Wednesday I was on the field again;

I went into Mrs. Caya's and there he was. He looked just like he did before, only he was alone, now, smoking a pipe this time and snapping the marbles about one of those slotted miniature pool tables in a glass box. He recognized me; I know he did, but he didn't even look at me until I said:

"Hello."

He looked at me. "Hello," he said. Then he looked at the table; he loaded the plunger carefully. "I soloed yesterday morning," he said.

"What?" I said. "What? Soloed?" He had told me Saturday he had been at it about a week. "That's fine," I said. "Good work."

He snapped the plunger carefully. "Yes," he said. "I got a kick out of it. The ship did too, I guess."

That was all. Later on I saw him and another lad about his age crossing the apron toward the airplane which he had learned to fly. They had a camera with them; later I saw that it had his name printed by hand on it, and I could imagine how he had probably approached Hayes with the notion of having his picture taken beside the airplane, asking Hayes whether he thought it would look too much like putting on side.

Mac Grider's story is not news to anyone in Memphis, I imagine; certainly not to anyone who ever read *War Birds*. He was in the first company of American air service candidates to go overseas. That was in 1917, when there were no airplanes for them to fly at home and when they took ship they did not even know where they were going and when they did arrive they immediately became military orphans without status or rank (and sometimes pay) while the other branches back home turned out officers complete to the spurs in 90 days or less.

This American company went to England and was sent to the British School of Military Aeronautics at Oxford and there broken up and posted to the Royal Flying Corps, progressing through the primary and advanced flight stages and then to Pilots' Pool, where in an anomalous state of neither fish nor fowl, with the status of enlisted men yet living as officers, American soldiers yet holding British pilot certificates, they languished again until the government back home remembered to decide what to do with them; whereupon one by one they emerged at last, with United States commissions and R. F. C. wings and were posted to British squadrons in France.

It was the spring of 1918 then. Maj. William Bishop led the R. F. C. lists with 74 Huns and his V. C. and his D. S. O. twice and his M. C. and he had now become too valuable to be risked in combat where some German tyro on his first flight might shoot him down by accident. So he was recalled to England and given a squadron; he was permitted to organize it himself and choose what men he wanted.

Three of the men he chose were Americans, Elliott Springs, Laurence Callahan and Grider. The squadron went out to France, where it became Sixty-five Squadron, S. E. 5's, single seater pursuit, and which had the peculiar honor to be commanded in rotation by three of the ranking British combat pilots of the war, the Canadian Bishop, the Englishman McCudden, the Irishman Mannock. Grider has an official record of enemy craft destroyed before he failed to return from patrol one day in August, 1918. His body was found in the crash near Lille, behind the German lines, and identified and buried by the German Red Cross.

So I stood on the apron, watching Grider's son and the companion fiddling with the camera, when Hayes came up to me.

"Listen," he said, "I want you to do something. Knock out something for the papers about this: Mac Grider's son. Twenty-two years old. Second year at Annapolis. Soloed in a week."

"In a week?" I said. "He actually soloed inside of seven days?"

"Yes. He stuck at it pretty close; he's got to be back at school on the twenty-eighth. So you knock out something. Something he won't be ashamed of."

"If I had soloed inside of a week I would want to be ashamed," I said.

"You know what I mean," Hayes said. "You do it."

They stood there beside the airplane, half playing with the camera, as people 22 years old would do.

"Ashamed," I said. "I don't know whether I can or not. I'll try it, though."

At last they had the camera ready, focused, whatever it was they were doing with it. He still wore the open shirt, the thin summer pants, the goggles of plain flat window glass that he had probably borrowed and that never cost much past $2 new.

That was it. If he had turned up with his student's permit and a pair of pursuit goggles with airproof bindings and calobar lenses you would not have been surprised. Or he could have come out even in a replica of his dead father's uniform, Sam Browne and boots and all, and a lot of women would have cried over the picture and even men would not have thought too hard of him.

But he didn't: he just stood there where the sun would fall on him good, in clothes he might have put on to mow

the back yard, while his companion squinted into the
camera, turning gadgets and such.

"Hurry it up," he said. "I'd hate to have my face freeze
like this."

[Memphis *Commercial Appeal*, September 23, 1934; reprinted, *Mississippi Quarterly*, Summer 1975. That text
is printed here.]

❈ ❈ ❈

Note on A Fable*

This is not a pacifist book. On the contrary, this writer holds almost as short a brief for pacifism as for war itself, for the reason that pacifism does not work, cannot cope with the forces which produce the wars. In fact, if this book had any aim or moral (which it did not have, I mean deliberately, in its conception, since as far as I knew or intended, it was simply an attempt to show man, human beings, in conflict with their own hearts and compulsions and beliefs and the hard and durable insentient earth-stage on which their griefs and hopes must anguish), it was to show by poetic analogy, allegory, that pacifism does not work; that to put an end to war, man must either find or invent something more powerful than war and man's aptitude for belligerence and his thirst for power at any cost, or use the fire itself to fight and destroy the fire with; that man may finally have to mobilize himself and arm himself with the implements of war to put an end to war; that the mistake we have consistently made is setting nation against nation or political ideology against ideology to stop war; that the men who do not want war may have to arm themselves as for war, and defeat by the methods of war the alliances of power which hold to the obsolete belief in the validity of war: who (the above alliances) must be taught to abhor war

---

* Title supplied by editor.

not for moral or economic reasons, or even for simple shame, but because they are afraid of it, dare not risk it since they know that in war they themselves—not as nations or governments or ideologies, but as simple human beings vulnerable to death and injury—will be the first to be destroyed.

Three of these characters represent the trinity of man's conscience—Levine, the young English pilot, who symbolizes the nihilistic third; the old French Quartermaster general, who symbolizes the passive third; the British battalion runner, who symbolizes the active third—Levine, who sees evil and refuses to accept it by destroying himself; who says 'Between nothing and evil, I will take nothing;' who in effect, to destroy evil, destroys the world too, i.e., the world which is his, himself—the old Quartermaster General who says in the last scene, 'I am not laughing. What you see are tears;' i.e., there is evil in the world; I will bear both, the evil and the world too, and grieve for them—the battalion runner, the living scar, who in the last scene says, 'That's right; tremble. I'm not going to die—never.' i.e., there is evil in the world and I'm going to do something about it.

[*Mississippi Quarterly*, Summer 1973; text based on a typescript from the files of his editor, for whom Faulkner wrote the piece late in 1953 or early in 1954, apparently either as dust jacket copy or as a statement to be used in publicity for the novel, which was published in August 1954.]

✳ ✳ ✳

SEVEN

Speeches

Funeral Sermon for Mammy Caroline Barr

MEMPHIS *COMMERCIAL APPEAL*, FEBRUARY 5, 1940

As oldest of my father's family, I might be called here master. That situation never existed between "Mammy" and me. She reared all of us from childhood. She stood as a fount not only of authority and information, but of affection, respect and security. She was one of my first associates. I have known her all my life and have been privileged to see her out of hers.

She was a character of devotion and fidelity. Mammy made no demands on any one. She had the handicap to be born without money and with a black skin and at a bad time in this country. She asked no odds and accepted the handicaps of her lot, making the best of her few advantages. She surrendered her destiny to a family. That family accepted and made some appreciation of it. She was paid for the devotion she gave but still that is only money. As surely as there is a heaven, Mammy will be in it.

[Upon the death on January 31, 1940, of the beloved family servant Mammy Caroline Barr, Faulkner gave her funeral sermon at Rowanoak on February 4. The text of the sermon, apparently what he delivered on February 4, was published in the Memphis *Commercial Appeal* on February 5. That text is printed here. (For a revised version of this text, see pp. 117–18.)]

Address to the Congrès pour la Liberté de la Culture

PARIS, MAY 30, 1952*

Allocution de M. William Faulkner

MR. CHAIRMAN,
LADIES AND GENTLEMEN,

I wish I could say this in French because it should be said in French by an American.

I am not a speech maker. I have not prepared a speech to make here. But this is something that should be said by an American. I have known for a long time that Americans in Europe behave badly.

I think that most Europeans do not know why. We still think in terms of a continent to be covered, not conquered, but completed, and of all the people who can have a star in the flag. It is difficult for us to think now of people who cannot have a star in our flag but we know

---

* On May 30, 1952, Faulkner gave a short speech, in English with a final paragraph in French, at a meeting organized by the Congrès pour la Liberté de la Culture under the title "L'Oeuvre du XXe Siècle." It was circulated, in English and in a French translation, in a pamphlet, reproduced from typescript, devoted to the conference. The French translation was published in *Arts* (Paris), June 1952. The

better that we all cannot; that our earth is bigger than our continent; that our earth is the whole world.

And we will or should behave better than we do and I believe that we will behave better than we do. I believe that in the intelligence of the French members here, and the muscle of Americans may rest the salvation of Europe.

Je pense que presque tous les Américains ont une dette de gratitude envers la France et je crois que, dans le monde entier, tous les hommes libres doivent un petit quelque chose à ce pays qui a été toujours la "Mère" universelle de la liberté de l'homme et de l'esprit humain. (*Applaudissements.*)

pamphlet text of the English (with the last paragraph in French) is printed here.

Address at the American Literature Seminar

NAGANO, JAPAN, AUGUST 5, 1955

In a discussion in Tokyo, a statement of mine was mis-construed, if not misquoted. This was to the effect that I believed that America had no culture, that we were all savages without intellect or spiritual tradition.

I did not say this because I don't believe it to be so. As I see it, no peoples have a mutual culture save those who happen to believe primarily in the same things, like the peoples who believe in freedom or the peoples who be-lieve in serfdom.

I believe that all racial and ethnic groups have their own individual cultures. The Japanese culture, for in-stance, is a culture of rationality, and the British culture one of insularity. That is, each one of these makes its cul-ture its national character.

Thus our American culture is not just success, but generosity with success—a culture of successful gener-osity. We desire and work to be successful in order to be generous with the fruits of that success. We get as much spiritual pleasure out of the giving as we do out of the gaining. All of these cultures are important, and in a way, they are interdependent.

A proof of this to me is the fact that we are meeting here in Japan, 10,000 miles from America, discussing in the English language American literature—that is, we are matching and comparing our two separate cultures which produce our national literature. Compared with the Japanese, we are clumsy and awkward and even bad-mannered. Yet out of this clumsiness and awkwardness has come that power which produced the American writers whom you consider worthy of being discussed here.

Out of our clumsiness and awkwardness there came that force which produced writers important enough to have a share in a seminar of intellects, the hosts to which are the people who have made a culture of the intellect.

I think it is our American culture of success and generosity which enabled our American writers to offer you something here today. I think that like our culture of material success, our writers are interested not merely in the success but in the generosity. We are as much interested in having what we have to offer acceptable to the writers of other nations as we are in being successful writers in our own country. I think we are much more interested in universal writing than we are in being American writers.

I think that our American culture causes our writers to think of themselves only secondarily as American writers, that we think of ourselves first as men and women dealing in the universal quality which is literature. I believe we are not really trying to produce American literature nor even to add to its prestige. I believe we are trying to increase the prestige of a universal literature. I believe that when we seem awkward and provincial, it is because we are provincial.

It is because our culture of the intellect is so new that

we have carried with us into the art of literature a certain naivete which we are too young in the craft as yet to have rid ourselves of. A proof of this American naivete is that there is no jealousy based on gender and very little even on material success among American writers. No American assumes it the man's prerogative to have more talent or to be more important in literature than a woman writer.

We have been, as a nation, a lucky people. We have escaped so much of the trouble and grief that other peoples have had to suffer and we are aware of this, and a part of our culture of success and generosity is a wish to share this good fortune with less fortunate people, if we can, through qualities of the spirit as well as of the pocketbook; that the American writer is quite proud of his position in universal literature without being jealous of any other nation.

I think that most other literary people can't quite conceive that the American can be a writer without being a man of ideas. The European writer, if he is a writer, is per se a member of all other correlative intellectual processes. The American writer can be a writer and not be a part of the universality of ideas at all. What serves him for an idea is not a rational process at all, but an emotional concept of and belief in the universal truth of man's heart, and its record in literature. It is this that we are proudest to participate in and share.

[In Japan in August 1955 Faulkner was frequently interviewed, and his comments were widely reported in the Japanese press. To correct or prevent misunderstanding of some of these comments, he wrote a statement that he gave as a speech at Nagano on August 5. In 1965 Joseph Blotner was given a typescript (not typed by Faulkner) of the speech, which he published in the Summer 1982 issue of the *Mississippi Quarterly*. Neither he nor the present editor, who edited that issue, was aware that a version of the speech had been published in the Memphis *Commercial Appeal,* August 28, 1955, "Distributed by International News Service." That published text was reproduced in *Each in Its Ordered Place: A Faulkner Collector's Notebook,* by Carl Petersen (Ann Arbor, Michigan, 1975). The text printed here is that of the typescript and *Mississippi Quarterly.*]

Address upon Receiving the Andrés Bello Award

The artist, whether he would have chosen so or not, finds
that he has been dedicated to a single course and one
from which he will never escape. This is, he tries, with
every means in his possession, his imagination, experience and observation, to put into some more durable
form than his own fragile and ephemeral life—in paint
or music or marble or the covers of a book—that which
he has learned in his brief spell of breathing—the passion and hope, the beauty and horror and humor, of frail

---

* On his trip to Venezuela in April 1961, Faulkner received from the
Venezuelan government the Order of Andrés Bello, first class. He
delivered his speech of acceptance in Spanish, translated from
Faulkner's original manuscript by Hugh Jencks, his interpreter on
that trip. This translation was published in the Caracas newspaper *El
Universal* April 7, 1961, and was reprinted in *A Faulkner Miscellany*,
ed. James B. Meriwether, University Press of Mississippi, 1974. With
it was a translation from the Spanish back to English by Muna Lee,
the Foreign Service officer who had arranged this trip.

Faulkner gave his original manuscript to his step-daughter, Victo-
ria Franklin Fielden, and her husband, William Fielden, who were
living in Caracas. It was acquired and published by Louis Daniel
Brodsky as "The 1961 Andrés Bello Award: William Faulkner's
Original Acceptance Speech," in *Studies in Bibliography*, 1986, vol.
39. That text is printed here.

and fragile and indomitable man struggling and suffering and triumphing amid the conflicts of his own heart, in the human condition. He is not to solve this dilemma nor does he even hope to survive it save in the shape and significance, the memories, of the marble and paint and music and ordered words which someday he must leave behind him.

This of course is his immortality, perhaps the only one. Perhaps the very drive which has compelled him to that dedication was simply the desire to leave inscribed beside that final door into oblivion through which he first must pass, the words "Kilroy was here."

So, as I stand here today, I have already tasted that immortality. That I, a country-bred alien who followed that dedication thousands of miles away, to seek and try to capture and imitate for a moment in a handful of printed pages, the truth of man's hope in the human dilemma, have received here in Venezuela the official accolade which says in effect: Your dedication was not spent in vain. What you found and tried to imitate, was truth.

Address at the Teatro Municipal

CARACAS, APRIL 6, 1961*

Anyone who had received as many honors as myself since reaching Venezuela, might have supposed no new one remained for him. He would have been wrong. In this performance of "Danzas Venezuela" he saw not merely another warm and generous gesture from one American country to a visitor from another one. He saw the spirit and history of Venezuela caught and held in a bright and moving instant of grace and skill, by young men and women who gave the impression that they were doing it from love and pride in the poetry and tradition of their country's history and the lives of its people, for the stranger, the alien, to see and understand and so carry back to his home with him a fuller knowledge of the country which he had already come to admire—never to forget the gesture nor the inspiration of it from the poetry of Blanco and the other poets, maybe even nameless ones, whose dedication it is to record the history of na-

---

* On the evening of April 6, 1961, Faulkner attended a performance of the "Danzas Venezuela" at the Teatro Municipal. For the occasion he wrote a brief speech of thanks to the dancers. It was translated into Spanish by Hugh Jencks, who read it to the dancers and the audience. Jencks provided this editor with a copy of Faulkner's original typescript, which was published in the *Mississippi Quarterly*, Summer 1974. That text is printed here.

tions and peoples, which senora Ossona translated into graceful and significant motion, nor senora Ramon y Riviera who directed it and the young men and women who performed it. He thanks them all. He will not forget the experience nor them who made it possible.

EIGHT

Introductions

Two Introductions

TO

*The Sound and the Fury**

INTRODUCTION TO
The Sound and the Fury, 1933

ART IS no part of southern life. In the North it seems to
be different. It is the hardest miner stone in Manhattan's

---

* In the summer of 1933, Faulkner wrote an introduction to *The
Sound and the Fury* for a proposed Random House edition. He sent it
to his agent Ben Wasson, who sent it to Bennett Cerf on August 24.
(See *Selected Letters of William Faulkner*, ed. Joseph Blotner, New York,
1977, pp. 71, 74.) The project was abandoned, but the introduction
was retained in the Random House files.

When plans were made in 1946 for a Modern Library double volume of *The Sound and the Fury* and *As I Lay Dying*, Faulkner's editor
Robert Linscott found the introduction and sent it to Faulkner in
the hope that it could be used, somewhat revised, in the new volume. Faulkner rejected the piece—"I had forgotten what smug false
sentimental windy shit it was," he wrote Linscott—but offered
to rewrite and shorten it. However, when the book was published
that December, there was no introduction in it. (*Selected Letters*,
pp. 235–36.)

Several complete and incomplete manuscript and typescript versions survived among Faulkner's papers. They represent at least
two quite different versions. The present editor edited and published two of the complete texts: the longer one, which Faulkner
dated "19 August 1933," first appeared in *Mississippi Quarterly*, Summer 1973, and is believed by this editor to be the one Faulkner sent
to Wasson; the much shorter one was published in *Southern Review*,
Autumn 1972, and this editor believes it to be the one Faulkner revised and rewrote in 1946. Those two texts are printed here.

foundation. It is a part of the glitter or shabbiness of the streets. The arrowing buildings rise out of it and because of it, to be torn down and arrow again. There will be people leading small bourgeois lives (those countless and almost invisible bones of its articulation, lacking any one of which the whole skeleton might collapse) whose bread will derive from it—polyglot boys and girls progressing from tenement schools to editorial rooms and art galleries; men with grey hair and paunches who run linotype machines and take up tickets at concerts and then go sedately home to Brooklyn and suburban stations where children and grandchildren await them—long after the descendents of Irish politicians and Neapolitan racketeers are as forgotten as the wild Indians and the pigeon.

And of Chicago too: of that rythm not always with harmony or tune; lusty, loudvoiced, always changing and always young; drawing from a river basin which is almost a continent young men and women into its living unrest and then spewing them forth again to write Chicago in New England and Virginia and Europe. But in the South art, to become visible at all, must become a ceremony, a spectacle; something between a gypsy encampment and a church bazaar given by a handful of alien mummers who must waste themselves in protest and active self-defense until there is nothing left with which to speak—a single week, say, of furious endeavor for a show to be held on Friday night and then struck and vanished, leaving only a paint-stiffened smock or a worn out typewriter ribbon in the corner and perhaps a small bill for cheesecloth or bunting in the hands of an astonished and bewildered tradesman.

Perhaps this is because the South (I speak in the sense of the indigenous dream of any given collection of men having something in common, be it only geography and climate, which shape their economic and spiritual aspirations into cities, into a pattern of houses or behavior) is old since dead. New York, whatever it may believe of itself, is young since alive; it is still a logical and unbroken progression from the Dutch. And Chicago even boasts of being young. But the South, as Chicago is the Middlewest and New York the East, is dead, killed by the Civil War. There is a thing known whimsically as the New South to be sure, but it is not the south. It is a land of Immigrants who are rebuilding the towns and cities into replicas of towns and cities in Kansas and Iowa and Illinois, with skyscrapers and striped canvas awnings instead of wooden balconies, and teaching the young men who sell the gasoline and the waitresses in the restaurants to say O yeah? and to speak with hard r's, and hanging over the intersections of quiet and shaded streets where no one save Northern tourists in Cadillacs and Lincolns ever pass at a gait faster than a horse trots, changing red-and-green lights and savage and peremptory bells.

Yet this art, which has no place in southern life, is almost the sum total of the Southern artist. It is his breath, blood, flesh, all. Not so much that it is forced back upon him or that he is forced bodily into it by the circumstance; forced to choose, lady and tiger fashion, between being an artist and being a man. He does it deliberately; he wishes it so. This has always been true of him and of him alone. Only Southerners have taken horsewhips and pistols to editors about the treatment or maltreatment of their manuscript. This—the actual pistols—was in the old days, of course, we no longer succumb to the impulse. But it is still there, still within us.

Because it is himself that the Southerner is writing about, not about his environment: who has, figuratively speaking, taken the artist in him in one hand and his milieu in the other and thrust the one into the other like a clawing and spitting cat into a croker sack. And he writes. We have never got and probably will never get, anywhere with music or the plastic forms. We need to talk, to tell, since oratory is our heritage. We seem to try in the simple furious breathing (or writing) span of the individual to draw a savage indictment of the contemporary scene or to escape from it into a makebelieve region of swords and magnolias and mockingbirds which perhaps never existed anywhere. Both of the courses are rooted in sentiment; perhaps the ones who write savagely and bitterly of the incest in clayfloored cabins are the most sentimental. Anyway, each course is a matter of violent partizanship, in which the writer unconsciously writes into every line and phrase his violent despairs and rages and frustrations or his violent prophesies of still more violent hopes. That cold intellect which can write with calm and complete detachment and gusto of its contemporary scene is not among us; I do not believe there lives the Southern writer who can say without lying that writing is any fun to him. Perhaps we do not want it to be.

I seem to have tried both of the courses. I have tried to escape and I have tried to indict. After five years I look back at *The Sound and the Fury* and see that that was the turning point: in this book I did both at one time. When I began the book, I had no plan at all. I wasn't even writing a book. Previous to it I had written three novels, with progressively decreasing ease and pleasure, and reward or emolument. The third one was shopped about for three years during which I sent it from publisher to publisher with a kind of stubborn and fading hope of at least justifying the paper I had used and the time I had spent writing it. This hope must have died at last, because one day it suddenly seemed as if a door had clapped silently and forever to between me and all publishers' addresses and booklists and I said to myself, Now I can write. Now I can just write. Whereupon I, who had three brothers and no sisters and was destined to lose my first daughter in infancy, began to write about a little girl.

I did not realise then that I was trying to manufacture the sister which I did not have and the daughter which I was to lose, though the former might have been apparent from the fact that Caddy had three brothers almost before I wrote her name on paper. I just began to write about a brother and a sister splashing one another in the brook and the sister fell and wet her clothing and the smallest brother cried, thinking that the sister was conquered or perhaps hurt. Or perhaps he knew that he was the baby and that she would quit whatever water battles to comfort him. When she did so, when she quit the water fight and stooped in her wet garments above him, the entire story, which is all told by that same little brother in the first section, seemed to explode on the paper before me.

I saw that peaceful glinting of that branch was to become the dark, harsh flowing of time sweeping her to where she could not return to comfort him, but that just separation, division, would not be enough, not far enough. It must sweep her into dishonor and shame too. And that Benjy must never grow beyond this moment; that for him all knowing must begin and end with that fierce, panting, paused and stooping wet figure which smelled like trees. That he must never grow up to where the grief of bereavement could be leavened with understanding and hence the alleviation of rage as in the case of Jason, and of oblivion as in the case of Quentin.

I saw that they had been sent to the pasture to spend

the afternoon to get them away from the house during
the grandmother's funeral in order that the three brothers and the nigger children could look up at the muddy
seat of Caddy's drawers as she climbed the tree to look in
the window at the funeral, without then realising the sym-
bology of the soiled drawers, for here again hers was the
courage which was to face later with honor the shame
which she was to engender, which Quentin and Jason
could not face: the one taking refuge in suicide, the
other in vindictive rage which drove him to rob his bas-
tard niece of the meagre sums which Caddy could send
her. For I had already gone on to night and the bedroom
and Dilsey with the mudstained drawers scrubbing the
naked backside of that doomed little girl—trying to
cleanse with the sorry byblow of its soiling that body,
flesh, whose shame they symbolised and prophesied, as
though she already saw the dark future and the part she
was to play in it trying to hold that crumbling household
together.

Then the story was complete, finished. There was
Dilsey to be the future, to stand above the fallen ruins of
the family like a ruined chimney, gaunt, patient and indomitable; and Benjy to be the past. He had to be an
idiot so that, like Dilsey, he could be impervious to the future, though unlike her by refusing to accept it at all.
Without thought or comprehension; shapeless, neuter,
like something eyeless and voiceless which might have
lived, existed merely because of its ability to suffer, in the
beginning of life; half fluid, groping: a pallid and helpless mass of all mindless agony under sun, in time yet not
of it save that he could nightly carry with him that fierce,
courageous being who was to him but a touch and a
sound that may be heard on any golf links and a smell
like trees, into the slow bright shapes of sleep.

The story is all there, in the first section as Benjy told it. I did not try deliberately to make it obscure; when I realised that the story might be printed, I took three more sections, all longer than Benjy's, to try to clarify it. But when I wrote Benjy's section, I was not writing it to be printed. If I were to do it over now I would do it differently, because the writing of it as it now stands taught me both how to write and how to read, and even more: It taught me what I had already read, because on completing it I discovered, in a series of repercussions like summer thunder, the Flauberts and Conrads and Turgenievs which as much as ten years before I had consumed whole and without assimilating at all, as a moth or a goat might. I have read nothing since; I have not had to. And I have learned but one thing since about writing. That is, that the emotion definite and physical and yet nebulous to describe which the writing of Benjy's section of *The Sound and the Fury* gave me—that ecstasy, that eager and joyous faith and anticipation of surprise which the yet unmarred sheets beneath my hand held inviolate and unfailing—will not return. The unreluctance to begin, the cold satisfaction in work well and arduously done, is there and will continue to be there as long as I can do it well. But that other will not return. I shall never know it again.

So I wrote Quentin's and Jason's sections, trying to clarify Benjy's. But I saw that I was merely temporising; That I should have to get completely out of the book. I realised that there would be compensations, that in a sense I could then give a final turn to the screw and extract some ultimate distillation. Yet it took me better than a month to take pen and write *The day dawned bleak and chill* before I did so. There is a story somewhere about an old Roman who kept at his bedside a Tyrrhenian vase which he loved and the rim of which he wore slowly away with kissing it. I had made myself a vase, but I suppose I knew all the time that I could not live forever inside of it, that perhaps to have it so that I too could lie in bed and look at it would be better; surely so when that day should come when not only the ecstasy of writing would be gone, but the unreluctance and the something worth saying too. It's fine to think that you will leave something behind you when you die, but it's better to have made something you can die with. Much better the muddy bottom of a little doomed girl climbing a blooming pear tree in April to look in the window at the funeral.

Oxford.
    19 August, 1933.

[*Mississippi Quarterly*, Summer 1973]

INTRODUCTION TO
The Sound and the Fury, 1946

I WROTE this book and learned to read. I had learned a little about writing from *Soldiers' Pay*—how to approach language, words: not with seriousness so much, as an essayist does, but with a kind of alert respect, as you approach dynamite; even with joy, as you approach women; perhaps with the same secretly unscrupulous intentions. But when I finished *The Sound and the Fury* I discovered that there is actually something to which the shabby term Art not only can, but must, be applied. I discovered then that I had gone through all that I had ever read, from Henry James through Henty to newspaper murders, without making any distinction or digesting any of it, as a moth or a goat might. After *The Sound and the Fury* and without heeding to open another book and in a series of delayed repercussions like summer thunder, I discover the Flauberts and Dostoyevskys and Conrads whose books I had read ten years ago. With *The Sound and the Fury* I learned to read and quit reading, since I have read nothing since.

Nor do I seem to have learned anything since. While writing *Sanctuary,* the next novel to *The Sound and the Fury,* that part of me which learned as I wrote, which perhaps is the very force which drives a writer to the travail of invention and the drudgery of putting seventy-five or a hundred thousand words on paper, was absent because I was still reading by repercussion the books which I had swallowed whole ten years and more ago. I learned only from the writing of *Sanctuary* that there was something missing; something which *The Sound and the Fury* gave me and *Sanctuary* did not. When I began *As I Lay Dying* I had discovered what it was and knew that it would be also missing in this case because this would be a deliberate book. I set out deliberately to write a *tour-de-force.* Before I ever put pen to paper and set down the first word, I knew what the last word would be and almost where the last period would fall. Before I began I said, I am going to write a book by which, at a pinch, I can stand or fall if I never touch ink again. So when I finished it the cold satisfaction was there, as I had expected, but as I had also expected that other quality which *The Sound and the Fury* had given me was absent: that emotion definite and physical and yet nebulous to describe: that ecstasy, that eager and joyous faith and anticipation of surprise which the yet unmarred sheet beneath my hand held inviolate and unfailing, waiting for release. It was not there in *As I Lay Dying*. I said, It is because I knew too much about this book before I began to write it. I said, More than likely I shall never again have to know this much about a book before I begin to write it, and next time it will return. I waited almost two years, then I began *Light in August,* knowing no more about it than a young woman, pregnant, walking along a strange country road. I thought, I will recapture it now, since I know no more about this book than I did about *The Sound and the Fury* when I sat down before the first blank page.

It did not return. The written pages grew in number. The story was going pretty well: I would sit down to it each morning without reluctance yet still without that anticipation and that joy which alone ever made writing pleasure to me. The book was almost finished before I acquiesced to the fact that it would not recur, since I was now aware before each word was written down just what the people would do, since now I was deliberately choosing among possibilities and probabilities of behavior and weighing and measuring each choice by the scale of the Jameses and Conrads and Balzacs. I knew that I had read too much, that I had reached that stage which all young writers must pass through, in which he believes that he has learned too much about his trade. I received a copy of the printed book and I found that I didn't even want to see what kind of jacket Smith had put on it. I seemed to have a vision of it and the other ones subsequent to *The Sound and the Fury* ranked in order upon a shelf which I looked at the titled backs of them with a flagging attention which was almost distaste, and upon which each succeeding title registered less and less, until at last Attention itself seemed to say, Thank God I shall never need to open any one of them again. I believed that I knew then why I had not recaptured that first ecstasy, and that I should never again recapture it; that whatever novels I should write in the future would be written without reluctance, but also without anticipation of joy: that in *The Sound and the Fury* I had already put perhaps the only thing in literature which would ever move me very much: Caddy climbing the pear tree to look in the window at her grandmother's funeral while Quentin and Jason and Benjy and the negroes looked up at the muddy seat of her drawers.

This is the only one of the seven novels which I wrote without any accompanying feeling of drive or effort, or any following feeling of exhaustion or relief or distaste. When I began it I had no plan at all. I wasn't even writing a book. I was thinking of books, publication, only in the reverse, in saying to myself, I wont have to worry about publishers liking or not liking this at all. Four years before I had written *Soldiers' Pay*. It didn't take long to write and it got published quickly and made me about five hundred dollars. I said, Writing novels is easy. You dont make much doing it, but it is easy. I wrote *Mosquitoes*. It wasn't quite so easy to write and it didn't get published quite as quickly and it made me about four hundred dollars. I said, Apparently there is more to writing novels, being a novelist, than I thought. I wrote *Sartoris*. It took much longer, and the publisher refused it at once. But I continued to shop it about for three years with a stubborn and fading hope, perhaps to justify the time which I had spent writing it. This hope died slowly, though it didn't hurt at all. One day I seemed to shut a door between me and all publishers' addresses and book lists. I said to myself, Now I can write. Now I can make myself a vase like that which the old Roman kept at his bedside and wore the rim slowly away with kissing it. So I, who had never had a sister and was fated to lose my daughter in infancy, set out to make myself a beautiful and tragic little girl.

[*Southern Review,* Autumn 1972]

Prefatory Note

TO

"APPENDIX: COMPSON, 1699–1945"

WHEN FAULKNER wrote *The Sound and the Fury* in 1928, he failed to finish it for anybody. In 1946, when Malcolm Cowley reached *The Sound and the Fury* in gathering and collating material for his portable Faulkner, Faulkner discovered that the book was not even finished for himself. Possibly he realised this in 1946 only because he was incapable of finishing it until 1946; that in 1928 and 1938 he still didn't know enough about people to finish out his own, and so the book was actually not unconsciously willful tour de force in obfuscation but rather the homemade, the experimental, the first moving picture projector—warped lens, poor light, undependable mechanism and even a bad screen—which had to wait until 1946 for the lens to clear, the light to steady, the gears to run smooth. It was too late then, though. The book was done. It was last year's maidenhead now. All Faulkner could do was try and make a key. He thought a page or two pages would do it. It ran nearer twenty. Here it is.

[Faulkner wrote "Appendix: Compson, 1699–1945," an addition to *The Sound and the Fury,* for inclusion in the Viking *Portable Faulkner,* edited by Malcolm Cowley, published in April 1946. It was republished in December 1946 in the Modern Library double volume of *The Sound and the Fury* and *As I Lay Dying*, and Faulkner sent an introductory note for the Appendix to his editor Robert N. Linscott, probably in May 1946. The note did not appear in the book, and the version he sent to Linscott has apparently not survived. However, a draft of it appears on the verso of a typescript page in an early draft of *A Fable*, and was published in "A Prefatory Note by Faulkner for the Compson Appendix," by James B. Meriwether, in *American Literature*, May 1971. That text is printed here.]

NINE

Book and Drama Reviews

[The first six reviews/essay-reviews in Part 9 of this Modern Library edition were originally published in 1920, 1921, and 1922 in the University of Mississippi student newspaper, *The Mississippian*. The author's name appears, variously, as: William F. [*sic*] Falkner; W. Falkner; and W.F. They were collected in *William Faulkner: Early Prose and Poetry,* ed. Carvel Collins (Boston: Little, Brown, 1962). In editing these pieces, Collins not only corrected a host of printer's errors in Faulkner's prose, but also made corrections in the quotations. Those corrected texts have been printed here with few changes.]

Review

OF

In April Once

BY W. A. PERCY

MR. PERCY is a native Mississippian, a graduate of the University of the South and of the Harvard Law School. He was a member of the Belgian Relief Commission in the early days of the war, then served as a lieutenant attached to the 37th Division. He now lives in Greenville.

Mr. Percy—like alas! how many of us—suffered the misfortune of having been born out of his time. He should have lived in Victorian England and gone to Italy with Swinburne, for like Swinburne, he is a mixture of passionate adoration of beauty and as passionate a despair and disgust with its manifestations and accessories in the human race. His muse is Latin in type—poignant ecstasies of lyrical extravagance and a short lived artificial strength achieved at the cost of true strength in beauty. Beauty, to him, is almost like physical pain, evident in the simplicity of this poem which is the nearest perfect thing in the book—

> I heard a bird at break of day
>   Sing from the autumn trees
> A song so mystical and calm,
>   So full of certainties,

> No man, I think, could listen long
>> Except upon his knees.
> Yet this was but a simple bird
>> Alone, among dead trees.

The influence of the frank pagan beauty worship of the past is heavily upon him, he is like a little boy closing his eyes against the dark of modernity which threatens the bright simplicity and the colorful romantic pageantry of the middle ages with which his eyes are full. One can imagine him best as a violinist who became blind about the time Mozart died, it would seem that the last thing he saw with his subjective intellect was Browning standing in naive admiration before his own mediocrity, of which Mr. Percy's "Epistle from Corinth" is the fruit. This is far and away the best thing in the book, and would have been better except for the fact that Mr. Percy, like every man who has ever lived, is the victim of his age.

As a whole, the book sustains its level of lyrical beauty. Occasionally it becomes pure vowelization, for it is not always the word that Mr. Percy seeks, but the sound. There is one element that will tend more than anything else to help it oblivionward, this is the section devoted to war poems. How many, many, many reams of paper that have been ruined with poetry appertaining to the late war no one, probably, will ever know, yet still the nightingales wear swords and Red Cross brassards.

Mr. Percy has not written a great book,—there is too much music in it for that, he is a violinist with an inferior instrument—yet (and most unusual as modern books of poetry go) the gold outweighs the dross. How much, I would not undertake to say, for he is a difficult person to whom to render justice; like Swinburne, he obscures the whole mental horizon, one either likes him passionately or one remains forever cold to him.

[*Mississippian*, November 10, 1920]

Review

OF

Turns and Movies

BY CONRAD AIKEN

IN THE FOG generated by the mental puberty of contemporary American versifiers while writing inferior Keats or sobbing over the middle west, appears one rift of heaven sent blue—the poems of Conrad Aiken. He, alone of the entire yelping pack, seems to have a definite goal in mind. The others—there are perhaps half a dozen exceptions— are so many loud sounds lost in a single depth of privet hedge; the others lay about them lustily with mouth open and eyes closed, some in more or less impenetrable thickets of Browningesque obscurity, others hopelessly mired in the swamps of mediocrity, and all are creating a last flurry before darkness kindly engulfs them.

Many of them have realized that aesthetics is as much a science as chemistry, that there are certain definite scientific rules which, when properly applied, will produce great art as surely as certain chemical elements, combined in the proper proportions, will produce certain re-actions; yet Mr. Aiken alone has made any effort to dis-cover them and apply them intelligently. Nothing is ever accidental with him, he has most happily escaped our na-tional curse of filling each and every space, religious, physical, mental and moral, and beside him the British nightingales, Mr. Vachel Lindsay with his tin pan and iron spoon, Mr. Kreymborg with his lithographic water coloring, and Mr. Carl Sandburg with his sentimental Chicago propaganda are so many puppets fumbling in windy darkness.

Mr. Aiken has a plastic mind, he uses variation, inver-sion, change of rhythm and such metrical tricks with skill-ful effect, and his clear impersonality will never permit him to write poor verse. He is never a press agent as are so many of his contemporaries. It is rather difficult to quote an example from him, as he has written with cer-tain musical forms in mind, and any division of his work corresponding to the accepted dimensions of a poem is as a single chord to a fugue; yet the three quatrains from "Discordants":

Music I heard with you was more than music,
And bread I broke with you was more than bread;
Now that I am without you, all is desolate;
All that was once so beautiful is dead.

Your hands once touched this table and this silver,
And I have seen your fingers hold this glass.
These things do not remember you, belovèd,—
And yet your touch upon them will not pass.

For it was in my heart you moved among them,
And blessed them with your hands and with your eyes;

And in my heart they will remember always,—
They knew you once, O beautiful and wise.

This is one of the most beautifully, impersonally sincere poems of all time.

The most interesting phase of Mr. Aiken's work is his experiments with an abstract three dimensional verse patterned on polyphonic music form: *The Jig of Forslin* and *The House of Dust*. This is interesting because of the utterly unlimited possibilities of it, he has the whole world before him; for as yet no one has made a successful attempt to synthesize musical reactions with abstract documentary reactions. Miss Amy Lowell tried a polyphonic prose which, in spite of the fact that she has created some delightful statuettes of perfectly blown glass, is merely a literary flatulency; and it has left her, reed in hand, staring in naive surprise at the air whence her bubbles have burst.

Mr. Aiken has never been haphazard, he has developed steadily, never for a moment at a loss, yet it is almost impossible to discover where his initial impulse came from. At times it seems that he is completing a cycle back to the Greeks, again there seem to be faint traces of the French symbolists, scattered through his poems are bits of soft sonority that Masefield might have formed; and so at last one returns to the starting point—from where did he come, and where is he going? It is interesting to watch, for—say in fifteen years—when the tide of aesthetic sterility which is slowly engulfing us has withdrawn, our first great poet will be left. Perhaps he is the man.

[*Mississippian*, February 16, 1921]

Review

OF

Aria da Capo: A Play in One Act

BY EDNA ST. VINCENT MILLAY

Something new enough to be outstanding in this age of mental puberty, this loud gesturing of the aesthetic messiahs of our emotional Valhalla who have one eye on the ball and the other on the grandstand. In newspaper parlance Miss Millay might be said to have scored a "beat"; truly so in the sense that her contemporaries (those of them who will ever become aware that she has done something "different") will each wonder to himself why he or she did not think of it first, which is very natural. Here is an idea so simple that it does give to wonder why under heaven no one has thought of it before. Its simplicity is doubtless the reason.

The play is a slight thing in itself; the surprising freshness of the idea of a pastoral tragedy enacted and concluded by interlopers against a conventional background of paper streamers and colored confetti in the midst of a thoroughly artificial Pierrot and Columbine suite alone makes it worth a second glance. Yet, this is an unjust statement; for about all modern playwrights and versifiers offer us is a sterile clashing of ideas innocent of imagination; a species of emotional shorthand. *Aria da Capo* possesses more than a clever idea skilfully carried out, yet it is difficult to put the hand on just what makes it go; there is no unusual depth of experience, either mental or physical, to be traced from it other than those characteristics acquired without conscious effort by every young writer, from the reading done during the period of his mental development, either from choice or compulsion. The language is good; the rhyme neither faltering through too close attention, nor careless from lack of it; the choice of words, with one exception—a speech of Pierrot's which I do not remember contains a word of inexcusable crudeness—is sound: and—heaven sent genius—the play is not too long; i.e., no padding, no mental sofa pillows to break the fall of the doomed and tiring mind. A lusty tenuous simplicity; the gods have given Miss Millay a strong wrist; and though an idea alone does not make or mar a piece of writing, it is something; and this one of hers will live even though Miss Amy Lowell intricately festoons it with broken glass, or Mr. Carl Sandburg sets it in the stock yards, to be acted, of a Saturday afternoon, by the Beef Butchers' Union.

[*Mississippian*, January 13, 1922]

American Drama:
Eugene O'Neill

SOME ONE has said—a Frenchman, probably; they have said everything—that art is preeminently provincial: i.e., it comes directly from a certain age and a certain locality. This is a very profound statement; for *Lear* and *Hamlet* and *All's Well* could never have been written anywhere save in England during Elizabeth's reign (this is proved by the *Hamlet*s that have come out of Denmark and Sweden, and the *All's Well* of French comedy) nor could *Madame Bovary* have been written in any place other than the Rhone valley in the eighteenth century; and just as Balzac is nineteenth century Paris. But there are exceptions to this, as there are to all rules holding a particle of truth; two modern ones being Conrad and Eugene O'Neill. These two men are anomalies, Joseph Conrad especially; this man has overturned all literary tradition in this point. It is too soon yet to be committed about O'Neill, though young as he is, he is already a quantity to make one wonder at the truth of the above assertion.

It is not especially difficult—after a man has written and passed on—to trace the threads which were drawn together by him and put on paper in the form of his own work. It can be seen how Shakespeare ruthlessly took what he needed from his predecessors and contemporaries, leaving behind him a drama which the hand does not hold blood that can cap; the German playwrights have obviously and logically followed their destinies according to the Teutonic standards of thought down to the work of Hauptmann and Moeller; Synge is provincial, smacking of the soil from which he sprang as no other modern does (Synge is dead now); while the one man who is accomplishing anything in American drama is a contradiction to all concepts of art.

This may be because of the fact that America has no drama or literature worth the name, and hence no tradition. If this be the reason, one must perforce believe that the Fates have indeed played a scurvy trick upon him in casting into twentieth century America a man who might go to astounding lengths in a land possessing traditions. Facts about Conrad, however, who is even more of a contradiction than O'Neill, supply a basis for hoping that chance is not diabolical enough to perpetrate such a thing; and also show what an incalculable, indefinable quantity genius—horrible word—is.

The most unusual factor about O'Neill is that a modern American should write plays about the sea. We have had no salt water traditions for a hundred years. The English are the wanderers, while we essentially are not. Yet here is a man, son of a New York political "boss," raised in New York City and a student at Princeton, who writes of the sea. He has been, through accident, a sailor himself: he was shanghaied aboard a South American bound vessel and was forced to make a voyage as an able seaman from Rio to Liverpool in order to get home. He is not physically strong, having congenitally weak lungs, hence must lead a careful life as regards hardship and exposure; and yet his first writing phase was dominated by the sea.

And he has written good healthy plays, and—a strange thing—New York has realized his possibilities. *The Em-*

peror Jones played there, and *The Straw* and *Anna Christie* are playing in New York this winter. These last two are later plays, not of the sea, but the thing that makes them go is the same that made *Gold* and *Diff'rent* go, that made the Emperor Jones rise up and swagger in his egoism and cruelty, and die at last through his own hereditary fears: they all possess the same clarity and simplicity of plot and language. Nobody since *The Playboy* has gotten the force behind stage language that O'Neill has. The Emperor Jones's "who dat dare whistle in de Emperor's palace?" goes back to the Playboy's "the likes of which would make the mitred bishops themselves strain at the bars of paradise for to see the lady Helen walking in her golden shawl."

He is still developing; his later plays *The Straw* and *Anna Christie* betray a changing attitude toward his characters, a change from a detached observation of his people brought low by sheer circumstance, to a more personal regard for their joys and hopes, their sufferings and despairs. Perhaps in time he will make something of the wealth of natural dramatic material in this country, the greatest source being our language. A national literature cannot spring from folk lore—though heaven knows, such a forcing has been tried often enough—for America is too big and there are too many folk lores: Southern negroes, Spanish and French strains, the old west, for these always will remain colloquial; nor will it come through our slang, which also is likewise indigenous to restricted portions of the country. It can, however, come from the strength of imaginative idiom which is understandable by all who read English. Nowhere today, saving in parts of Ireland, is the English language spoken with the same earthy strength as it is in the

United States; though we are, as a nation, still inarticulate.

[*Mississippian*, February 3, 1922]

American Drama: Inhibitions

—— 1 ——

ONLY BY means of some astounding blind machination of chance will the next twenty-five years see in America a fundamentally sound play—a structure solidly built, properly produced and correctly acted. Playwrights and actors are now at the mercy of circumstances which must inevitably drive all imaginative people whose judgment is not temporarily aberrant, to various conditions of fancied relief; to a frank pandering to Frank Crane's market—holding a spiritual spittoon, so to speak, for that stratum which, unfortunately, has money in this country—to Europe; and to synthetic whiskey.

Writing people are all so pathetically torn between a desire to make a figure in the world and a morbid interest in their personal egos—the deadly fruit of the grafting of Sigmund Freud upon the dynamic chaos of a hodge-podge of nationalities. And, with characteristic national restlessness, those with imagination and some talent find it unbearable. O'Neill has turned his back on America to write of the sea, Marsden Hartley explodes vindicative fire crackers in Montmartre, Alfred Kreymborg has gone to Italy, and Ezra Pound furiously toys with spurious bronze in London. All have found America aesthetically impossible; yet, being of America, will some day return, a few into dyspeptic exile, others to write joyously for the movies.

— 2 —

We have, in America, an inexhaustible fund of dramatic material. Two sources occur to any one: the old Mississippi river days, and the romantic growth of railroads. And yet, when the Mississippi is mentioned, Mark Twain alone comes to mind: a hack writer who would not have been considered fourth rate in Europe, who tricked out a few of the old proven "sure fire" literary skeletons with sufficient local color to intrigue the superficial and the lazy.

Sound art, however, does not depend on the quality or quantity of available material: a man with real ability finds sufficient what he has to hand. Material does aid that person who does not possess quite enough driving force to create living figures out of his own brain; wealth of material does enable him to build better than he otherwise could. No one in America—no writer—can detach himself from the national literary shibboleths and pogroms to do this, though; those who are doing worth while things really labor infinitely more than the results achieved would show, for the reason that they must overcome all this self torture, must first slay the dragons which they, themselves, have raised. An apt instance was

related to me by a dramatic critic on a New York magazine: Robert Edmund Jones, a designer of stage settings,
discovered that, for some time, he had been subject to
an intangible ailment. He found that the quality of his
work had been mysteriously deteriorating, that his sleep
and appetite were being undermined. A friend—perhaps
the one who assisted him in discovering his alarming
condition—advised him to repair to a certain practitioner
of the new therapeutic psycho-analysis. He did so, was
"siked," and immediately recovered his appetite, his un-
troubled slumber, and his old zest in stage designing.
This is what all writers who are exposed to the prevailing
literary tendencies in America must combat; and, so long
as socialism, psycho-analysis and the aesthetic attitude
are profitable as well as popular, so long will such conditions obtain.

One rainbow we have on our dramatic horizon: language as it is spoken in America. In comparison with
it, British is a Sunday night affair of bread and milk—
melodious but slightly tiresome nightingales in a formal
clipped hedge. Other tongues are not considered here:
the Northman is essentially the poet and playwright, as
the Frenchman is the painter, and the German the musician. It does not always follow that a play built according
to sound rules—i.e. simplicity and strength of language,
thorough knowledge of material, and clarity of plot—will
be a good play as a result; else playwriting would become
a comparatively simple process. (Language means nothing to Shaw: except for the accident of birth he might well
have written in French.) In America, however, with our
paucity of mental balance, language is our logical savior.
Very few authors are able to say anything simply; these ex-
tremists fluctuate between the manners of various dead-
and-gone stylists—achieving therefrom a vehicle which

might well serve to advertise soap and cigarettes—and sheer idiocy. Those who realize that language is our best bet employ slang and our "hard" colloquialisms in order to erect an edifice which resembles that of a mason who endeavors to build a skyscraper with brick alone, forgetting the need of a steel skeleton within it.

Our wealth of language and our inarticulateness (inability to derive any benefit from the language) are due to the same cause: our racial chaos and our instinctive quickness to realize our simpler needs, and to supply them from any source. As a nation, we are a people of action (the astounding growth of the moving picture industry is a proof); even our language is action rather than communication between minds: those who might be justly called men of ideas take their thinking consciously, a matter of mental agility like an inverted Swedish exercise, and they frankly and naively call upon all near them to see and admire.

This is the Hydra which we have raised, and which we become pessimists or idiots slaying; who have the fundamentals of the lustiest language of modern times; a language that seems, to the newly arrived foreigner, a mass of subtleties for the reason that it is employed only as a means of relief, when physical action is impossible or unpleasant, by all classes, ranging from the Harvard professor, through the gardeniaed aloof young liberal, to the lowliest pop vendor at the ball park.

[*Mississippian,* March 17 and 24, 1922]

Review

OF

Linda Condon—Cytherea—The Bright Shawl

BY JOSEPH HERGESHEIMER

NO ONE since Poe has allowed himself to be enslaved by words as has Hergesheimer. What was, in Poe, however, a morbid but masculine emotional curiosity has degenerated with the age to a deliberate pandering to the emotions in Hergesheimer, like an attenuation of violins. A strange case of sex crucifixion turned backward upon itself: Mirandola and Cardinal Bembo become gestures in tinsel. He is subjective enough to bear life with fair equanimity, but he is afraid of living, of man in his sorry clay braving chance and circumstance.

He has never written a novel—someone has yet to coin the word for each unit of his work—*Linda Condon,* in which he reached his apex, is not a novel. It is more like a lovely Byzantine frieze: a few unforgettable figures in silent arrested motion, forever beyond the reach of time and troubling the heart like music. His people are never actuated from within; they do not create life about them; they are like puppets assuming graceful but meaningless postures in answer to the author's compulsions, and holding these attitudes until he arranges their limbs again in other gestures as graceful and as meaningless. His tact, though, is delicate and flawless—always a social grace. One can imagine Hergesheimer submerging himself in *Linda Condon* as in a still harbor where the age cannot hurt him and where rumor of the world reaches him only as a far faint sound of rain. Perhaps he wrote the book for this reason: surely a man of his delicacy and perception would never suffer the delusion that *Linda Condon* is a novel.

For this reason the book troubles the heart, the faintest shadow of an insistence; as though one were waked from a dream, for a space into a quiet region of light and shadow, soundless and beyond despair. *La figlia della sua mente, l'amorosa l'idea.*

Cytherea is nothing—the apostle James making an obscene gesture. Rather, the apostle James trying to carry off a top hat and a morning coat. A palpable and bootless attempt to ape the literary colors of the day.

The Bright Shawl is better. The sublimated dime novel peopled, like *Cytherea,* with morbid men and obscene women. But skilful; the tricks of the trade were never employed with better effect, unless by Conrad. The induction to *The Bright Shawl* is good—he talks of the shawl for a page or so before one is aware of the presence of the shawl as a material object, before the word itself is said; it is like being in a room full of people, one of whom one has not yet directly looked at, though conscious all the time of his presence.

These two books have swung to the opposite extreme from *Linda Condon.* Hergesheimer has tried to enter life, with disastrous results; Sinclair Lewis and *The New York Times* have corrupted him. He should never try to write about people at all; he should spend his time, if he must write, describing trees or marble fountains, houses or cities. Here his ability to write flawless prose would not be tortured by his unfortunate reactions to the apish imbe-

cilities of the human race. As it is, he is like an emasculate
priest surrounded by the puppets he has carved and
clothed and painted—a terrific world without motion or
meaning.

[*Mississippian,* December 15, 1922]

Review

OF

Ducdame

BY JOHN COWPER POWYS

To LIVE means to vegetate. That is all that nature requires. All the fretting and stewing over this and that is
man's own invention. And when people are put in a natural setting which in any way intrigues the eye, the importance of the characters becomes negligible: they are not
convincing. Imagine a Punch and Judy show without a
hooded stage.

Characters like Rook and his women, and Lexie and
the women he did not have, should be put in play form—
just the dialogue, to be read. But to write them in against
a background of quiet, lovely English country defeats its
own ends. Why is it that Americans don't seem to feel
that part of the earth's surface in which their roots are?
Joseph Hergesheimer, a decayed Pater, must go to Ha-

vana to write lovely prose; and when we try to describe our surroundings we do verbal calendars, lithographs on linoleum.

Material and aesthetic significance are not the same, but material importance can destroy artistic importance, in spite of what we would like to believe. Here is winter and the last rumor of Indian summer like a blonde, weary woman with reverted gaze done so well that Mrs. Ashover and her problem and Lexie with his imminent death become quite peppy, for suffering the compulsions of air and temperature and season as man does, everything is imminent, particularly death at this season, so both of them lose their significance. Where is the man who can die as grandly as December? Lexie should have died with December and so have lived, taking thereby an immortality, as Napoleon's old soldiers took an immortality from him. He was dead at Elba: and they were dead, regardless of the fact that they lingered in inns afterward.

But Lexie, living, does serve an end. . . . "There sounded from some neighboring tree invisible to them both the world-old Cuckoo! Cuckoo! of the unconquerable augur of sweet mischief.

"Lexie's face relaxed. . . . 'It hasn't changed its tune yet!' he cried, 'the summer is only beginning!' "

Hoarding his coppers of days, of hours and minutes. The only time that Lexie really lives as a character. And certainly he should live: the very passion for breath of a man shadowed by imminent and certain death, should live.

This neurotic age! People are still children. Sophistication is like the shape of a hat. Think of what, say Balzac or O. Henry, could have done with a man foredoomed to near and unavoidable death. He could have robbed trains, committed the indiscretions which one who is afraid that he will live to see ninety cannot and dare not. But Lexie does none of these things: he does not even grandly seduce anyone.

> If it do come to pass
> That any man turn ass,
> Leaving his wealth and ease
> A stubborn will to please,
> Ducdame, ducdame, ducdame:
> Here shall he see
> Gross fools as he,
> An if he will come to me.

To gather fools into a circle: God has already done that. God and Balzac. Fools answer the same compulsions that we of the (so-called) intelligentsia do. And why gather fools into a circle? Unless you have something to sell them like Henry Ford.

Rook Ashover, Lexie his brother, Netta and Ann and Nell and the parson, seeing the new year in: Let the bird of loudest lay on the sole Arabian tree: death and division, and love and constancy are dead. Yet still the bitter days draw on, and Horace with one eye on Menelaus thinks Eheu! fugace!

"Susannah and the Elders!" murmured Lexie. . . . "but aren't they provocative and tantalizing? I wish we could hide ourselves in the weeds and see it making love to Leda."

There is Lexie. And here is Netta, descendants of barmaids with a passion for gentility. Abnegation. She gives over her lover for the lover's sake. Do women do this? Perhaps their amazing ability for using chance to serve their own ends causes them to do quite obscure things (obscure to men, that is). But to think of women giving up anything which can or may be of use! Perish the thought.

Katharsis: a loved shape purged of dross; a lingering scent or a single glove after the music itself has faded away. Grand to read, but not inevitable, in this day of money motives and keyhole excitements. And surely, women do not have to bother with this. Man invented chastity as he invented security—something for his particular temporary woman to wear.

So he says: "Chastity is important, as my fathers believed. They sentimentalized over chastity. But I do not believe this: I do not believe that anything is true: people are shadows of a shade, serving some obscure end. Therefore I sentimentalize over the fact that I am not sentimental."

People like the sexton, Pod—"if the holy Lord had meant us to sleep single He would never have put it into our brains to hammer up these here double beds"—and Mr. Twiney—certainly they would not make a book; but, being of the earth earthy, they make the Rooks and Anns seem more futile than ever.

These people are not dramatic material. What we want in our reading is people who do the things we cannot or dare not do, or people that motivate stories in us. Or people in whom the compulsions of climate reveal themselves only when the action itself is completed.

Gathering people into a circle is like removing your overcoat at a Childs restaurant—you do it at your own risk. For sometimes you get a novel, and sometimes you don't. From a successful novel you get a sense of completeness, of form: that is, the people in it do the things which you would do if you were, one by one, these people. We are all fools, probably; and most of us know it: but it is unbearable to believe that the things we do are not significant. And the things these people do are not significant, for they do things which we do not like to believe we would do.

> . . . . Here shall he see
> Gross fools as he
> If only he come with me.

To be gross fools: being a gross fool is as hard as being a saint. Being a gross anything is rather grand— bootlegger or politician or courtesan. One who can sincerely lie, or squeeze every potato before buying it; to be sincerely unpleasant to live with—this is something. But these people are not sincerely fools, none of them are. In the sense of having their actions change the trend of somebody's life. They dub along without significance. But perhaps this was what Mr. Powys wanted. But surely they do not do those things that we as individuals would like to do to preserve that world of fine fabling in which we live.

[This review appeared in the *Times-Picayune* (New Orleans), March 22, 1925, signed "W. F." It was discovered and confirmed as Faulkner's by Professor Carvel Collins in 1950, and republished in the *Mississippi Quarterly,* Summer 1975. That text is printed here.]

Review

OF

Test Pilot

BY JIMMY COLLINS

(The uncut text)

I WAS disappointed in this book. But it was better than I
expected. I mean, better as current literature. I had expected, hoped, that it would be a kind of new trend, a literature or blundering at self expression, not of a man,
but of this whole new business of speed just to be moving
fast; a kind of embryo, instead of the revelation by himself of a man who was a pretty good guy probably and did
it pretty well and had more to say than some I know and
in a sense was just incidentally writing about flying. Instead the book turns out to be a perfectly normal and
pretty good collection of anecdotes out of the life and experience of a professional flyer. They are wide in range
and of varying degrees of worth and interest, and one, an
actual experience which reads like fiction, is excellent,
the best thing in the book, concise and ordered and not
only sustained but restrained. The others fall into groups,
ranging from anecdotes of crashes which were not fatal,
anecdotes over which flyers themselves laugh with what
Laurence Stallings once called "that bizarre and macabre
humor of flyers" and to which nonflyers would listen with

horrified and aghast bewilderment. There is another group of hangar yarns, shop talk of pilots which some nonflyers would enjoy and others find merely dull and still others actually incomprehensible. Then there is a third group of stories. I mean, manufactured tales: some the kind of air stories you might find in a boys' magazine, one a tale of poetic retribution, one after the classic Greek where man is destroyed wilfully and without reason by the gods—in this case Chance and Terror—and there is one sentimental piece which you might find in a magazine for ladies.

None of them are long and none overtold—his sense of restraint along with his gift for narrative are the author's best qualities—though I feel that some of them never warranted the telling to begin with—and most of them are tinged with a kind of sentimental journalese— that reportorial rapport which seems to know at once and by sheer instinct when any public figure enters town and where to find him—which shows especially in his nature descriptions. You are never arrested by a single description of night sky or night earth or sunset or moonlight or fog; you have seen it before a hundred times and it has been phrased just that way in ten thousand newspaper columns and magazines. But then, he contributed to a newspaper column I understand. But even if he had not, this could justly be excused him because of the sort of life a test pilot would have to lead: a life which would never dare solitude, whose even idleness must take place where people congregate, which would not dare retire into introspection where it might contemplate sheer language calmly or it would have to cease to be that of a test pilot. But he has undeniable narrative skill; he would doubtless have written whether he flew or not. In fact, the book itself indicates that he apparently wanted to write, or at least that he flew only to make money to support his family. And he was a Communist; he said himself, with an admirable calm simplicity, that he saw no other economic belief for one to hold: and so he would be the only Communist aviator outside of Russia because the idea of an American professional flyer and ex-Army officer professing Communism hardly makes sense. And "Return to Earth" will both speed your breathing and stop it, and "Back-Seat Pals" will split your sides, and "High Fight" will make any husband roar; and granted that one of a writer's jobs is to show man in his always ludicrous and not always successful clashes with the world which he created, he did his job well.

Because it was not Collins who hurt his book. He is dead, killed in the crash of an aeroplane which he was testing for the Navy, it being the custom of the Military to not permit its own pilots to test new aeroplanes. The last chapter in the book is entitled "I Am Dead" and consists of an obituary which Collins wrote himself. I dont mean this as any commentary on twentieth-century publishing methods, the crass come-on schemes of modern day publishing for whose benefit by an almost incredible fortuity he wrote the document, dared to it, I believe jokingly, by a friend, and I believe jokingly, complying because the book states that the dive which killed him was the last of a series on the last aeroplane which he intended to test, having perhaps gradually built up an assured income through his writing. It should have been a private document, shown you privately by the friend with whom he left it. You are sorry you read it in a book. It should not have been included. It should have been quoted from at most, quoted from not as the document which it is but for a figure which it contains, the only figure or phrase in the book which arrests the mind with the fine shock of poetry:

The cold but vibrant fuselage was the last thing to feel my warm and living flesh

But there is still another reason why it should not have been included. Because this time he overwrote himself, the only time in the book. Because, though he may have begun it jokingly, he did not continue since no man is going to joke to himself about his own death. So this time he overwrote. But I suppose this may be forgiven him too, since though a man stops sentimentalising about love probably the day he discovers that both he and his first sweetheart not only can desire and even take another but do, he probably never reaches that day when he no longer sentimentalises over his own passing.

But this is not what I hold against the book. What I hold is, it is not what I had hoped for. I had hoped to find a kind of embryo, a still formless forerunner or symptom of a folklore of speed, the high speed of today which I believe stands a good deal nearer to the end of the limits which human beings and material were capable of when man first dug iron, than to the beginning of those limits as they stood ten or twelve years ago when man first began to go really fast. Not the limits for the machines but for the men who fly them: the limit at which blood vessels will burst and entrails rupture in making any sort of turn that will keep you in the same county, not to speak of co-ordination and perception of distance and depth, even when they invent or discover some way to alter further the law of top speed ratio to landing speed than by wing flaps so that all the flights will not have to start and stop from one of the Great Lakes. The precision pilots of today even must have absolutely perfect co-ordination and depth perception, so perhaps, being perfect, these will function at any speed up to infinity. But they will still have to do something about his blood vessels and guts. Perhaps they will contrive to create a kind of species or race like they used to create and nurture races of singers and eunuchs, like Mussolini's Agello who flies more than four hundred miles an hour. They will be neither stalled ox nor game chicken, but capons: children culled by rules or even by machines from each generation and cloistered and in a sense emasculated and trained to conduct the vehicles in which the rest of us will hurtle from place to place. They will have to be taken in infancy because the precision pilot of today begins to train in his teens and is through in his thirties. These would be a species and in time a race and in time they would produce a folklore. But probably by then the rest of us could not decipher it, perhaps not even hear it since already we have objects which can outpace their own sound and so their very singers would travel in what to us would be a soundproof vacuum.

But it was not of this folklore that I was thinking. That one would be years in the making. I had thought of one which might exist even now and of which I had hoped that this book might be the symptom, the first fumbling precursor. It would be a folklore not of the age of speed nor of the men who perform it, but of the speed itself, peopled not by anything human or even mortal but by the clever willful machines themselves carrying nothing that was born and will have to die or which can even suffer pain, moving without comprehensible purpose toward no discernible destination, producing a literature innocent of either love or hate and of course of pity or terror, and which would be the story of the final disappearance of life from the earth. I would watch them, the little puny mortals, vanishing against a vast and timeless void filled with the sound of incredible engines, within which furious meteors moving in no medium hurtled nowhere, neither pausing nor flagging, forever destroying themselves and one another, without love or even copulation forever renewing.

[The original published text of Faulkner's review of *Test Pilot*, by Jimmy Collins, in *American Mercury*, November 1935, was included in the first edition of this collection, and is found here on pp. 188–192. Subsequently, Faulkner's typescript was found. It had been heavily edited: nearly three hundred words had been omitted and a title, "Folklore of the Air," had been added. The typescript text was published in the *Mississippi Quarterly*, Summer 1980. That text is printed here.]

TEN

Public Letters

LETTER TO THE NEW ORLEANS *Times-Item**

"What is the matter with marriage?" I do not think there is anything the matter with marriage. The trouble is with the parties thereto. Man invariably gains unhappiness when he goes into a thing for the sole purpose of getting something. To take what he has at hand and to create from it his heart's desire, is the thing. Men and women forget that the better the food, the quicker the indigestion.

Two men or two women—forming a partnership, always remember that the other has weaknesses, and by taking into account the fallibility of mankind, they gain success and happiness. But so many men and women when they marry seem to ignore the fact that both must keep clearly in mind that thing which they wish to create, to attain, and so work for it together and with tolerance of each other.

None of us will believe that our sorrows are ever brought about by ourselves. We all think that the world owes us happiness; and when we do not get it, we cast the blame upon that person nearest to us.

The first frenzy of passion, of intimacy of mind and body, is never love. That is only the surf through which one must go to reach the calm sea of real love and peace

---

* In the spring of 1925, the New Orleans *Times-Item* offered a prize of $10 each week for the best letter answering the question, "What Is the Matter with Marriage?" Faulkner wrote a winning letter, published with an introductory note about his poetry on April 4.

and contentedness. Breakers may be fun, but you cannot sail safely through breakers into port. And surely married people do want to reach some port together—some haven from which to look backward down golden years when mutual tolerance has removed some of the rough places and time has blotted out the rest.

If people would but remember that passion is a fire which burns itself out, but that love is a fuel which feeds its never-dying fire, there would be no unhappy marriages.

There is nothing wrong with marriage. If there were, man would have invented something else to take its place.

[New Orleans *Times-Item,* April 4, 1925]

✄ ✄ ✄

LETTER TO THE EDITOR OF THE MEMPHIS
*Commercial Appeal**

In the matter of W. H. James' letter on lynching in the *Commercial Appeal* Feb. 2.

---

* The Memphis *Commercial Appeal,* February 2, 1931, published a letter from W. H. James, a black man from Starkville, Mississippi, praising a recently organized anti-lynching women's group in Mississippi. In it James stated: "How strange it seems that history never gave a record of a single lynching until after the days of reconstruction."

In a letter signed "William Falkner" and published in the *Commer-*

History gives no record of lynching prior to reconstruction days for several reasons.

The slave-holders and slaves of the pre-Civil War time,
out of whose relations lynchings did, or could, take place,
were not representative of either people, any more than
the Sicilian expatriates and shopping women in Chicago
stores, out of whose accidental coinciding the murder of
innocent bystanders (or fleers) occurs, are representative
of European emigrants or American women and children, or of the General Cooks and the George Rogers
Clarks who made Chicago possible.

Secondly, there was no need for lynching until after reconstruction days.

Thirdly, the people of the black race who get lynched
are not representative of the black race, just as the people who lynch them are not representative of the white
race.

No balanced man can, I believe, hold any moral brief
for lynching. Yet we in America have seen, ever since we
set up to guide our own integral destiny, miscarriage of
elementary justice on all hands. Like all new lands, not
yet aware of our own strength, we have been the prey of
opportunist and demagogues; of men whose sole claim
to rule us was that they had not a clean shirt to their
backs. So is it strange that at times we take violently back
into our own hands that justice which we watched go
astray in the blundering hands of those into which we put
it voluntarily? I don't say that we do not blunder with our

---

cial Appeal, February 15, Faulkner responded at some length. This
reply, with James's letter, was included in an essay by Neil R. McMillen
and Noel Polk, "Faulkner on Lynching," *Faulkner Journal*, Fall 1992
(i.e., Spring 1994). That text is printed here.

"home-made" justice. We do. But he who was victim of our blundering, also blundered. I have yet to hear, outside of a novel or a story, of a man of any color and with a record beyond reproach, suffering violence at the hands of men who knew him.

It will be said that the standard for a black man is stricter than that for a white man. This is obvious. To make an issue of it is to challenge and condemn the natural human desire which is in any man, black or white, to take advantage of what circumstance, not himself, has done for him. The strong (mentally or physically) black man takes advantage of the weak one; he is not only not censured, he is protected by law, since (and the white man the same) the law has found out that the many elemental material factors which compose a commonwealth are of value only when they are in the charge of some one, regardless of color and size and religion, who can protect them.

It requires a certain amount of sentimentality, an escaping from the monotonous facts of day by day, to make a lynching. Note the crimes in compensation of which lynching occurs. Sacredness of womanhood, we call it. Not a thing, but a reaction: something so violent and so nebulous that even all the law words can not pin it down, since the law words were all invented in lands and by people who had had time to outgrow (or who could not afford) our American susceptibility to vocal resonance.

Lynching is an American trait, characteristic. It is the black man's misfortune that he suffers it, just as it is his misfortune that he suffers the following instances of white folks' sentimentality.

Let James go to his county tax collector, who will tell him (his county being fairly representative of Mississippi hill country as distinct from the delta) that there is more white-owned land sold up for taxes than colored-owned, though the delinquent list be the same. There may be reason for this, white man's reason: as, for instance, it will be proved that the colored man had never had title to the land at all, having used, as they do, two or even three separate names in making trades or borrowing money from the government loan associations, and so having used the land tax-free for a year and made a crop and moved on. Thus: Joe Johnson arranges with a white man and a bank to buy a piece of land. He is about to make a good crop; he is a hard worker; maybe he runs the neighborhood blacksmith shop; he is getting ahead. Then one day the cashier of the bank and the Farm Loan secretary compare notes and they find that a certain John Jones has borrowed $700 on land identical in description with that in the temporary possession of one Joe Johnson. There's nothing to do. Joe Johnson, or John Jones, tricked two white men. "Oh, well," the white men, the cashier and the secretary say, "he's a good man. He may make out." And he not only may and will, but he perhaps does make a good crop by hard work. But he has first committed one felony in person and a second one by proxy in permitting to compound it one of that unwitting race which holds with the Bible that justice is a matter of violent and immediate retribution on the person of the sinner: a sentimentalist.

There is a colored man, a friend who has helped me in my need and whom I have helped in his, who has eaten of my bread and between whom and myself the crass material balance of labor and recompense has long since faded from our ken, to be perhaps totted and receipted for in some better place, he hopes, who tells me now and then of his brother. They are sons of a slave. The brother went to Detroit years ago, where, he writes back, "he has not done a lick of work in 15 years, because the white folks up there give him food. All he has to do is, fall in a line at a designated place on a designated day, and receive the food or its equivalent in a printed form, which he sells to wop and bohunk immigrants who have not yet learned to talk enough English to save the middleman's profit."

In Europe they don't lynch people. But think of a man living for 15 years and doing nothing at all, in France say, or Italy. It cannot be done anywhere under the sun except in America.

James speaks of "as humble and submissive as. . . ." Let him think about this. Humility and submissiveness is usually the part of a weak person waiting to take his advantage, without regard to color. Humility and submissiveness are as false a part of a black man's social equipment as of a white man's. He does not need them. And the black man who is a valuable integer in the social fabric (property owner, merchant; any one who does a fair day's labor and receives a fair day's wage and applies it toward the comfort of his present life and the security of his old age) has no reason to assume humility. And he does not do it. In fact, there is a certain class of colored people who trade in humility just as there is a certain class of people who trade in man's other weaknesses and vices; it just happens that the colored man is better fitted to trade in humility, as the Irishman is for politics.

James reminds us that history records no lynchings prior to reconstruction days. Neither does history record any peculiar and noticeable removal to, and sojourn in, the south of Yankees until that period. Particularly New

Englanders, who had some time since begun to practice the custom of hanging people of whose conduct they did not approve. I have lived in Mississippi all my 30 years, yet most of the lynching[s] with which I am acquainted have occurred in outland newspapers; vide three I read of in French newspapers in Paris during a period of nine weeks, one of which happened at Oregon, D.C., Washington, the second at Halma, Alabama, D.C., America, and the third at a place called NveZique. They had photographs, flames and all, and the men there, looking at the camera. Most of them wore smock coats, and one man near the front had on wooden shoes.

I hold no brief for lynching. No balanced man will deny that mob violence serves nothing, just as he will not deny that a lot of our natural and logical jurisprudence serves nothing either. It just happens that we—mobber and mobbee—live in this age. We will muddle through, and die in our beds, the deserving and the fortunate among us. Of course, with the population what it is, there are some of us that won't. Some will die rich, and some will die on cross-ties soaked with gasoline, to make a holiday. But there is one curious thing about mobs. Like our juries, they have a way of being right.

WILLIAM FALKNER.
Oxford, Miss.

[Memphis *Commercial Appeal*, February 15, 1931]

❌ ❌ ❌

BLURB FOR *Men in Darkness,* BY JAMES HANLEY*

A damned fine job. That's language: not British, not American, not South African, not Ebury Street nor Chicago: just language. It's almost like a good clean cyclone or a dose of salts, since most books nowadays sound like they were written either by pansies or stallions.

※ ※ ※

BLURB AND PROMOTIONAL USE OF LETTER TO CLIFTON CUTHBERT**

"I have just finished your book," William Faulkner writes to Clifton Cuthbert, author of JOY STREET, just published by William Godwin. "I hated to put it down even to sleep. I would not have believed (save for that unmistakable quality of freshness) it to be a first book. In fact, as regards craftsmanship, knowing what to tell and what not to tell, it's one of the best first books I have ever read."

[*William Faulkner: The Carl Petersen Collection,* Berkeley, 1991]

---

* This blurb by Faulkner appeared on the dust jacket of the first American edition of James Hanley's novel *Boy* (New York: Knopf, 1932).

** On the dust jacket of the first edition of the novel *Thunder without Rain,* by Clifton Cuthbert (New York: William Godwin, 1933), appears a blurb by Faulkner praising Cuthbert's first novel, *Joy Street.* The text of the blurb is taken from Faulkner's letter to Cuthbert, probably written in late 1931 or early 1932, which appeared in an

"The story is very exciting; I hated to put it down even to sleep. I would not have believed (save for that unmistakable quality of freshness) it to be a first book. In fact, as regards craftsmanship, knowing what to tell and what not to tell, it's one of the best first books I ever read."

WILLIAM FAULKNER

[Jacket of *Thunder without Rain*, New York, 1933]

❋ ❋ ❋

———

CLASSIFIED AD IN THE MEMPHIS
*Commercial Appeal**

I will not be responsible for any debt incurred or bills made, or notes or checks signed by Mrs. William Faulkner or Mrs. Estelle Oldham Faulkner.

WILLIAM FAULKNER

❋ ❋ ❋

---

unidentified New York newspaper. A clipping of the published letter was quoted in *William Faulkner: The Carl Petersen Collection,* compiled by Peter B. Howard, Berkeley, Calif., 1991. That text of the letter, with the publisher's notations, is printed here, as is the dust jacket blurb text, which differs slightly.

* This classified ad appeared in the Memphis *Commercial Appeal,* June 22, 1936, and was reprinted in the *Oxford Eagle,* June 25, soon after Faulkner's return from a script-writing stint in Hollywood, where he and Meta Carpenter had become lovers. He wrote to her

INSCRIPTION ON THE MONUMENT TO LAFAYETTE COUNTY'S WORLD WAR II DEAD[*]

AFRICA ALASKA ASIA
EUROPE THE PACIFIC
DEC. 7, 1941   SEPT. 2, 1945
THEY HELD NOT THEIRS,
BUT ALL MEN'S LIBERTY,
THIS FAR FROM HOME
TO THIS LAST SACRIFICE.

✻ ✻ ✻

that Estelle, in spite of his warnings to local merchants, "had managed to charge up to about a thousand dollars during his absence." (See *A Loving Gentleman: The Love Story of William Faulkner and Meta Carpenter*, by Meta Carpenter Wilde and Orin Borsten, New York, 1976.) Joseph Blotner included the *Commercial Appeal* text in *Faulkner: A Biography*, vol. 2, New York, 1974. That text is printed here.

[*] Faulkner was the anonymous author of the inscription on the monument to Lafayette County's World War II dead. Erected in 1947, it stands on the north side of the courthouse in Oxford. The text was first published in the *Oxford Eagle*, February 13, 1947, where it was attributed to Faulkner. One change was made in the text for the monument: the date "Sept. 2, 1945" had been "Aug. 15, 1945" in the *Eagle*.

The *Eagle* text, and the change for the monument, appeared in James B. Meriwether, "Faulkner and the World War II Monument in Oxford," in *A Faulkner Miscellany*, ed. James B. Meriwether, University Press of Mississippi, 1974.

LETTER TO THE MEMPHIS
Commercial Appeal

I have just received a letter from a citizen of Chickasaw County, where the killing occurred and the parties to it lived, about the Chickasaw-Calhoun County tragedy in which three white men are said to have dragged an unarmed Negro farmer from his wagon and, in the presence of his wife and children, beat him to death with an automobile tool, the trial of which was transferred by change of venue to Calhoun County, where the defendant was declared not guilty on the grounds of self-defense.

The letter is not signed.

I think I understand why: those who, even at odds of three to one, were reduced to that extremity for self-preservation, will probably not hesitate to use more of the same kind of self-defense on any critic of their behavior.

So I don't quote the body of the letter at this time. There is no need for it, since the men's lawyers have already implied the same thing in achieving a change of venue from the county and the people who knew the clients best.

But I will quote this:

"The people (of Chickasaw County) knew Malcolm Wright.

"The man whose place this Negro rented had arranged that the place should go to him in the event that the landlord died first; that is, the small farm which Wright had worked for years was to be his as provided by will.

"My little colored maid, a young married woman, said, 'Mama always told us children that if we kept our place and did right, nothing would ever harm us. But Malcolm Wright kept his place and always tried to do right.' "

That's the important part, not just tragic but terrifying. All that the Negro has, he got from us, the white people. That is, his ways and habits are our ways and habits, because he had to learn and ape our ways and habits in order to live among us. We taught him to speak a language, and read it, to eat and think as we eat and think, to wear the same clothes, to want the same automobile, the same pleasures, to farm the same land by the same methods to raise the same cotton and corn; we even invented and taught him his religion and his vices; the homely and primitive worship, the malt whisky and the dice.

And now we seem to be offering him a postgraduate course. And if this—not just the murdering of little children in their beds at night, or the dragging of unarmed fathers out of wagons on public roads and beating them to death with iron rods while their wives and children watch, but the seed, the heritage of desperation and hatred in the blood of their kin and descendants—is what we have set out to teach them now, then, ladies and gentlemen, we had better be afraid.

Some of us already are—fear and grieve both. But so far all some of us either dare or can do is raise anonymous voices like the above: to which tragic pass has come this country, this land, America, founded by oppressed people that there shall be forever a refuge where no man shall oppress another, which only yesterday took share in a bloody war on the principle that every man's life and liberty shall be safe and secure, Mason, Methodist, Jew, Republican, Atheist, Vegetarian or Swedenborgian:—to what tragic pass, when that condition is not only condoned but even supported and so perpetuated by precedent, for whatever supported and so perpetuated by precedent, for whatever the reason—ignorance or big-otry or—basest of all—the employment of the ignorance and bigotry for preferment or money, wherein a citizen dare not raise his voice against outrage and injustice for fear of martyrdom.

WILLIAM FAULKNER

[Memphis *Commercial Appeal*, April 30, 1950]

❋ ❋ ❋

BLURB FOR *The End of the Affair,*
BY GRAHAM GREENE[*]

. . . for me one of the most true and moving novels of my time, in anybody's language.

WILLIAM FAULKNER

❋ ❋ ❋

---

[*] From the rear panel of the dust jacket of the first edition of Graham Greene's novel *Loser Takes All* (London: Heinemann, 1955). It was taken from a letter Faulkner wrote to Harold Raymond, senior partner of Chatto and Windus, his English publisher, January 22, 1952. The letter is published in *Selected Letters of William Faulkner*, ed. Joseph Blotner, New York, 1977.

DRAFT OF SEPTEMBER 15, 1957, LETTER TO THE
EDITOR OF THE MEMPHIS *Commercial Appeal**

The undersigned agrees with writer M. J. Greer (Letters to the Editor, Sept. 1st.) in his practical evaluation of the segregation problem. All the laws in the world will not make white and non-white people mix if one of the parties doesn't want to, just as all the laws in the world cant keep them separate if both parties want to mix.

I still dont believe the Negro wants to "mix" with white people. I dont believe he likes white people that much. But, from three hundred years of association with white people, he has become enough like the white man to rebel at a culture which holds him inferior and second class simply because of his race and color—which, because of his pigment, denies him privilege which anyone else with a different color of skin, possesses by natural right. He doesn't want to be in the white man's churches and schools anymore than he wants the white man in his: he simply wants the right to *choose* not to enter them.

A few years ago the Supreme Court rendered a decision which we white Southerners didn't like, and resisted. As a result, last month Congress would have passed a bill containing ramifications and implications a good deal more threatening than the presence of a Negro child in a white school or a Negro vote in a white ballot box, if there hadn't been one expert on hand to see it in time. So

---

* Faulkner's letter to the Memphis *Commercial Appeal,* September 15, 1957, was included in the first edition of this collection, and is found here on p. 229. An unfinished but much longer draft of the letter appears on the verso of two pages of *The Mansion*'s typescript, and it was published in "Faulkner's Typescripts of *The Town,*" by Eileen Gregory, *Mississippi Quarterly,* Summer 1973. That text is printed here.

we escaped—that time. But as long as the Negro continues to be held inferior and second class in citizenship—
that is, subject to taxes and military service, yet denied
the economic and political and educational equality giving him at least the right and competence to vote for,
even if not represented among, them who tax and draft
him—Congress will continue to be offered bills containing these ramifications and implications visible only to an
expert, until some day that expert wont be on hand to
save us, and one of them will pass. But at least we will have
the satisfaction of knowing that we have nobody to blame
but ourselves.

If we really want to make admission to our schools selective and restrictive and still stay clear of Congress and
the Supreme Court, all we need do is raise the standards
of the grades and classes to that level where the schools
themselves will exclude the inferior and the unfit—
which we would have done long ago if we had wanted
really to train and educate our children. But that would
exclude some white pupils too so

[Unfinished]

※ ※ ※

ESTATE ADMINISTRATOR'S NOTICE

STATE OF MISSISSIPPI COUNTY OF LAFAYETTE ADMINISTRATOR'S NOTICE TO CREDITORS OF MAUDE BUTLER FALKNER

Letters of Administration having been granted on the 18th day of October 1960 by the Chancery Court of Lafayette County, Mississippi, to the undersigned upon the estate of Maude Butler Falkner, deceased, notice is hereby given to all persons having claims against said estate to present the same to the clerk of said Court for probate and registration according to law within six months from this date, or they will be forever barred.

This 17th day of October, 1960.

William C. Falkner, Administrator
Jesse J. Hardin, Clerk
By Mary Wilson, D.C.

[Faulkner's mother died October 16, 1960. This estate administrator's notice was published in the *Oxford Eagle,* October 20, 1960, and repeated on October 27 and November 3.]

JAMES B. MERIWETHER got his undergraduate degree at the University of South Carolina and began his graduate studies at Princeton, intending to make Shakespeare his major field of study. Upon earning his M.A., Meriwether spent three years in the Army Security Agency during the Korean War. He later returned to Princeton, and realizing that he had mostly read American literature during those three years, he determined to write a dissertation on William Faulkner, believing Faulkner to be the most challenging and important American writer. Meriwether subsequently met Faulkner's editor at Random House, Saxe Commins, who also lived in Princeton. Meriwether assisted Commins in various editorial projects, including the copyediting and proofreading of *The Town*. Faulkner, having left a trunk of his manuscripts and typescripts at Random House, agreed with Commins to their deposit at the Princeton University Library, early in 1957, for Meriwether to catalog. This he did, resulting in Meriwether's first book, *The Literary Career of William Faulkner: A Bibliographical Study,* Princeton, 1961. Following the death of Saxe Commins, Meriwether assisted Faulkner's new editor, Albert Erskine, in editing *The Mansion, The Reivers,* and new editions of *Sanctuary, As I Lay Dying, The Town,* and *The Hamlet*.

Meriwether pursued teaching jobs at the University of Texas and the University of North Carolina before returning to teach at his South Carolina alma mater in 1964. Of his many Faulkner publications and projects, he believes those that made the most significant contributions to the field were the twenty-four annual Faulkner issues of the *Mississippi Quarterly*, which he edited beginning in 1964, and which included many previously unpublished writings by Faulkner. In addition, he has directed a number of doctoral dissertations on Faulkner, most of which were subsequently published as books. James B. Meriwether lives in South Carolina with his wife, Anne, also a scholar.

MODERN LIBRARY IS ONLINE AT
WWW.MODERNLIBRARY.COM

MODERN LIBRARY ONLINE IS YOUR GUIDE TO CLASSIC LITERATURE ON THE WEB

THE MODERN LIBRARY E-NEWSLETTER

Our free e-mail newsletter is sent to subscribers, and features sample chapters, interviews with and essays by our authors, upcoming books, special promotions, announcements, and news.

To subscribe to the Modern Library e-newsletter, send a blank e-mail to: **sub_modernlibrary@info.randomhouse.com** or visit **www.modernlibrary.com**

THE MODERN LIBRARY WEBSITE

Check out the Modern Library website at
www.modernlibrary.com for:

- The Modern Library e-newsletter
- A list of our current and upcoming titles and series
- Reading Group Guides and exclusive author spotlights
- Special features with information on the classics and other paperback series
- Excerpts from new releases and other titles
- A list of our e-books and information on where to buy them
- The Modern Library Editorial Board's 100 Best Novels and 100 Best Nonfiction Books of the Twentieth Century written in the English language
- News and announcements

Questions? E-mail us at **modernlibrary@randomhouse.com**
For questions about examination or desk copies, please visit
the Random House Academic Resources site at
www.randomhouse.com/academic